In Anguish

Trial and Error: A family's nightmare
over sexual assault allegations

Melanie Metcalfe

DayOne

Copyright © 2003

All scripture quotations are from The New International Version © 1973, 1978, 1984,
International Bible Society. Published by Hodder and Stoughton.

British Library Cataloguing in Publication Data available

ISBN 1 903087 40 -6

9 781903 087404

Published by Day One Publications
3 Epsom Business Park, Kiln Lane, Epsom, Surrey KT17 1JF.
01372 728 300 FAX 01372 722 400
email—sales@dayone.co.uk
web site—www.dayone.co.uk
North American—email-sales@dayonebookstore.com
North American web site—www.dayonebookstore.com

This is a true story. In order to protect the identities of those involved, names and
some details have been changed.

Designed by Steve Devane and printed by CPD

'God whispers to us in our pleasures, speaks in our conscience, but shouts in our pain: it is his megaphone to rouse a deaf world.'
C.S.Lewis *The Problem of Pain*

1999 was a very traumatic year for the Metcalfe family.
This book has been written as an illustration of how great God is; and of how a very ordinary family were preserved in a most extraordinary way through the care and prayer of others.

Contents

T his is an unusual, perhaps unique story about the nightmare experience of a very ordinary family with very special qualities, written with powerful honesty and gripping potency. But it is far more than just an interesting story and good read.

Law makers should read this book to realise how unreasonable the whole issue of the anonymity and impunity of those who level maliciously false accusations, and how unjust the 'presumption of guilt' syndrome can be. Law enforcers should read it to be warned of the damage caused by heavy-handed, insensitive and even ignorant methods of police investigation, that could irreparably wound a family. Society should read it to appreciate the unfairness of a legal aid system that could leave an innocent family homeless and bankrupt. And all who work at any level in the voluntary sector among children and youth, should read it to be alerted to the dangers of innocent, but naïve or unwise conduct being manipulated in a court of law by vicious and evil minds; this story should put all youth workers on their guard.

I recall preaching at Nick's church on the Sunday before the fateful Wednesday when he knew that, within a few days, he could be sentenced to many years in prison with an indelible stain on his character and his family. After the service he was happily playing Christian songs with a group of teens and twenties gathered round the piano. Even knowing the fun-loving character of Nick and the strong support of Melanie and their church, I wondered how on earth he could be so relaxed. Together they told me: it was a mixed story of absolute integrity, total trust in one another, loyal, coherent and courageous friends – and an excellent barrister; but above all, it was a story of a firm belief that God is in control and that he has plans behind all the events of this world.

So, this is far more than just a moving story brilliantly written. The word 'insight' in the title is significant: Melanie opens a window on her family, and the wise will look and learn. The story enshrines a host of messages of love, support, faith and trust as well as warnings of injustice, false assumptions, and unwise (albeit innocent) behaviour. If we do not listen to the message of this book—and learn from it—we will be very much poorer and far more vulnerable.

Brian H Edwards Surbiton Surrey February 2003

The start of the story

W e are a couple probably very similar to you or to someone you know. We thought of ourselves as young, but at the time were in fact in our late thirties. We did not consider ourselves rich, although my husband had a good job with Mainwave. We lived a tranquil, law abiding, unadventurous, middle class life, had a good sized house in Oxted, a reasonable garden, and four children; which was probably the reason we didn't view ourselves as wealthy, as the accompanying expenditure always seemed to be endless. We also had two cats, thoroughly spoilt and totally adored, Sooty and Sweep.

Nick, brought up in Crawley, was the second of three boys. I also had lived there all my life and was youngest of two girls. We'd met at the local church youth group when only eighteen and sixteen and when Nick still worked for the GPO. We both came from Christian families, and had been baptised at the same service in 1973.

But that was all years ago now. We were married in 1982 and lived briefly near both sets of parents. By then, Nick, frustrated with the lack of prospects in the Post Office had changed job to work for Mainwave. He enjoyed his computer based work, did well and two house moves then resulted, instigated by Nick's employer. However, being fond of a change and being hyperactive in approach to life, the moves were no hardship to either of us and on each occasion we'd been able to buy a larger house.

Over the years, and along with so many of our contemporaries, our children arrived. First, Emily, studious, co-operative, impractical and serious; then Jessica who'd been a foul baby but transformed over the years to a kind, practical and sensitive child. Felicity was perhaps the one most like Nick, fun loving, mischievous and enjoying a life of constant activity. Lastly Esther in 1991, totally different from the others, more affectionate, more tactile, more chatty by far, feeling that as number four it was difficult to get her views heard: consequently she was the one who shouted loudest and talked constantly.

Nick is the shortest of three brothers, being only five foot eight. His complexion is dark, a tanned skin giving him an Italian appearance. He has deep brown eyes and almost jet black hair. He has a prominent nose, a genetic feature inherited by all four girls, and poor eyesight necessitating the wearing of glasses. Now, as the years advance, his shape has become more portly, though he is by no means fat, and a tell tale bald patch is beginning to appear, as are a few grey hairs.

Ever since his teenage years he'd lived a life of hectic activity. When he wasn't decorating his grandmother's flat, he was cycling round England with his friend, and when he wasn't taking a life saving course, he was helping with canoeing and sailing on a children's camp organised by our local church. Kind hearted and compassionate to a T, with a passion for water sports, he was always helping someone, even after he and I were married. Sometimes it frustrated me that he was always keen to help with children's clubs, camps and their water sports; and was not at home to help with our own children quite as much as I would have liked. But I fully recognised that was where his gifts and abilities lay and was gratified to see just how much his skills, energy and enthusiasm were appreciated.

With each move we'd found and joined a local church and quickly become involved. At the first, Nick decorated the manse for the new pastor, regularly drove the minibus, went on children's camps and became a deacon. The second move had been to Oxted, and although the church was different in many ways, it too needed practical help. Nick was straight in there, playing the piano, driving their minibus and running the young people's work. We were both involved and it was hard work, but on the whole rewarding and great fun. Saturday evenings involved something recreational ranging from bowling, swimming, or ice skating to more tranquil activities such as board games, cooking and quiz nights. Sunday evenings were rather different. The group congregated at our house after the church evening service for coffee, squash and chat, and then would settle down for some teaching from the Bible, often led by Nick, a discussion or a constructive video.

Although we'd initially taken on the work short term, months turned into years. Recognising that at some point it would be necessary to extricate ourselves from the work and pass it on, we resolved that once Emily was old enough to attend, we'd call a halt. We told the minister of our plans and he seemed quite happy with that concept. As we were nearing that point and the end of our seven-year stint of youth work and wondering what we would then do, a hundred and one possibilities went through our minds. We could take a break from church work, we could help with the older folk's groups, we could even move house to be nearer Nick's work. For the first time in years we had no fixed commitment holding us down. Of course, a change appealed to Nick who always had itchy feet, but then there were the girls to consider who had loads of local friends and seemed reasonably settled in their schools. Admittedly Esther was moving from Infants to Juniors, and Jessica was allegedly in the worst tutor group in the school, but Felicity was very settled with a close knit group of friends, and Emily likewise.

However, it was while we were mulling over these and similar thoughts that a new headmaster came to Emily and Jessica's school. Initially all was excitement and anticipation as rules were changed, uniforms altered and routines readjusted. But as time went on we wondered whether the change had really been for the best. The idea of putting children into 'sets' according to their ability was disposed of, as being too discriminatory and selective. Youngsters were encouraged to complain about the staff if they felt there was a problem. Several of our friends began talking about removing their children and we too foresaw the school deteriorating into chaos and anarchy.

One evening around that time Emily came down stairs late, long after she'd said goodnight and Nick and I both glanced up quizzically. It was obvious from her expression and the tears trickling down her cheeks that all was not well. 'Whatever is the matter?' I asked with concern, and Emily then proceeded to explain how she felt she'd have to change schools as hers was going down the plughole. Astute as ever and concerned for her academic future, she'd been keeping a close eye on things ever since the new headmaster had arrived. After much thought and consideration she felt things weren't as they should be and the only solution was to move school. That conclusion upset her on a number of fronts. She, unlike her father, didn't relish the prospect of change; in a multitude of ways she liked her school, its location and its facilities, and worst of all she didn't want to leave her friends.

No rushed decision was made that night, but from this point onwards, we began to contemplate a house move, and to investigate other schools in the area, and indeed in the environs of Nick's work location on the outskirts of Guildford.

The summer of 1998 was a frenetic one. Having settled on relocating, we then had to find schools we were happy with and indeed a house to move to. Our friends in Oxted were sad, particularly church friends who, over the period of ten years we had lived there, had become very close, and one or two of them begged us to reconsider our decision. Felicity was particularly concerned, being in a cluster of three close friends and apprehensive at the thought of starting to build new relationships.

At last however, a lovely house was found, ours was sold, new schools were visited and approved of, applications accepted and everything began to happen. Not quite in the order we had hoped; for the September term was upon us long before contracts were exchanged, necessitating a long journey each day for Nick delivering all four to their new schools in the morning before work and for me collecting them all each afternoon.

Finally contracts were signed, exchanged and completion took place on November 17. Great was the whole family's delight when we realised that the long mooted move was at last a certainty. Within weeks we were happily settled, surrounded by cardboard boxes requiring attention, but delighted to be in our new house, nearer Nick's work and with all four girls happily ensconced in their new schools. Even Felicity was content as she'd made friends with a bright little girl called Rosie who'd started at the same time as her.

Christmas was upon us before we knew it, and I felt rather out of control as I tried to prepare for the festivities and having the family to stay, whilst still having a fair proportion of books and clobber stowed away in boxes. Thankfully the chaos wasn't noticed by the relatives who just admired the house and appreciated the catering; or if it was, they had the sense not to draw attention to it. My parents from Herefordshire stayed over Christmas and were shown Nick's work place and the girls' schools, followed by Rebekah and Chris, their three children and dog, (my sister and her family). It was chaotic, crazy, noisy and busy but enjoyed by all. 'Indeed,' I thought as I looked back once everyone had left, 'considering how quickly after the move Christmas had come upon us, everything had gone exceedingly well.'

'But all that was in a previous life,' I shuddered as I reminisced. The girls were just happily back at their new schools for the Spring term when the lightning struck.

Chapter 2

Life turned upside down

It was Wednesday, just over twenty four hours after the bomb had dropped, that I was walking along the Surrey hills. Wrapped up in my inward pain, hardly noticing the weather, the scenery or even the constant drizzle of rain. I kicked dejectedly at the squelchy leaves: 'This can't be happening, it just can't.' Involuntarily I let out a loud anguished groan and burst into another flood of tears. Totally oblivious to the drip of the spring rain on the already saturated beech, firs, brambles and undergrowth, I marched aggressively on, unaware of the mud, the puddles and the deplorable state of the footpath.

The path along the Surrey Downs levelled a little and became firmer. I kicked a stick out of the way, came to a clearing and dumped myself down on a bench placed there 'in loving memory of Edith Bradford to enable walkers to rest, relax and enjoy the view'. 'The view, what view? Who cares about the view? What did it matter? What did anything matter? How can life have been good? How can it have been happy and relaxed? It would certainly never ever be the same again.'

Many more tears, and then at last a state of numbness. Emotion was drained out of me and I could cry no longer. Even my thoughts seemed dull, with no edge to them. Lethargy engulfed me and I felt that 'Now more than ever seems it rich to die.' Time stood still, as I sat there hunched up, lifeless and blank. But somehow I knew deep down inside that life must go on, and so, with an effort I heaved myself up and forced my legs to amble along.

Was it only Monday that all had been fine? I thought back, for it felt like a previous existence, a different life, aeons away. I remembered the washing being done, the bedrooms were tidied, always an unenviable job after the weekend chaos, and the children went to school. My friend Fiona had called, I'd done a little shopping, I just couldn't believe that that had happened only on Monday. The children had come home from school, Jessica had had a headache, Felicity had been given a certificate for good work; Esther had, as always, talked non-stop, and Emily had been her usual quiet self, getting on with life, school, music.

'Only Monday?' I thought. 'Oh yes, and there was the mouse.'

Half a mild smile crept over my tear stained, pale face as I reminisced. Just at teatime Sooty had leapt through the cat flap with a field mouse in his mouth; I had screamed and Jessica, ever anxious to help, had reassured me. 'Don't worry Mum, I'll deal with it.' Giving the cat a hefty shake, the mouse had dropped to the floor. 'You hold the cat Mum,' Jessica had said, purposefully thrusting Sooty into my arms. But then looking down, the audacious rodent had not only come back to life, but scarpered. I had thought it must be in the dark under the stairs, but the girls hunted assiduously to no avail. Then I saw a movement in the hall and two tiny beady eyes looking at me from behind the bookcase. Grabbing saucepans, plastic pots and cake tins to catch it in, we'd all advanced towards it and it darted into the study. 'Oh that wretched little creature,' I recalled, 'it seemed so important at the time, and I was so insistent that it had to be caught, and there was no way I was going to tolerate a mouse in the house. As if that mattered. If we'd known what was going to happen, it was a nothing and I made such a fuss.'

Then Nick had come home. Initially he had found the whole thing funny. But he hadn't been able to catch it either. I had finally trapped it between cupped hands and the little monster had bitten me, so I'd involuntarily let it go, Esther had dissolved into tears and Nick had got cross. But he and the other three had caught it in the end; we'd all peered through the opaque top of the Tupperware at the cute little creature and voted to release it into the field out the back: after putting up such a brave fight it definitely deserved a second chance. 'A second chance, if only we could have one, if only the clock could be put back. But what was the point of thinking that?' I pondered. 'The clock can't be put back, it has all happened, and where on earth are we to go from here?' My shoulders visibly sank as the weight of the recent memories pressed on me all over again. And again the tears began to fall.

The sun came out, a watery misty sort of pallor filled the sky. The drip drip of the moisture off the trees and bushes became less persistent. Soon I would have to make my way home, I knew that: wash my face, change my clothes, put on a bright face for the children and be supportive of Nick. How? I'd manage somehow, I would cope, a stalwart, but oh, if only the anguish would go away. I groaned again out loud as I turned left towards the house and an elderly gentleman walking his dog looked somewhat strangely at me. What did I care? What did it matter what anyone thought now? Perhaps he thought I was unstable, neurotic, I really couldn't give a fig. The world had changed. The door was shut on happiness, maintaining appearances, enjoying a happy social life. Overnight our whole existence had been turned upside down and whatever the outcome I knew, deep down, that life would never ever be the same again.

'Fade far away, dissolve and quite forget … the weariness, the fever, and the fret.' For a second I was diverted by my recollection of school. Empathising with Keats for the first time in my life, and appreciating that he too must have suffered severely to write such poignant words. But now I knew, oh yes, now I knew. I wished I could fade far away. I wondered what the future held. How many more days, weeks, months there were to live? I felt distracted, unable to concentrate, giving hypocritical smiles when people asked how I was.

'I just can't bear it.' I burst out totally regardless of whether or not anyone could hear.

On Sunday night there had been problems with the car alarm; although we had not noticed a thing sleeping up the other end of the house, Emily had heard it four times. Being only half awake Emily had ignored it until the morning and then told Nick over breakfast quite nonchalantly, 'The car alarm went off four times last night.' Nick nearly choked on his muesli. 'Why on earth didn't you come and tell us?' Adolescent, self righteous, knowing smile. 'I don't think I was awake enough.'

So on Monday night Nick had knocked on the neighbours' door and apologised for the noise. After all, we'd only just moved in and the last thing we wanted to do was upset anyone in the road. Yes, the friendly faced, middle aged man told us, they had heard it, (that was embarrassing,) but it hadn't woken their granddaughter, (that was a relief). Nick had begged them, if it happened again, to come and ring the doorbell, but said he thought the seat belt had been caught in the door and did hope it wouldn't occur again. Many apologies, and thankfully we were all still friends.

Consequently, when the doorbell rang at 6.30 am the following morning, I surfaced and, glancing at the clock, I roused Nick and muttered: 'Your car alarm must be going off.' He was out of bed in a flash and down the stairs.

Voices. Back up the stairs three at a time. Puzzled expression. 'It's the Police.' Before I had got further than a confused 'What? Why?' he was pulling on clothes, and I did the same.

'Mr Metcalfe, what are you doing?'

A large figure in dark clothing loomed at the bedroom door. I still shudder to think about it. I can't remember what I had on, but hope it was decent. 'Getting dressed' was Nick's retort, I remember the moment vividly and indignantly. 'I mean what did they think he was doing? Playing draughts?' He hurried down the stairs and into the lounge. I followed a couple of minutes later. Two policemen and a police woman were standing there. Nick's face was indescribable. Pale, distorted with anguish, sort of twisted, puzzled like a child, tortured like a soldier dying on the battlefield. I'll never forget it. It will always be with me, that look of total devastation and bewilderment.

'They think I've raped Anita and assaulted Penny,' he gasped. Almost flying across the room, I ran to his side, grabbed his arm and said, 'That's crazy, there's obviously been some terrible mistake.'

My mind leapt around at random, like a firework display wildly out of control. Why should two of our good friends from our old youth group back in Oxted allege such crazy things? What did other people in the church think? Did they know? Why hadn't they warned us?

The policeman obviously felt it was all a bit emotionally charged and came out with:

'Nick Metcalfe, we're arresting you on suspicion ...' I can't remember the exact words and terminology, but walking into the lounge on that Tuesday morning was like walking into your worst nightmare. At some point I asked them if they'd like a coffee. Good job they declined, my hands were shaking so much I'd never have managed to make any drinks. Nick was taken off with the two officers to search the house, and I was left with the policewoman. Young, attractive and polite, but had she any idea what she was doing to our family? Walking in and turning life upside down?

'I'd like to talk to you and then the girls if I may?' she'd announced.

'If I may?' I'd thought angrily. 'What would have happened if I'd said "no"?'

I ran upstairs and woke the girls up. It was a horrific wakening for them.

No mother would ever want to do what I had to do that morning. I barged into the bedrooms of four peacefully sleeping girls and turned their tranquil world upside down.

'Get up,' I ordered, 'the police are here, they say Dad's done something wrong. Get dressed, they want to talk to you.' I saw complete bewilderment on each of their faces as I broke the news, confusion on the two little ones, something more closely resembling panic on the two older ones.

Back downstairs, 'I'm sorry to have to come to see you like this,' said the WPC with a half hearted attempt at a smile. She wasn't half as sorry as I was. She was wearing a Child Protection Unit badge which made my stomach churn.

'No, no she can't take the kids.' I screamed inwardly as I clutched the settee to steady myself. I didn't know what was going on, I didn't understand what was going on, but I knew they just couldn't take my girls.

'Tell me a little about yourself and the family.'

What could I say? One minute we were the happiest family in middle-class Britain, and the next minute it was shattered into a thousand fragments and would never be the same again.

'Yes, yes Nick and I get on really well.' I managed to say after an apprehensive pause.

'No, we have no problems. Yes, the children are happy at school and by the way Nick wouldn't ever harm anyone. Only last night he spent two hours chasing a field mouse round the study to humour me and then released it because he felt sorry for it.'

The WPC probably wasn't very interested in the field mouse bit but it was too bad, it just came out. 'Could I speak to each of your children?' she'd asked. What could I say? They were the police. They called the tune.

'You may accompany them if they wish.' I was outraged.

'If *they* wish,' I'd thought. 'What about if *I* wish? I just happen to be their mother, but that is clearly irrelevant.'

They were all four sitting round the breakfast table like lambs, and I explained to them that they each had to see the policewoman. Did they want me with them? I'd asked. Poor loves, of course they wanted their mother with them, they had even less of a clue what was happening than I had. Emily was in first. Scared, tense, sitting on the edge of her seat. The lady officer introduced herself: 'I know it's rather unusual to have to talk to a police woman.' I can still recollect my outrage. It was 6.30 in the morning, we, as individuals and as a family, had never been in trouble with the law and now Emily's father was being marched round the house by two policemen watching it being torn apart. Cupboards were wrenched wide, drawers yanked open and the contents of wardrobes strewn liberally across the floor and the bed.

'But I just need to ask you a few questions.' The WPC continued. Pause. I had wondered what on earth was coming next?

'How do you get on with your dad?'

Anger surged within me, 'What sort of question is that?' I wondered. 'She adores him, thinks the world of him, would do anything for him.'

Emily's response came hesitatingly: 'I like him.' It must have been the shock of everything that caused her restrained response.

'Do you get on well with your sisters? Do you like school? Do you have friends?'

Then, in my view, another stupid question. 'Do you have any one you could go to if you had any problems?'

Of course she had her parents. But she listed form teachers, friends from church etc. which was probably just as well, now that Nick and I had unexpectedly entered the world of villains. In the last fifteen minutes our role as parents had become irrelevant and insignificant so that our help clearly wouldn't be of much value. Emily seemed to have done OK and she was asked to send in her next sister.

In came Jessica, the sensitive one. In tears before she'd even sat down.

'I'm sorry this has upset you,' murmured the policewoman.

'So she jolly well ought to be,' I remember thinking. 'What long term psychological effect is this going to have on my girls?'

'Why are you crying?' persisted the policewoman.

It makes me tingle with anger even now as I recall the conversation. 'What a moronic question. She's an ordinary twelve year old girl who isn't exactly in the habit of being woken up by a dawn raid from the police.' The answer was just about intelligible between the sobs:

'Because my dad wouldn't do anything wrong.' Same questions as before, and soon the tearful Jessica was discharged and Felicity came in.

I still remember back to the moment when suddenly my poor stupefied brain began to function again, having been numbed by the shock of the events unfurling before me. Nick would need a solicitor! Yes, it took all that time for the penny to drop. But at last I came to my senses. Leaving Felicity with the policewoman, I telephoned, well who could I telephone? We'd just moved house and the only solicitor I knew was our conveyancer. Poor fellow, I got him out of bed. He sounded terribly sleepy and I had to repeat three times who I was before he even began to take it in. I'm not sure even now that he really remembered who we were, but it didn't really matter; rape wasn't his line, he explained, but he gave me Mr Green's number. I gratefully rang Mr Green, who although surprised at being contacted at such an early hour was thankfully available and willing to assist Nick. Quickly asking the police where Nick would be taken I gave Mr Green the address and begged him to get there as soon as he possibly could. His voice, despite being disturbed at 7 am, sounded calm and confident. It was clear to me that he'd walked this way before. He carefully instructed me to tell Nick to ring him once at the police station. 'Write down my phone number,' he ordered, 'so that Nick can contact me. Don't give it to your husband on a piece of paper, it's amazing how such things have a habit of disappearing in police hands; make sure you write it on his hand before he leaves.'

It was a relief to have just a little support as our whole world crumbled before us; when apparently every person we'd ever known had turned against us, at least this unknown solicitor would advise Nick to a certain extent. Back to the lounge. Felicity was calm and the policewoman had made an effort to make friends.

'Well she might, with an audacious intrusion into our lives like this, the least the wretched woman could do was try to be pleasant.'

Then came the same questions and similar answers. Finally Esther came, holding my hand extremely tightly, she was only seven after all. Same questions, and then it was all over, and the girls could go back to their Shreddies.

I returned to the family room, off the kitchen. The police were loading videos into big brown paper bags.

'What is happening?' I cried in my head. 'This happens on telly, in *The Bill*, but not in our ever so average, law abiding, middle class set up.'

The police were taking videos Nick had recorded at Christmas for the children; home videos of their cousins in Australia; videos Nick's dad had made of us on holiday. They took Nick's computer too, discs, an unexposed film from Esther's camera and then the policewoman gave me a card with all their names on. She told me they were taking Nick to Horsham Police station, she didn't know the number but it would be in Yellow Pages.

'You'll need a solicitor.' I said to Nick, trying to sound efficient, 'I rung Robert Marshall who recommended Mr Green. I'll give you his number.'

One of the policemen gave an impatient cough. I grabbed a pen, pulled Nick's hand towards me and announced: 'There's no point in giving you a silly slip of paper you'll only lose it.'

I wrote the number clearly on the back of his hand, Nick was bemused, but had the sense not to comment.

The girls were upstairs brushing their teeth and hair, the police were anxious to take Nick away, but I remember I suggested a kiss for the girls. Nick quickly ran upstairs, closely followed by a policeman. 'I mean, what was Nick likely to do? Jump out of the window?' He returned, face contorted with grief. I'd never seen him cry before.

'They're all so sad,' he muttered.

I recall asking the police to look after him as they went to leave the premises, in retrospect it was a stupid thing to do, he was yet another criminal in their minds. I gave him a hug and a kiss, which was all very public, with three police people watching, but I didn't care, and then I watched him walk up the drive with a police officer on either side and one just behind. The sense of abandonment and isolation was overwhelming. I was left alone on the doorstep wondering: 'Will I see him again? Is he going to be locked away? What in heaven's name is happening?'

Waiting

I had tried to reassure the girls—no lies—explaining that obviously some huge mistake had been made, and that they had to get off to school now or they'd be late. All four were in tears. Emily and Jessica were adamant they didn't want to go. 'It's the best thing for you, keep everything as normal as possible.' I said reassuringly. 'Normal? Our lives will never be normal again.' flashed through my mind. It was a crisis of gargantuan proportions and I remember saying to the girls: 'We must pray about it.' Whether I had any confidence in God at that point I really don't know. But we all sat down where we were, there on the landing and I prayed straight from the heart. 'God, we don't know or understand what is happening. Please, please look after Dad and be with him and help us all to get through today. Amen.'

It reminded me of when Fluff, our first kitten, had been run over and the neighbour arrived to tell us. We sat on the floor of the hall, there in Oxted, all five of us in tears asking God to be with Fluff and help her either recover quickly or else not to suffer much pain. It had felt like the end of the world at the time, but it was nothing compared to what was happening now.

After the prayer it was a matter of putting on shoes and coats and getting into the car. I have no idea how we reached school. I cannot remember anything about the journey at all and am convinced that a guardian angel must have driven the car. I do remember as we climbed on board sensing something was wrong, but my brain wouldn't connect as to what it was, then it dawned on me that I still had my fluffy slippers on. 'Good grief, in all the confusion I'd forgotten to put on my shoes. Still no one's likely to notice and on a day like today it really doesn't seem significant.' On any other day I'd have been horrified at the omission, but today it made no impact on me whatsoever. The journey started. Initially silence: then Emily, my dear deep thinking one said, 'This is just like *The Railway Children*, isn't it Mum?'

'Yes, yes I s'pose it is.' I replied. But deep inside I thought how played down the shock, horror, stress and trauma was on the film when the father was taken away and hoped to goodness that we weren't in for the years of anguish that Roberta, Phyllis and Peter experienced.

'What is ahead of us?' I wondered. But for the life of me, I couldn't imagine. It was just dark, dark, oh so dark. The girls asked me what to say at school, and how to explain their distressed state. 'Don't say anything,' was my advice, 'absolutely nothing, act normal.' What a farce. But as the journey progressed, they settled down. Children are so stalwart. I think we even played I-spy.

Back home to an empty house. Everything, the walls, doors, carpet, windows, looked so normal. Did it really happen? I grabbed the telephone and rang my sister Rebekah. 'Hi, it's me.'

'Is everything all right?'

'No, are you on your own?'

'Well, the children are here … hold on a minute … OK. No one's listening, what's the matter?'

Rebekah was absolutely wonderful, she always had been good in a crisis. Bossy, overbearing and dominant at times, my older sister could quite easily crush me. On this occasion it was the reverse. She was aghast, shocked, and horrified at all I had to tell her, but concerned and comforting. She instantly took control.

'Put the kettle on,' she said firmly. 'Do it now, while I'm talking to you.'

And a little later she carefully instructed me to make a strong black coffee, which I did. I was shaking like a leaf and howling fit to burst.

Less involved and far more objective Rebekah discussed succinctly the need for a solicitor. On explaining that I had already found one, Rebekah was adamant, 'No, no I mean a proper one. One who knows what he's doing, deals especially with cases like this. Leave it with me, I'll ring Chris and he'll sort it out. Now do you need money for bail?'

'I've no idea,' I wept.

'Well ring me if you do,' she instructed. 'Now go and find something to do and I'll ring you back when I've spoken to Chris.'

What to do had been a problem that Tuesday morning after ringing Rebekah. In a crisis you usually turn to the police for help. The great macho British bobby was always there to save the day? Except on this occasion, the problem *was* the police. I was stunned: 'How could they believe such a thing? How many people supported these wild accusations?' But my most pressing concern was to find out what on earth was happening to my husband. Grabbing Yellow Pages I located Horsham police station. I got through to the custody suite and was told the solicitor had arrived and was with Nick.

The day dragged tortuously on; I tried to do some ironing. I put on the television in an effort to distract myself, but couldn't concentrate on it, couldn't cope with the noise and turned it off again. I rang the station again, Nick was being interviewed. I walked from room to room, dazed, shocked, crying; 'This can't be happening, it can't be true, everything yesterday seemed so fine, so normal.'

For a while I perched on the landing windowsill, tears streaming down my face.

'What are they doing to him?' I wondered. 'What is going on?'

My mind jumped wildly from one terrifying thought to another. 'Why had the girls said such things? Nick would never hurt anyone. Was there any truth in it? Why hadn't our friends warned us? Did everyone in Oxted believe them? How many people knew? What would our families think?' The chaotic mental state I was in made life almost unbearable. I couldn't settle and paced the floor.

'Nick had always been a friendly sort of person, but rape? It was inconceivable, impossible, ridiculous. Or was it? Was it just possible that in the hectic life style we had when the girls were tiny that he'd been frustrated, felt unloved, and looked for affection elsewhere?' It was the worst thought of all, and as quickly as it surged into my mind I endeavoured to crush it, but it took firm residence and refused to be dislodged. 'Surely I knew my husband well enough to know? He just wouldn't do anything of the sort. But men are strange, and perhaps when I was up to my ears with babies something went desperately wrong?' There was no one to talk to, no one to turn to and I screamed at God to help me in the awful mess I was in.

Lunchtime came and I tried to eat. The bread looked unattractive and tasted like cardboard. After what seemed like a hundred chews I swallowed my mouthful down and gave up the idea of eating. At 2pm the telephone rang, I pounced on it and was told that the solicitor was leaving the station and Nick would be brought home shortly. I took up my perch on the windowsill again. Never had time dragged more. I was desperate to find out what had happened, to be reassured that all was well, to be put in the picture, to learn how Nick had got on, but the clock hands were cemented in place and refused to move. An age later, when my mind was almost blank from exhaustion, he eventually arrived at 2.40pm, looking tired and shaken. Still escorted by the police, but only two this time, who came back into the house and took his work laptop and accompanying paraphernalia, then they finally left us alone.

What had happened at the police station, as Nick recounted it, sounded tedious, tortuous and devastating. Firstly, having handed over the contents of his pockets and removed his belt and shoes, Nick had been locked in a cell with 'Metcalfe assault' scribbled on the board outside. 'Why, oh why should an innocent man be taken from his home at the crack of dawn and locked in a cell?' I couldn't begin to understand it and was baffled, I'd seen it happen innumerable times on television, but never in my wildest dreams had I thought it might ever happen to *my* husband.

Nick had been left to stew for a short while and was offered breakfast and a drink of coffee by the custody sergeant. Eventually he was allowed to speak on the telephone to his solicitor who had already conferred with the officers and had ascertained a few basic facts regarding the accusations. He told Nick they were allegations surrounding Anita and Penny from as far back as nine years previously. He told Nick to demand a pencil and piece of paper and try to get down some pertinent dates. Nick, relieved to have something to do, spent an hour or so in his cell drawing a time line from when he had moved to Oxted to the present day with any possible relevant events he could remember. Incredibly, despite his rude awakening and pressurised surroundings, Nick had managed a very accurate set of facts which the police reluctantly allowed him to keep in the subsequent interview. Eventually he was called from his cell, and after a brief chat with the solicitor who was now at the station he was led to the interview room.

The police had then grilled Nick about youth work, all that he'd done, trips he'd made to Italy, demanded specific dates from years back and been aggressive in their questioning about anything he'd had to do with Anita and Penny. There were clearly multiple allegations of rape and sexual assault from Anita, several sexual assaults of Penny and to his surprise he also discovered that on a trip to Italy, Anita claimed she had seen him sexually assault another girl, Debs, although strangely the police had no statement from this girl to confirm the allegation. Repeatedly looking back over notes from previous interviews with the girls in question, the policeman bombarded Nick with a constant stream of questions referring to the alleged incidents. Nick was baffled. He hadn't been given the opportunity to read the accusations, and the continual curdling of fact and fiction made trying to answer the questions almost an impossibility. But at every hesitation DC Stephens, apparently assuming guilt, became more aggressive. Nick felt thoroughly threatened, how could he answer questions about incidents which he could not recall simply because they had never happened? Furthermore, who could accurately remember dates, times and conversations which were said to have taken place eight or nine years previously? Real events and conversations which he did remember had been subtly changed and embellished. Consequently each individual question involved him in deep thought and subsequent hesitation as he endeavoured to distinguish in his own mind the truth from the fantasy. It was a gruelling process which lasted for several hours. At the end of it he felt physically drained and mentally exhausted. He was totally confused as to how these bizarre fabrications had ever become a reality in anyone's mind. He'd told them the truth as far as he could remember it, denied rape, sexual assault and anything else in that line ardently and had eventually been discharged. He was on police bail, he told me, which meant he was free as long as he obeyed the conditions, which were that he had no contact with the two girls. The police also advised him to have no contact with anyone from Oxted, no telephone calls, letters, emails, or visits. The only parting instruction Nick had been given was to reappear at Oxted police station in eight weeks' time.

The police's advice was devastating. All we yearned to do was call our friends in Oxted and beg them to explain what was going on. We were desperate to get a fuller picture, to understand how the arrest had come to be made and what had been happening prior to it. We'd had little chance to form new friendships in Cranleigh, only having been there six weeks, with Christmas in between, so ninety per cent of our close friends were 'out of bounds' to us. It was bewildering, and frightening in the extreme and made both of us feel as if we couldn't be more lonely if we'd been stranded on a desert island.

Tuesday evening had been bizarre. We were trying so hard to do the 'mummy and daddy' bit with comments such as 'Had a good day?' emerging from our mouths with minimal meaning, focus or relevance as our daughters returned from school. Whether the girls noticed how distracted their parents were, is difficult to say. Emily and Jessica were quietish and clearly anxious; Felicity and Esther, oblivious to the gravity of the whole situation, chattered on merrily. Try as hard as I could, I was unable to get my mind round what to cook for dinner, and in the end it was a question of opening the freezer and grabbing the first thing that came to hand. Chicken nuggets, chips, beans and then ice cream. It all tasted like sawdust to us anyway, but the children enjoyed it.

Once the girls were in bed, we huddled together on the settee, words seeming pointless. Our world had fallen apart. The happy family that had been admired, respected and even envied by so many friends and neighbours had been shattered. Tears fell. At last Nick hoisted himself onto one elbow and said, 'You do realise how serious this whole business is, don't you?'

'Today's hardly been a joke.' I retorted indignantly.

'But the charges are cleverly concocted. It's not just any old sexual assault, you know, it's sexual assault of a thirteen year old. In the eyes of the law that's a child.'

'And?' I queried anxiously.

'Therefore,' continued Nick in a subdued tone of voice, 'according to the police I had sexual intercourse with a thirteen year old girl, so it's considered as rape, whether it was with or without consent.'

'But you didn't do it anyway.'

'I know that and you know that, but the police didn't seem convinced, I can assure you.'

'Do you mean,' I asked as my tired mind frantically tried to follow what Nick was telling me, 'that Anita, or whoever's behind her, has deliberately said these assaults were years ago to get you into more trouble?'

'Exactly,' replied Nick emphatically, 'and of course it's far more difficult to prove I'm innocent as it all allegedly happened so long ago. But it's an incredibly serious crime to be charged with, triple rape of a 'mere child'.'

'What exactly are you trying to tell me?' I enquired, with an added note of tension in my voice. There was a pause and I just knew something unpleasant was coming, though my exhausted and numbed brain had no idea what it was.

'I think what I'm getting at is, if this comes to court and if I'm found guilty, it's automatically a custodial sentence.' I looked at Nick, my eyes wide open in horror, my mind weaving this way and that in a tangled knot of confusion and fear, not knowing what to say or how to say it.

'Prison?' I thought. 'Please God.' I prayed desperately. 'No.' And I felt physically very sick.

I knew I just had to ask him, the question that had haunted me throughout the day, I couldn't live with it a moment longer, and although it seemed tortuously cruel after the day he'd been through it simply couldn't wait.

'Nick?' I said tentatively.

'Yes,' came the reply in a voice so fatigued that I wanted to cry.

'Can I ask you something?'

'Why not, the police have been asking me things all day, you might as well keep up the good work.' His tone was loaded with sarcasm, frustration and exhaustion. Deciding not to beat around the bush which would have been unfair to both of us and prolonged the agony, I came out with:

'Can you honestly put your hand on your heart, look me straight in the eye and promise me there is absolutely no truth in any of this nonsense? Because if there's even a hint of anything I think you ought to tell me. I'll stand by you whatever, but I need to know exactly how the land lies.' I'd said it and felt much more at ease having got the burden off my chest. But what would the response be? I waited anxiously, but wasn't kept long.

'Absolutely no truth whatsoever, I can assure you.' Nick was adamant. 'It's a complete load of nonsense. Half the facts are incorrect, the dates are miles out, and I would never ever commit the gross acts I'm being accused of, it's ridiculous.' Nick was vehement in his defence and I accepted his answer completely, partly because it was what I so desperately wanted to hear, and partly because I knew deep down that he was telling the truth.

That night we couldn't settle. We prayed as never before. Clasping each other tight we took turns in expressing our utter devastation, confusion and pain to The Almighty. Could he, would he help? Neither of us were certain. After what felt like hours I gave the quilt a huge tug and sighed.

'You can't sleep either?' Nick asked. 'Do you want a drink?'

'No, I'm fine. I just keep going over everything in my mind.'

'So do I,' replied an anything but sleepy Nick beside me. 'Try and get some sleep' he murmured lovingly, then after a pause, 'I don't know what we're going to do.'

The despair in his voice scared me and I bit my lip in a determined effort not to sob. Hours passed, I curled up nearer Nick and heard steady breathing. At last he'd settled, at least for a bit, but my mind was in the fast lane and refused to take a break. We hardly slept a wink, we tossed, turned, got up for a drink, for the bathroom, and all the turmoil churned away within. The anxiety bubbled, festered, subsided and then resurfaced again as thought after thought reared its ugly head.

At breakfast on Wednesday we made a supreme effort to install a semblance of normality; and whilst the children's banter irritated us, the choice of cereals bemused us and the burnt toast exasperated us, the children were eventually deposited at the correct schools and we were together again. Still in a state of shock, still envisaging imminent prison, still aghast at the turn of events and not knowing which way to turn.

It was that Wednesday that I had gone for a walk, when Nick had gone in to work to talk to his manager about the situation. He'd hardly known what to say. For twenty years Nick had worked for Mainwave without so much as a hiccough, and there he was confronting his manager with the fact that the day before he'd been arrested for rape and sexual assault. It was an embarrassing, humiliating and worrying session. Nick's manager was aware of the problems before Nick even opened his mouth, because the police had been in the day before and taken copies of all his work discs, but he had no idea of the extent of the accusations and was horrified to hear them.

He was largely conciliatory with: 'Mistakes are often made, Nick, and quite regularly in the police force from what I hear. I can imagine a little what you're going through because about fifteen years ago, believe it or not, I was arrested on suspicion of being the Yorkshire ripper. I was an engineer at the time and serving the area the ripper worked in. My car was seen several times right near to where crimes had been committed. Thankfully all my records could be checked and my customer invoices, and so after going through the arrest and interview stage I was released, but it was scary stuff I can tell you. Take whatever time off you need until this blows over, but give me a ring if I can do anything. I can assure you very few people have an inkling about it and I'll ensure it stays that way.'

Nick had returned downcast and dejected. Was this the end of his career at Mainwave? What would people think? No one wants to work with a sex maniac. We'd both felt desperately unhappy, unsettled and frightened, and with no sleep the night before our spirits sank lower and lower as the day progressed. In the evening Nick announced he was going for a walk, on the theory that it would give him some exercise and help him sleep. He was never one for sitting around moping, and I knew that a vigorous route march might at least make him physically tired; if only that would help his poor overactive mind to stop whirring. I retreated to bed overwhelmed with confusion, fatigue and desperation, and cried quietly into my pillow. 'Don't let him do anything silly, please bring him back.' I was full of fear, apprehension and dread. Might he try and take his life? No, he was strong, he was made of sturdy stuff. But the doubts haunted me, I'd never seen him more miserable. He was beside himself with grief; he could see far enough ahead to know the effect this would have on the family, so might he just try and take a short cut, finish it all so that the rest of us could get on with our lives?

'Please, please God,' I mumbled into my tear soaked pillow, 'send him back. Don't let anything at all happen to him. We need him, we love him, please God.'

At 11.30pm to my immense relief I heard the key in the lock and knew he was home. He had sad bags under his eyes, looked pale and drawn, but he was home and we could face the future together.

Reminiscences

T he following days crept forward. Occasionally the telephone rang and each time I willed it to be the police acknowledging that they'd made a huge mistake and apologising. I also longed to hear from Rebekah with information about a solicitor. Nick had rung his work's legal department asking how to find a good solicitor and had been given the strange advice 'go and hang about at the law courts and see who you can find.' The idea was preposterous. Our total ignorance of anything legal meant that even if we were to visit a law court we wouldn't know what we were looking for or who to ask.

Mr Green had been supportive at Horsham police station but Nick had felt, as Mr Green had looked things up again and again in a manual he'd brought with him, that he really needed a specialist in the area. After all, it appeared as if it was going to be a case of Nick's word against that of the two girls', as the alleged events took place so long ago. We were desperate for expert advice, words of comfort and encouragement, we felt so ignorant of the legal field we'd unwittingly entered. We both longed for someone with knowledge to map out what lay ahead.

At last the telephone call came, about a week after the arrest. Rebekah informed me that Chris had located a Mr Dixon in Croydon who'd been recommended to him and she duly passed on the telephone number. Nick rang him instantly and after explaining his situation was promptly told: 'I think you'd better come and see me.' An appointment was made.

We felt as if life was on hold, as if the everyday things had become strangely irrelevant and insignificant. Meals held no challenge for me, though I normally love cooking, and had no interest for Nick, who generally enjoyed a good dinner. Meetings at work were tedious and he found cheerful communication with colleagues difficult to maintain. Nick's vital projects and important undertakings lost their urgency and became a bore on which it was hard to concentrate. For me, the housework was achieved on a good day, but it didn't seem to matter if not a lot was accomplished. The mechanism of living ground on, but held no fascination or interest for either of us.

On the Sunday, we went to church. I have absolutely no recollection of what was said, but I do remember during the first hymn noticing marks appearing on my hymn book and realising tears were streaming down my face. Glancing sideways at Nick, I realised that he too was similarly affected. We hoped no one would notice.

Perhaps the first week was the worst; children to school, Nick to work and then I would return home to a strong black coffee and a free fall of tears. One day it would only be for the duration of the drink, other days they just fell and wouldn't stop falling. It was at this point that I prayed as never before. 'God, I *know* you allow suffering, and I *know* it's for our good. But it hurts, Lord, so much. Please, please help Nick, and help me get through today.' Then with a huge effort I would get up after my coffee and do something. Tidy the house, put the washing in; I drifted around in a nebulous way unable to concentrate, no motivation and minimal willpower. Often cascades of sorrow gushing over my pale cheeks throughout the activity. Of course, the lack of concentration had its consequences. Out shopping I ambled round the supermarket picking up this and that without a clue as to what was needed in the cupboard for the next week. Strange occurrences on the housekeeping front became a normality. One day there was no toilet paper. The girls were told 'not to fuss, just use tissues'. Food went off in the fridge because it was forgotten about instead of eaten up. Clothes were left in the washing machine instead of being hung out to dry, and in the tumble dryer instead of being put away. All the time the weight of the recent occurrences, the pressure of the unknown future, weighed down on me like an oppressive black sack resting on my shoulders. Occasionally it seemed a little lighter, but generally it was there, heavy, imposing, restricting every action, limiting rapid movement and forcing rests, oh, so frequently. The only freedom I had was to think, and that I did night and day, drifting forward into the future and the potential horrific scenario; remembering back to that fateful Tuesday morning and drifting far far further to my earliest memories of Anita, of Penny, and pondering for hours on end how our friendship could possibly have resulted in this.

I remembered that it wasn't long after Esther was born that we'd started running the youth group. The Oxted church was a bit short of young couples at the time and even before we were asked it was obvious that it was coming. We loved youngsters and despite the fact that we had little experience, our four being seven or under, we'd taken it on. I recalled that it had all been rather hectic. Planning a programme, something active on a Saturday night, quite often out and about, and then a more civilised session on a Sunday evening, usually in our lounge. Yes, the youngsters had felt at home in the lounge, treated it like home, let their hair down, made their own drinks, got out the biscuits. There'd been many good times, happy relaxed sessions, discussions often rotating round the teenage interests: music, drugs, drink, sex, boyfriends, girlfriends, television and the inevitable moan about parents. My shoulders relaxed a little as a flood of happy memories filled my mind. Some of those Saturday trips were wild; a midnight swim in the sea, overnight hikes, sleeping under the stars; some were less adventurous, badminton, swimming, ice skating, bowling, first aid. 'How did we cope with all that and four young children?' I questioned, and then reminded myself; 'Still we were younger then and fitter.' It had been incredibly busy, never a spare moment, no television, rarely socialising, just work for Nick and then planning outings in the evenings and housework and kids for me and trying to provide back up for all he did. It was certainly a challenge. Then of course, the youngsters would pop in and chat, often for a whole evening, or during the day if they were at college. They seemed to have nothing to do while we were up to our ears. I wondered how many cups of coffee and drinks of squash I had provided over the years? How many biscuits were eaten? I remembered that I never offered home-made cakes because they were always eaten far too quickly!

As I reminisced I involuntarily sighed. The young people often chatted to me when they popped in during the day over a cup of something. Invariably I was doing something else at the time, ironing, cooking or had a child tucked under one arm. It was so chaotic, Emily doing play dough, Jessica colouring, Felicity in the process of being potty trained whilst I was trying to supervise all that and discuss intelligently GCSE options, or the latest boyfriend crisis or how unreasonable parents were. I grinned at the recollection, and then my shoulders dropped again. 'And where does Anita fit into all this?' I wondered .

I thought back to Anita's first attendance. Alice brought her, of course.

Alice was in to bringing friends, she'd brought loads of new people, some had continued sporadically, others just came the once, and one day she turned up with Anita and her twin sister, Jasmine. Years ago that was, Jasmine was more organised, dominant, and self possessed. Anita had seemed a bit scatter brained, very sweet, but needing to rely on people. When was the first time she'd come? Oh yes. That memorable day trip to the Isle of Wight. But the fact that two new girls had joined them on that occasion had paled into insignificance because of the way other events had taken over. 'That was a day and a half,' I recalled. Nick had arranged for everyone to meet at our house at 5.am, an unearthly hour. They'd all duly appeared and set off shortly afterwards for Portsmouth. But it hadn't been much later, I had gone back to bed when the door bell rang and there stood Esther Brookes in dressing gown and slippers.

'Have they gone?' She asked.

'Tony's left behind his insulin and I don't know how he'll manage without it.' She said in a frantic tone.

'Oh right,' I'd replied firmly, trying to sound tranquil and in command of the situation,

'I'll ring the ferry port and make sure Nick knows, they might be able to get him something at a chemists en route?'

'Perhaps,' she had responded doubtfully.

'Esther was a lovely lady,' I thought back. 'but a born worrier and having a son like Tony didn't exactly help. Poor Tony!' Tony Brookes, a severe diabetic as an infant, had spent most of his early childhood years in hospital and even after that, had had quite a number of crises in which an ambulance had been summoned and the poor lad had been rushed to hospital. So now, he'd gone on a day trip to the Isle of Wight without his insulin and Esther was clearly extremely anxious. From then on the day had gone from bad to worse. I rang Wightlink, and a very pleasant young man informed me that one ferry had just left with no Nick Metcalfe checked in and another was due to leave in an hour. They'd ring back, he'd assured me, if Nick checked in for that one. I had wondered how the whole group had managed to miss the first ferry, traffic jam perhaps? And then I'd decided to ring the harbour police to ask them to look out for Nick's party too. They were very sweet and promised to keep an eye open for Nick's van. What make was it? What colour? As soon as they spotted it they'd get him to ring me.

For a brief while all seemed under control. But no telephone call came. Wightlink were adamant that a Nick Metcalfe hadn't boarded any ferries before midday and the police hadn't seen the van. 'That day was one of the slowest in my whole life,' I remembered. 'At least it was until all this mess had happened.' I had willed the telephone to ring but nothing had happened. All I could think was that Tony had been taken ill before they ever reached the ferry terminal and that the whole group of them were sitting, worried to bits, in a waiting room at a casualty department somewhere. Or that there'd been a car crash. But surely I would have heard if there had been?

That day had crawled by, the children blissfully unaware of the turmoil in my mind. By lunchtime when the telephone hadn't rung, I had tried desperately to persuade myself that no news was good news, but I wasn't really convinced. The afternoon was equally tortuous with a frantic act to appear normal for the kids but alarmed and anxious underneath. Once the children were in bed all I could do was wait. I found it strange how I couldn't concentrate because I was so wound up. The programmes on television didn't hold an atom of interest and as for reading, the book could just as well have been in Arabic as the latest John Grisham for the interest I took in it.

I remembered at last hearing the van chug into the drive at 11pm that night and flying out to meet Nick to find out what had happened. 'How's it all gone?' I asked anxiously hoping I didn't look as traumatised as I felt.

'Fine,' Nick had replied with one of his schoolboy grins. 'One of the best trips we've ever had. Everything went according to plan and everyone seemed really happy.'

A wry smile crept over my face, as I remembered opening and shutting my mouth like an astonished gold fish before stuttering, 'Was Tony OK?'

'Fine, why shouldn't he have been?'

Out it all came in a torrent of tension and tears. Nick could hardly believe it. He'd caught the early ferry, but being foot passengers they didn't have their tickets closely examined; the group had just waived them in front of a ticket collector and been signalled on board. And as for the police not seeing the van, they'd parked right behind the police station! 'If the officer you'd spoken to had bothered to look out of the window he'd have seen the jolly van parked right outside!'

Tony had been fine too. He'd realised he'd forgotten his insulin, but wasn't a bit bothered. He was careful what he ate and had had a great day. He did say if his mother realised he'd forgotten it she'd go ape; but then, in his words she was a professional panicker anyway, so he wasn't going to worry!

What a relief it had been hearing Nick talk like that, and realising that all the problems and anxiety had been at this end, and the trip itself had been a huge success. 'That's probably why Anita and Jasmine had continued to come, because their first experience had been such a good one,' I pondered. They'd been intermittent that first year, not always together, more often on Saturdays and occasionally on Sundays. Everyone liked them, perhaps Anita in particular because she was forgetful, needed encouraging and supporting; Jasmine was far more independent.

'Then there was the sponsored swim,' I recalled. It was nothing to do with the youth group, it was Emily's brainchild. She'd been told about the Charity Swim at the local pool by her school teacher and was anxious to participate. She needed a team of six. With the gift of hindsight I realised they were all a bit young; but at the time we wanted to support their enthusiasm and the good causes. Emily had got her friends Keri and Nicky to swim, and Jessica, only nine, had been very keen. Nick had said he'd do it and they'd need a sixth swimmer. I can't remember if we'd asked anyone before Jasmine; probably we did as we didn't know Jasmine and Anita that well then. But in the end we were getting desperate and Nick rang the twins up. Jasmine tended to be more sporty, so Nick had asked if she was willing to be the final member of the team. She wasn't free on the appropriate night and had suggested Anita. Not only was Anita available that night but seemed really enthusiastic. So Emily had the requisite number of swimmers to make a team and signed up to participate.

The great day came and the girls were buzzing with excitement. Nick began to wonder what he'd taken on, and how many lengths he'd end up swimming when the girls flagged: but there was no turning back and off he set, leaving me with the little ones. But they managed it; they reached the target of forty lengths in the time, though it hadn't been easy. Jessica was stalwart but alarmingly slow, Emily had the stamina but not the speed, Keri and Nicky had done OK and poor old Anita had got cramp and had had to be hauled out leaving Nick to do the lion's share in quite a short amount of time. He'd torn up and down the pool and done it. 'Of course he'd done it, he was always one to accept a challenge.' I thought. 'Gracious me, he wouldn't have been running the youth group if he hadn't wanted a challenge.' He'd done it and returned with some very tired little girls and looking like death warmed up himself. But Anita's cramp had proved more of a problem than we'd realised.

Apparently a lady had appeared claiming to be a physiotherapist and had tried to massage the foot, causing Anita a lot of pain. She'd then hyperventilated and an attendant at the pool, supposedly trained in first aid, thought she was having an asthma attack and had given her oxygen. An ambulance had been called, but in the end she'd been helped home and not felt hospital was necessary. No one was aware that ankle problems were to plague her for the next eighteen months or so.

Support

As I tidied the bedroom I punched a pillow irritatedly and plonked myself on the bed. What had I achieved since the girls went to school? Dusted two bedrooms ineffectively and absentmindedly, oh yes and washed the breakfast things. I used to whistle round the housework and then have friends round, go visiting, help at school and generally live a hectic and fulfilling life. But that was before, in the previous life, the life that would never be lived again in the same haphazard and frivolous manner. Now social contacts were kept to a minimum; after all if people saw my pale, distracted face they wouldn't have to be Sherlock Holmes to guess there was a problem. The police had told us not to contact our friends in Oxted and having lived there for nine years and only recently moved it was obvious that that was where the majority of our associates were, but they were out of bounds.

So all I could do was think, and thinking wasn't helpful or uplifting. Thinking drove you mad, trying to work out why Anita had done such a thing, or whether she had been encouraged to do it. Was she persuaded by someone else? And if so, who? The whole thing was crazy. What did she expect to get out of it? Financial remuneration? Was there such a thing in a rape case? Surely not. If Nick was found guilty the punishment was a custodial sentence not a fine. What was to be gained by concocting these lies? What had induced her to go to the police with such bizarre allegations? Had she fantasised, or perhaps hallucinated in hospital as a result of the drugs she had been given for her foot?

My mind drifted back again to the Swim. Following that incident at the swimming pool Anita had been in and out of hospital for nearly a year. It was terrible. At times her foot had swollen up, sometimes it went really black, and certainly at one point amputation had been mentioned. Poor Nick had felt responsible. He hadn't been, of course, all he'd done was ask her to swim, but he felt he'd somehow contributed to the year of pain she'd suffered. I completely understood how he felt, I'd probably have been the same or worse, we were both soft hearted and caring under our robust exterior. Nick had visited Anita quite regularly in hospital often taking other young people, including Emily once which made her feel very grown up and privileged. Then after her hospitalisation Anita had been on crutches for a while and in and out of the doctors. But at last her foot seemed to right itself which was a great relief to everyone in the group. She continued regularly coming to the meetings, enjoying them as much as ever. We had photos of them all playing water games in the back garden, dressing up for the Christmas party, singing silly songs in the Talent night. 'What on earth went wrong?' I thought.

My mind hopped on to Penny. She'd joined when she was considerably older. Fifteen? Or was it sixteen? Natasha had brought her, there was some connection with the Guides but I couldn't remember exactly what. So she must have come ages after Anita; again she enjoyed it instantly and rapidly became a regular. She got on well with everyone, was envied by quite a few because she was extremely musical. She played the piano without music, the violin grade eight and the clarinet. She certainly was exceptionally gifted. That was possibly why she hit it off with Anita, who was musical too, could sing like a lark and play the piano. They used to sit at our piano and play the most amazing duets, could pick up a tune just like that and were always in demand to accompany any singing we did. 'It gave them a good link with Nick too,' I thought. 'Well, not so good with the gift of hindsight.' The three of them, often with Andrew Townsend who was also musical, used to talk music together; Anita would sing new songs through for Nick so that he could teach them to everyone else more easily and Penny would accompany them on the clarinet to emphasise the tune. I remember those Sunday evenings being great fun with music and singing; everyone participating to a greater or lesser degree, but it did mean that Anita and Penny spent a lot of time with Nick. 'But there was always a room full of people all the time, nothing could possibly have happened, unless it was all in their minds? What they had wanted to happen? Had they had a crush on him, and regarded him as Mr Perfect because he could identify with them in their enjoyment of music? Aagh,' I thought thoroughly frustrated, 'this is insane. I've absolutely no idea what in heaven's name induced them to concoct their stories and trying to guess does not help. I must distract myself, go out shopping, choose what to have for dinner, put the radio on, anything rather than go round and round this crazy circle, it's getting me absolutely nowhere.'

But it was when I tried to do anything that the effort really began. My body felt weighed down by a thousand weights, movement was slow and I stopped regularly, flinging myself onto the nearest chair or bed, not because I was genuinely physically tired but more that the mental exertion of keeping my mind focused on what I should be doing was overwhelming. I had so much whirring round in my head that to propel my body forward adequately required such mammoth effort it was often just too much. Climbing the stairs was the worst. 'Never in all my life,' I thought, 'have I had to heave myself up these stairs hanging on to the rail like I am now.' But there was no alternative, jobs had to be accomplished, though inadequately and painfully slowly, and somehow life had to go on.

Nausea too afflicted me. My first panicky thought was that I might be pregnant, then gradually appreciating that that was highly unlikely I assumed it was strangely somehow due to the strain and stress. Sometimes it was worse than others, but much of each day I felt sick. Food had no appeal and maintaining the pretence of producing decent meals for the family proved nigh on impossible. Some days it was all instant stuff straight from the freezer, other days I'd manage to put together an omelette or shepherds pie: by the time it was ready I never fancied it and ate the meal simply as a matter of discipline and to appear normal to the girls. There were days when we all suffered from my lack of concentration and enthusiasm and the family were greeted as they sat down to eat with a somewhat lethargic: 'I'm sorry folks I started making spaghetti bolognaise before I realised I didn't have enough mince, so it's more tomato than anything else, you'll just have to make do!' If Felicity or Esther so much as opened their mouths to complain Nick was on them like a ton of bricks. He understood. Emily and Jessica had too much sense, ate what they were given and kept quiet.

Time dragged itself forward and help and support came from a marvellous selection of friends and relatives. Gradually news came trickling in from Oxted. The police had told people there not to ring us, but after the first few days there came first one and then another tentative telephone call.

'We were told not to contact you, but we did want to say …'

'The police said we shouldn't ring you but we needed to know how you were.'

Those telephone calls began to pump the life blood back into us. Slowly but surely we realised that our Oxted friends had not abandoned us and our spirits gradually lifted. We appreciated that God hadn't abandoned us either.

The first visitors who braved our company were Brian and Joyce Darnell, co-workers in the youth group in Oxted with us. The Saturday after the police raid, they came down. It was an amazing, stunning and encouraging day for the whole family. Brian and Joyce believed in us. They were going to stand by us, they thought the allegations ridiculous and had told the police so. On being interviewed by the police and told to have no contact with the Metcalfe household, Brian had been most indignant. 'Are you telling me it is against the law for me to visit my friends?' He'd asked, outraged. 'No,' had come the reply. 'But we're advising you against it at present.' 'Well, as it happens,' continued the exasperated Brian, 'I've arranged to go down this Saturday and collect their greenhouse, I assume you won't stop me?' Without further ado Brian and Joyce had picked up the telephone, rung us and informed us of their imminent visit. The greenhouse had long been promised to the Darnells but no date prearranged. Now we were only too thankful that it provided a legitimate excuse for us to see our friends and learn how everyone at Oxted felt about us. We'd been so isolated, felt so alienated and at last some physical contact was being made. We were so encouraged and thanked God for greenhouses for days afterwards!

Brian and Joyce were predictably wonderful. Older than us by ten years or so, they provided the stability we so desperately needed. Reassuring us again and again that many, probably the majority, of our friends in Oxted had total confidence in us and would support us come what may. It was an uplifting day. Joyce brought down sweets and cakes for the children. Nick and Brian worked together dismantling the greenhouse and it was almost a 'normal' Saturday for the girls. Many hugs were exchanged as Brian and Joyce left and our hearts were slightly lifted by the visible affirmation of faith in us. After four long, tortuously long, days feeling totally isolated, alone, alienated and probably despised by those in Oxted we were now reassured that was not a fair picture and there were those prepared to stand by us.

But Brian and Joyce also brought other more disquieting news of the day of Nick's arrest; it had also been 'swoop day' in Oxted. The police had visited all the homes of the girls who'd attended the youth group and interviewed the girls. They'd been asked loaded questions and the police had clearly been looking for support for the allegations. In fact they'd refused to take statements from the majority of girls, because they supported Nick and had nothing condemnatory to say. The church leaders had also been interviewed and the news had, of course, spread like wildfire.

Those in Oxted were simply astonished by the turn of events, horrified and confused; but the majority we were assured by far, much to our vast relief, didn't believe a word of the allegations. Cards then started arriving and flowers. A couple of the cards stated 'The police told us not to make contact with you, but we wanted to anyway.' I wondered just how far the deviousness of the police would take them. The flowers were beautiful: bouquets, pot plants, even some freesias from Jersey. In the end I lost count of how many Interflora callers I had, but it was so encouraging to know that so many people believed in us and had gone out of their way to demonstrate the fact. I didn't dare stand the cards up on the mantelpiece, anyone calling would be sure to notice them and enquire whose birthday it was and no one in the vicinity had an inkling what was going on in the Metcalfe household, we felt it was better that way. No one locally had any idea what we were going through. The flowers were a bit of a give away, but I carefully distributed them around the house in case of suspicion. Anyway, there weren't many callers and certainly none who made any curious comments.

As I cycled to school with Esther each morning I kept my head down and maintained a low profile. I didn't want to get involved in conversation with the locals and avoided everyone at all costs. Life had been shut down. No mums from school to coffee; how could you make trivial chit chat about schools, teachers, toddlers' potty training and SATS when a ten ton burden is sitting on your shoulders? We had few friends from the new local church to meals, for either we lied through our teeth when they asked how we were, or else we were obliged to pour it all out, and what would they think, people who hardly knew us? Neither option appealed, so it was best to keep visitors to an absolute minimum.

One or two stalwart friends from years back visited, listened, commiserated and made rather futile efforts at distraction, telling us how their Christmas had gone or what course their kids were hoping to do at University. But it fell on rather deaf ears. Not that the effort wasn't appreciated, it was; but it was so hard to concentrate, to drag our perception beyond ourselves, with foul slander and accusations behind us and a possible prison sentence ahead.

Then there was dear Auntie Grace, my father's sister. She'd always been close to me, interested in all I'd done as I'd grown up, fond of Nick and really very keen on the children considering she was a spinster. Being the older generation it might have been expected that Auntie Grace would not be able to handle the concept of police raids and allegations of rape. But not a bit of it, she was the most supportive of all. She rang daily just past nine, once I had delivered the girls to school and talked for as long or as short as was required. She was there to whinge at, to shout at, to cry to, or simply to be a diversion by recounting her latest successes in her local charity shops, or the antics of her elderly neighbours. Auntie Grace was a godsend, I appreciated her care, concern and interest so much, and came to rely on those telephone calls as lifelines to help me through each day. Even though Auntie Grace had never had much to do with men, she was genuinely anxious for Nick, sent him cheering and amusing cards and was keen to help in any way she could.

But all the help, cards, bouquets and telephone calls in the world didn't take the pain away. That nagging heavy burden which just wouldn't diminish at all. Nor would it stop the stream of anguished thoughts that flowed almost constantly. Perhaps the intensity eased a little as time went by, but the load never lifted, just lightened a fraction.

The day at last came for Nick to meet Mr Dixon. He was pleased to be doing something to start his vindication and I was comforted that, finally, someone would be looking at events from our perspective. Nick had the afternoon off work and knowing his way round Croydon a little, seemed unconcerned as to locating Mr Dixon's office. As I waived Nick off cheerily just after lunch I prayed fervently that he and Mr Dixon would build a good rapport and that we had found someone able to help Nick out of this crazy mess.

Nick returned about 6.30pm and sat down to eat with the family. It was exasperating for me to have to put the myriad of questions I had on hold, until Felicity and Esther had gone to bed and Emily and Jessica were busy with their homework. But, eventually, some peace arrived and Nick filled me in.

He'd found the office with no problem, sat in a waiting room for five minutes and then been shown into Mr Dixon's office. What was he like? Tall, slim, forties, mouse hair, moustache, friendly, perhaps a little obsequious. He'd treated Nick courteously and honestly which he'd appreciated. He'd said early on that he had confidence in Nick's innocence just from his whole demeanour, but also explained that cases like this were extremely difficult, the 'offences' having taken place so long ago and it resulting in a case of one person's word against another.

However, he gave Nick a vast list of jobs to do to start creating his defence, if the whole thing ended up in court, and also assured him he'd take him through every stage and ensure he wasn't trampled on by legalities. Nick had felt positive following the interview. He liked Mr Dixon, felt he was very 'on the ball' and was confident we were now in contact with someone who really knew his subject.

'How much is all this going to cost?' I enquired.

'A lot,' replied Nick. 'Mr Dixon will bill us in stages but if it goes to court it's in tens of thousands.'

'Good grief!' I exclaimed. 'Where are we going to get that sort of money from?'

'I've no idea.' said Nick emphatically, and I gathered that certainly, in the immediate, the matter was closed.

It was awful. In great missionary stories, super-Christians pray and money seems to drop out of heaven. But we weren't super-Christians, we were ordinary, anxious, scared and stressed Christians. Would God really help us through? Deep down, we knew he would. But quite where all the money would come from, if it were needed, was a different question. We prayed fervently that the case would be dropped, the lunacy and inaccuracies of the statements become apparent, and the whole thing disposed of once and for all.

Another police raid?

What had Nick done to upset Anita so much? What could be her reasons for concocting such a story? Apparently many of Nick's misdemeanours had taken place in Italy. But why there for goodness sake? He'd been stressed out beyond measure and wouldn't have had a moment to get diverted or distracted by the girls on the trip.

Nick had arranged two trips to Italy; taking the young people, but only those over sixteen, on working parties to alter a campsite in northern Italy so that it could be used for disabled children, to give them a break, a holiday and a feel for the big outdoors. The site was miles from anywhere, even the roads were dust tracks ten miles in any direction and the area was peace and tranquillity personified. Set in the centre of a vast deciduous forest, land had been cleared, wooden huts erected and a huge pond discovered. Many wild birds flocked to it, frogs were abundant, it was superb for swimming and various water sports for the more energetic in each party.

Each time Nick had gone, the group had been allocated different tasks. The first year it had been to creosote the huts and construct some play equipment for the children; the second time round it had been to get hot showers working and cut trees back to clear an area for football, rounders etc. The first trip had gone really well, so when another was mooted it was enthusiastically supported. But it had been a bit of a disaster from the start. The morning they were due to set off there was a telephone call to Nick from Esther Brookes. Tony had lost his passport, what should they do? Why was it always Tony? Clearly without a passport he couldn't go, that would leave an empty space and extra expense for the rest of the party unless it could be filled. A ridiculous thought at that short notice, but Penny had been round the night before wishing now she'd joined up; she'd enjoyed the previous trip so much she really wasn't sure why she'd held back on this one. I had given Penny a ring, 'You know you said you wished you could have gone to Italy last night?' 'Er, yes.' ' Well Tony's lost his passport and there's a free space. If you can be here in an hour all packed, plus passport, you're on'. And to our amazement her parents had given her the OK and there she was, large as life, beaming, less than an hour later.

But then Tony had managed to get a replacement passport, and the whole group had had to divert after their ferry crossing from Dover, to Zurich airport to pick him up. It was just after that detour that the gear box had gone on the van. It was horrendous for Nick, there he was stuck in Switzerland, responsible for thirteen teenagers with a vehicle whose gear box could only manage 1st, 2nd and 3rd gear. In the end they'd decided to potter on and reach their destination, which they did eventually, only to find the electricity supply had failed to the campsite so there was no hot meal or drinks or even hot water to wash in when they arrived.

'I don't think it was all bad,' I mused. I recalled that they got most of the work done and the youngsters had a whale of a time. It was only Nick who was stressed out trying to persuade the Italians to fix the van in double quick time. They didn't seem used to the concept of hurrying and even the night before they were due to come home the local Italian garage hadn't sorted it out. But somehow or other it was fixed and the group set off home, only to find the majority of tunnels through the Swiss mountains were out of action. They were held up again and again, their final delay being a lorry that had shed its load within sight of the dock. Nevertheless they'd managed to catch the boat by the skin of their teeth and had arrived home safely.

I remember they'd been on such a high when they eventually reached Oxted, that none of them had wanted to go home. They'd had squash and cakes and maintained the holiday spirit for as long as possible. In fact Anita, Penny and their friend Debs had lingered even longer than everyone else, playing the piano, the organ, singing and generally larking around. The atmosphere had been positively festive, triumphant and merry; so I was totally baffled as to what on earth had induced these girls to turn tail on Nick. After all, he'd worked so hard getting the trip arranged in the first place, accommodating Penny at the last moment, picking up Tony, getting the van fixed, and negotiating blocked tunnels and traffic jams. So why did they now maintain he'd been busy sexually harassing them whilst abroad? He'd not had time to give such a thing a thought. Surely the other young people would bear witness to that fact? Surely they'd all stand up for him and say he'd been busy with all the arrangements rather than assault? Anita maintained he'd put his hand down Deb's trousers, Penny reckoned he'd groped her bottom while plumbing in the showers. I felt it was all so crazy, it just didn't add up.

But then I worried; 'What if they didn't stand by him? What if no one took his side? What if rumours have been spreading over recent months and the stories are believed? What if our friends have turned against us? Aargh', I moaned out loud, causing the cat which was busy washing itself to jump and look mildly disconcerted for a full ten seconds, 'I can't handle this, I just can't.'

But I had to. Day after day there was the routine of getting the girls off to school, the jobs to be done, the neighbours to be smiled at and the shop assistants to be assured that, 'Yes, I'm fine, thank you. How about you?'

About a month after the raid, Emily and Jessica both played in a netball match at their school one Saturday morning. Not only was it an honour to be in the team, but it was good distraction for all the family. While the eldest two girls leapt around, marked partners and scored goals, Nick, I and the two younger ones went into Croydon shopping. We'd been given money for Christmas and had meant to spend it in the January Sales, but of course, with other distractions there'd been no opportunity. Felicity and Esther were not impressed with the shopping, played tag round the clothes stands and came alarmingly near breaking some valuable china ornaments near the kitchen department. But our purchases were finally made, two triumphant netball players retrieved and we made our way home. The car was full of incessant noise. Emily and Jessica bubbling over with: '…and she was really tall Mum, and I never thought I'd get the pass, but I did, and gave it to Ramona and she scored. Wasn't that brill?' 'And Dad, at one point Emma fell over, just imagine if she'd had to go off, we'd never have won, but she didn't. She had blood all down her leg, but she was OK and it was really good …' And on and on. The little ones pulled each other's hair, squabbled, squealed, I pleaded with them to behave all to no avail, and the riot continued. That is, until the car pulled into the drive. There, right in front of our house, was a police car.

'Oh no, what now?' exclaimed Nick in a despairing tone. I felt my heart rate increase and my legs weaken. Trying desperately to regain some sort of composure I suggested to Nick that we went in first and left the girls in the car. 'Good idea' he agreed. Once the front door was open Nick called out, 'Hello, anyone here?' No answer. He came out again and had another look at the police car, definitely empty. A pause. 'I think they must have gone next door.' He said with audible relief. Sure enough forty minutes later the car had gone with no intrusion into our household. It had been a truly frightful moment driving up the road and seeing that police car there. Would we ever be able to feel comfortable with the police again?

After the police car incident, the next hurdle was my birthday. It fell on a Saturday so there was no ignoring it as I had wanted to, and indeed had told a friend on the telephone, 'I wish I could forget about my birthday until this mess has been dealt with. I mean how are we meant to be even remotely happy with all this hanging over us?' However a birthday's a birthday to children whatever the circumstances and we both knew it. I had been dreading it; but in the end it had gone remarkably well. Presents in bed, a beautiful top and skirt from Nick, sweets from the littl'uns, note paper from the older two, many many lovely cards with understanding comments in like 'Do try and have a good day despite everything' and ' We do hope you have a special time, we'll be thinking of you.'

The morning had drifted by pleasantly enough, Nick had put up the climbing frame in the garden, something he'd been meaning to do for ages but hadn't been able to get his mind round; the girls did homework, Esther had her dolls' pram up and got under everyone's feet while Felicity had found a whistle and was provoking wrath on all sides. In the afternoon Nick had to sort out the indicators on the van which were singularly erratic; so the girls and I explored Godstone market and went to Tesco. There on Nick's instruction a large toffee pavlova was bought as a birthday gateau, carefully chosen by the four girls. Once home Felicity spent a happy half hour putting thirty nine candles into thirty nine holders and delicately arranging them on the cake. The others had suggested fewer candles now that Mum was over twenty one, but no other alternative was even faintly acceptable to the indomitable Felicity.

At tea, Nick had the job of lighting them, which he managed admirably without setting fire to anyone or anything and without even burning his fingers. A cacophonous serenade of 'Happy Birthday to you' followed and then I blew them all out in one go amidst shouts and cheers from the family. 'Weird,' I reflected, 'how there most definitely can be moments of merriment whilst sailing in a sea of sadness.'

The evening was good, too. Emily had happily baby-sat while we went to the video hire shop. Bewildered by choice and with very different interests a selection suiting both of us proved quite a challenge. Nick was keen on action packed drama, James Bond or something more light hearted whilst I wanted a good story, perhaps with a tinge of romance, nothing too slushy or sexy but a good yarn. In the end we settled on 'Six days and seven nights.' The stereotypical story of an unlikely couple getting stranded on a desert island, who have opposing views on everything, but nevertheless end up falling in love. It suited both of us. Snuggled up next to Nick on the settee it was possible to put life on one side and just enjoy the birthday evening together.

Coping—or trying to

'Those moments were good,' I thought back. 'When you could be normal, not haunted by recent happenings, relaxed, settled.' But now six weeks on I realised they hadn't come very often and the tension and stress we were under was beginning to show. Not on the surface I hoped, but in a hundred and one niggling ways. Concentration and motivation continued to be a challenge for me at home. I would still stop halfway through dusting a room and gaze uncomprehendingly out of the window, or flop into an arm chair and dissolve into tears. Everything was such an effort. I'd been an enthusiastic netball player as a teenager, and housework, whilst it hadn't been particularly relished, had always been done with a zest and a vigour that was now completely lacking. Instead of bounding up the stairs two or three at a time, I hung on to the banisters and heaved myself up, dragging one leg ponderously after the other. Instead of hoovering briskly with the vacuum cleaner in one hand and a cup of coffee in the other, I'd take a break, plonk down in a chair with a numb mind and look blankly ahead. Instead of having the radio on loud while cleaning the kitchen floor, and commenting out loud if a point was made in a discussion that I happened to disagree with, I couldn't raise the enthusiasm for the radio and plodded round in silence, pushing the floor mop backwards and forwards with the motion of a mechanical moron.

Also there were the headaches. I rarely told Nick about those, but a day hardly went by without one. Still, I had to keep going for his sake, and the girls', so the Paracetamol and Nurofen were regularly raided and I kept up a brave face. Not that Nick was exempt physically: two fearful fluey colds—he'd only ever had one before in the sixteen years we'd been married—and what was perhaps worse, itching. It carried on all day, he said, but was worst in the evening. No rash, just intense itching on the chest and hips. When he finally got round to telling me I poured systematically over all our medical books and came to the obvious conclusion. It was stress related. But what could I do about it? I was desperate to relieve even the slightest pressure on Nick and knew he'd never visit the doctor.

I trundled down to the local chemist the next day and saw the pharmacist, a grey haired man with half glasses on the end of his nose. He listened attentively and picked up a packet of Piriton. 'These are what he needs,' he pronounced. 'One when he gets in from work and one at bed time for three to four days, by then it'll hopefully be easing off and he can just have the one when he gets in from work. Of course,' he added wryly, looking me straight in the eye, 'if it's stress related, the only real answer is to remove the stress.' 'That's easier said than done' I retorted smiling. 'Little do you know,' I thought quietly to myself as I paid and made my way out of the shop.

Church friends, both locally and from Oxted continued to show love and concern in a variety of ways. A fact that really kept us both going. Knowing that we weren't in the battle alone, although it felt like it at times, was so reassuring. One friend came for coffee every two or three weeks and always brought a huge box of 'goodies' with her. These ranged from shower gel and floor cleaner to packets of cereal and jars of marmalade. It was fun unpacking the box, and indeed we greatly enjoyed sampling the various products, but what meant the most was that she understood. Kate knew what an effort it was to concentrate on shopping, running the home and feeding the family, and consequently helped to lift the burden whenever she could. Not only that, but it also saved us valuable pounds, something we were desperate to do as the legal expenses were ever increasing. Other friends too would arrive on the doorstep and say; 'I'm not stopping, but I just thought this might come in handy,' and pass across a home-made fruit cake, chocolate cake or tin of biscuits. Such gestures of love meant more to us than words can ever say.

On one occasion an Oxted friend, Anne Darlington brought us a delicious fish pie. We ate it with relish that night. That is, all except Felicity, who, fussy at the best of times did not enjoy it and made a point of saying so. A few weeks later we met up with the Darlingtons for a country walk and we were relating the multitude of gifts we'd received. Felicity, never backward in coming forward, joined in the conversation with; 'You won't believe what someone gave us. Fish pie, it was disgusting!' Although I tried to smother her mouth with my hand, the damage was done and I was totally mortified! Thankfully Anne found it highly amusing and roared with laughter, and I think we were forgiven, but the embarrassment lived with me for weeks. On another occasion Nick's parents were down for the day and try as I might I could not think what to give them to eat. The more I thought about it the more my mind drew a total blank. It was frustrating and exasperating and just one of the many side effects of the tension we were under. It was mid morning, and the in-laws were due at lunch time, when Godfrey and Davina Smythe, a middle aged couple from the Oxted church, unexpectedly called by. They claimed they were just passing and wanted to bring us 'a little something.' Davina presented me with a casserole containing eight beautiful steaks, all ready cooked and in a delicious gravy. I was breath taken, but before I had a chance to say anything Davina came out with; 'I've no idea how much you all eat, so I do hope I've done enough.' I was almost in tears and totally unable to express my gratitude, but in that and in a hundred and one incidences we saw God's caring and loving hand at work in a most extraordinary and inexplicable way.

When I returned from doing the weekly shop seven or eight weeks after Nick's arrest I found a piece of paper lying on the mat. Snatching it up I read it with increasing anxiety and a mild air of suppressed excitement. It was headed; 'Surrey Constabulary', and stated: 'Mr Metcalfe, your computer is now ready for collection, please give me a ring.' It was signed by the detective constable on the case. Of course, the police wouldn't have found anything because there was nothing to find however hard they looked. So might we be nearing the close of this foul chapter of our lives? I was frantic with anxiety, abandoned the shopping and grabbed the telephone. Of all the days Nick had to work in Birmingham, why did it have to be this one? Why had he switched off his mobile and left his answer telephone on instead of responding? What if the DC's shift finished soon, then we'd have to wait until tomorrow and we've had enough of waiting. Answer your telephone Nick, please. Desperately trying to keep calm I put the kettle on, resolved not to try ringing for another fifteen minutes, and went out to the van to retrieve the shopping.

Fifteen minutes proved far too long to wait but however many times I dialled Nick's number all I heard was: 'Hello, this is Nick Metcalfe on Tuesday the third of March. I'm sorry I'm unavailable at the moment but if you would like to leave a message I'll get back to you as soon as possible.

Thank you.' The shopping was slowly put away and by the time that was done and there was still no contact with Nick, I assumed his telephone wasn't working. I rang Directory Enquiries and then a Mainwave help desk, all to no avail. I stamped my foot with irritation on the kitchen floor. 'Why, oh why, when at last something was happening did Nick have to disappear off the face of the earth?' Unfortunately the help desk had no success in tracking Nick down, they were courteous and helpful, but the telephone call proved to be a futile one. All they could promise was to put a message on his system. 'But surely,' I felt, 'if he's looking at his system he should be answering his phone?'

None of my days seemed to pass particularly quickly, but this one dragged exceptionally slowly. At last when the shopping was all put away and I had had my lunch, the telephone rang. I pounced on it. To my immense relief it was Nick and I relayed the news. It did not come as a surprise to him as someone at work had contacted him earlier that day saying that his home computer equipment had been dropped off at work along with various bits the police had confiscated from Mainwave. 'Nevertheless,' said Nick a little breathlessly, 'I'll still give DC Stevens a ring, we might at last find out what's happening. I'll ring that solicitor Chris recommended too and give him an update.' But I was too impatient to wait for Nick to make two telephone calls and insisted on being contacted after the first. 'After all,' I argued, 'I'm in this fix as well and as desperate as anyone to know what is going on.'

I'd hardly put the telephone down when it rang again. 'It's only me' said Nick's voice.

'You were quick.'

'Yes well it doesn't take long to say the stuff's been dropped off at work.'

'But didn't you ask …?'

'Yes, yes, course I did', interrupted Nick a little impatiently. 'But the rat reckons he's not at liberty to disclose any further information. I'll call the solicitor and ring you again.'

'OK thanks' I said in a rather subdued tone. So we were none the wiser after all that. Still it was good to have the computer back, Nick would find that invaluable at work and Emily and Jessica would be delighted as it was a near essential aid to homework, not to mention with their music, as Nick had typed in piano accompaniments for their clarinet and violin pieces, and they'd been hard pressed without it and had tried desperately not to moan. It was good to have that back anyway. But what were the police playing at? Why wouldn't they enlighten Nick a bit? After all they couldn't possibly believe the wild accusations made against him, could they?

The telephone rang again. 'Hi, it's me,' came Nick's voice. 'I've spoken to the solicitor and it looks as if he's had a hand in getting all the computer stuff back, because of the girls needing it. What's more, surprise, surprise, they found there isn't anything dodgy on it.'

'I could have told them that,' I said indignantly.

'I know, but at least nothing's been planted on it. With everything else that's going on, anything could happen. Anyway,' he added with a touch of humour, 'I just hope he benefited from reading all my youth group epilogues that were on there.'

'I don't imagine he bothered to read any of that.' I replied despondently.

'Also,' he continued. 'we've got a definite date for me to go to Oxted police station, it's March the 12th.' Before I could comment he went on, 'That's the good news, the bad news is that there're three allegations now against me.'

'There can't be!'

'Well there are.'

'Who's the third?'

'No idea, Stevens wouldn't even tell the solicitor, goodness knows why, he'll have to at some point.'

'This is ridiculous.'

'I know, it's crazy, isn't it? But the solicitor said the police might well be prepared to disclose the accusers' statements on request a week or so before I attend the police station, so he's asked for them and will chase it in a few days' time. So, in a week or so hopefully I'll know a bit better what exactly I'm up against. He did say it was another minor complaint, not a major one.'

'Well I s'pose that's a good thing.' I said, frantically trying to be positive and supportive, but feeling deep down, despair overwhelming me, engulfing me in a terrifying way I'd never previously experienced.

I put the telephone down and sank to the floor exactly where I was. These last weeks I'd felt I'd been imprisoned within a tortuous box with no escape. Then today I'd just glimpsed a ray of light, of hope, as I'd imagined the lid of the box beginning to give a little; but instead of hope and light; things had become even blacker than before and I sobbed pitifully as I felt the walls of my box closing in on me.

Cleared or charged?

A week before the 12th March the police chose not to reveal the identity of the third witness. According to Mr Dixon, Nick's solicitor, the police felt that the Oxted church was such a close community that the witness might be put under pressure. The confusion and anguish was set to continue right up to the very last moment, when all would be revealed at the next interview.

'This week will be a long one,' I anticipated, 'it's going to stretch like a piece of elastic, like a kid's chewing gum, stretch and stretch and then, oh help, it'll go ping. I've got to help Nick, it'll be so tough for him waiting and waiting. I must think of something.' So, the following day I said in an assertive voice: 'You need a target, Nick.'

'What?' He asked quizzically.

'An achievable target to work at this week, and I've got the answer.'

'Go on,' he replied slowly with a wry grin. He hadn't been married to me for sixteen years without knowing that when I had the bit between my teeth there was absolutely no stopping me.

'You know how awful the spare room looks with the green paint?'

'Err, yes.'

'Well in case anyone comes to stay, I think it should be the first room we, well you really, decorate. You know Kate's been down here quite a few times since we moved? Well she's told me exactly what colour it should be, so I reckon you could go out tomorrow and get the paint. I can show you which shade she recommended from the Dulux chart.'

'OK.'

Kate was a close friend of mine, a mother of three and passionate about home decorating, colour co-ordination, textures, fixtures and fittings. She'd been the perfect person to advise us, particularly as Nick and I were far too distracted to be able to think about such things.

Normally Nick would have argued. He wasn't the sort of man you dictated to, and he certainly never encouraged me to take the upper hand. To be fair, he used to listen to my opinions and rarely dismissed them out of hand, but liked to be the final decision maker, even if it was concurring with his wife. But at the moment he was subservient, submissive, passive to a point of worrying me, but I knew that once he got his teeth into the decorating, he'd come up again. A little bit of his old spirit would return.

I was right too! The week leading up to the 12th wasn't the pure hell I'd envisaged. There was the rubbing down to do, filling, undercoating, the coving to paint, the new light to put in, and each night after work, Nick beavered away. He was going away for work, three days after the 12th, so he knew the job had to get done. He worked late, one o'clock one night, one forty five another. 'Probably,' I thought, 'he might as well be doing that as coming to bed and tossing and turning half the night.' Certainly he was getting tired; and one night he fell fast asleep while I was still talking to him.

At last the long awaited day came. The arrangements were all in place. Angie, one of the few local church people who knew what was going on and who'd been so supportive, would have the children after school, excluding Felicity who was going to a sleep over at a friend's. She'd pick them up, look after them, feed them and hang on to them until Nick or I rang. What a blessing it was, I thought, that we'd made such good friends at our new church so soon after moving house, otherwise we'd be completely stuck now.

What was more, Angie and her husband Peter seemed to totally accept Nick's innocence. It was peculiar, but wonderful, that people who we hardly knew, who we'd met only a couple of months previously, were prepared to be so incredibly supportive.

As Nick's visit to the police station approached, the church members at Oxted and indeed other family and friends were daily constant in fervent prayer. Many of them hoping and praying, as I was, that the whole thing would soon be dropped. But they too envisaged the larger picture, a thing it was impossible for us to do. They prayed earnestly that this case would remain out of the newspapers, for everyone's sake, Nick's, mine, the church, but especially for Emily, Jessica, Felicity and Esther's sake. Godfrey Smythe's letter of spiritual encouragement arrived before March 12th. Nick and I valued this, and a number of others he wrote, very highly indeed.

Chapter 8

Woodpecker House
Forest Lane
Hurst Green
Surrey

5 March 1999

Dear Nick and Melanie,

Hello, here I am again. Just wanting to let you know that you are not forgotten and that Dav and I are still thinking and praying for you. And of course, wanting to lead you to Jesus.

I have so wanted to write to you as you face the long agonising wait until 12 March. I have prayed and prayed that God would tell me what to write, and one text only has come to me '…they who wait upon the Lord shall renew their strength; they shall mount up with wings as eagles; they shall run and not be weary; and they shall walk and not faint.' (Isaiah 40 v.31 KJV). Or as in the NIV '…they who hope in the Lord …'. Now I do not know why this particular verse came to me, for, to be honest, I reckon that you feel like anything but eagles at this time. I guess that you feel in the mire at the bottom of a pit. So I, and you, will just have to take it as it says, or else call God a liar.

Let's have a look at it backwards. 'they shall walk and not faint.' That's you, Melanie. Many a day you feel so down, so low, that you cannot face the walk around the Supermarket. When it is just too much to keep up that 'smile' when your heart is hurting fit to break. When you dread meeting an 'acquaintance' who asks you 'How are you?' – and you cannot, dare not reply. Oh to be able just to WALK.

And 'they shall run and not be weary'. That's you Nick. Always under pressure at Mainwave to run, run, faster, faster. Oh for stronger legs.

Listen. God is saying you shall mount up on wings as eagles. How? When? If you hope in the Lord and wait on Him. Do you hope in the Lord? DO YOU? I tell you, you can have, you need have no other hope but in the Lord. Of yourselves you are nothing. You have no power and no prospect. Friends are no good either, no matter how understanding or well-meaning they may be. Only the Lord is going to get you out of the pit.

First of all you must hope. That means trust- believe what He says. Then you must wait. Wait for His timing. Can you do that? Can you hang in there, until He wants you out?

But, you say, why does God want me in this pit? What is there in it for me? It is horrible and I don't like it. WHY DOESN'T GOD GET ME OUT NOW? I cannot answer that. But I plead with you to trust Him and wait on Him, for I am convinced that He WILL bless you through even this most horrible experience.

Last night I prayed 'Lord, what am I doing here? Is this really the right verse? Am I helping with all this prattling on?' He said, 'Carry on—stick it out'.

So what's all this about eagles wings? Well, eagles rely on the wind to sustain them. The wind of the Spirit?? Is there wind down the bottom of a pit? (I really had trouble with this one, for God would not let me change the first part of this letter where I had said you were in a pit.) Well maybe there are eddies of wind…. But you have to launch yourself and flap your wings to get airborne again.

Baby eagles do exercise to strengthen their wings. They eat the food their parents give them, and they stretch up and flap. Maybe God is saying that if you feel you haven't enough power to face next Friday, then you should exercise your wings of faith and eat the food of God, and He will build you up strong. So trust Him for today. Don't get het up for tomorrow or next week. Do your exercises TODAY. Eat the food God brings you. Flap your wings in Satan's face. All is NOT lost.

Finally (and I went back to the Lord on this one too) maybe you have fallen out of the nest and your wings are injured. Then I am certain and sure that as you cry to Him, the Lord Himself will lift you up out of the pit of despair and onto a ledge in safety, where your broken bones will heal in time.

Do not despair, little eagles. God knows all about you. (I have told Him!!) He is near and He will not forsake you, for He loves you. Hope in Him, wait on Him, flex those wings of faith. You WILL fly.

Down in the pit my Saviour is with me
I will not despair.
For I know He will not test me
More than I can bear.

I will trust him, I will praise him
'till my wings are strong
To lift me out of this horrible pit
To the place where I belong.

God Bless—I am looking for you in the sky.
Godfrey and Davina Smythe

When I am low

When I am low
    All gets too much for me.
I cannot hope or think; or see
    The way ahead.
The days are endless battles that I lose
    And I sink so low that I would choose
    Any way out of the pit of despair
    To know that somewhere, someone cares…
Believe me, I get *so* low.

When I am low,
    Then Jesus comes to me.
It seems that somehow, only He
    Knows how I feel.
He talks to me and helps me face each day.
    The battles go on, but when I pray
    He strengthens and arms me for the fight.
    I know he understands my plight.
He cares, when I am low.

Do you get low?
    Does life get you on the run?
I tell the truth- there is only One
    Who can help
You must learn to accept the fact that you
    Have not the power to pull yourself through.
    You are defeated. He alone can give
    The strength to enable you to live.
But he's *near*, when you are low.

Are you low now?
    Then yield yourself to him.
Open your heart and let him in
    To take control.
Own him as Saviour and Lord of your life,
    To serve and follow him, even through strife.
    The Glorious Master, who sets you free
    To be the person he wants you to be—
At *peace*—no longer low.

G. E. Smythe
29 Jan 1998
Hebrews 13 v 20 & 21

'May the God of Peace ... equip you ... for doing his Will'

It was Red Nose day, possibly that helped for it provided plenty of distractions. Esther had been up early getting dressed in red trousers, red T-shirt, sweat shirt, hair ribbon, and, of course, a red nose. Felicity's school had been a little more restrictive; socks and hair ribbons only were to be red. Felicity, being the independent type, didn't fancy red socks, but duly had a red ruffle round her pony tail. Emily and Jessica's school didn't seem to acknowledge Red Nose day, which perhaps made them more aware of the activities of their parents. Nevertheless, they were all safely dispatched to school, Nick returned and changed. How smart should he be for an appearance at a police station? Perhaps jeans would make him look as though he were an older man trying to look young? Surely a suit was too formal? In the end Nick settled for smart casual, blue trousers and an open necked striped shirt with a navy fleece jacket. We downed a quick coffee, opened the post; quite a few letters from friends only too aware that it was the big day, and gathered the essentials. These included Nick's mobile phone to spread the news afterwards, notes that Nick had jotted down late the night before pointing out why the bizarre accusations were so unreasonable, money and sweets that I had bought. 'After all', I reflected, 'Nick's blood sugar must be maintained, and sucking a wine gum never did anyone any harm.'

Chapter 8

The journey to Oxted was uneventful. To my surprise Nick seemed calm, there were no erratic actions in his driving or impatient splutterings at traffic lights that seemed inclined to linger too long on the red.

'What exactly are the arrangements you've made with Mr Dixon?' I asked.

'I'm meeting him outside at 10 to 11.'

'Good, because I'd like to meet him, so I'll just pop over, shake his paw and introduce myself. After all it can't harm his opinion of you to see a real live wife standing by you.'

'OK'.

In the police station car park there was one vacant space which Nick adeptly reversed into, though it left us both wondering where the solicitor would park if he wasn't there yet. We were five minutes early so we sat in the car in thoughtful silence before climbing out. 'Somehow,' I remember thinking, 'it can all seem quite distant and one can be detached from the reality and the gravity of all this until you actually arrive. But now we're here, it's really going to happen. The police are going to re-arrest poor old Nick, grill him, treat him like dirt and then either let him go or take him to court.' My stomach churned as these thoughts went through my mind, and I wondered how Nick was feeling. Holding hands on the gear stick we both prayed, 'Dear God, we don't understand why all this is going on. But please, give us strength and help Nick through this.' We had very little idea what lay ahead or how things would pan out.

'Can you see Mr Dixon?' I asked.

'No, I'll hang around outside 'til a couple of minutes to, then go inside. It won't impress the police much if I'm late, even if my solicitor is. Though, of course, he might be inside already talking things over, he said he might do that.'

'I'll wait until you go in, I'd like to see Mr Dixon if he comes.'

'Thanks.'

The square red brick building looked dour and ominous to me as we stood outside and as it began to drizzle we sheltered in the porch way of the police station. A car drove into the car park, and our heads quickly turned, I was aware that both our hearts were racing and our nerves jangled. 'Is that him?' I asked seeing a middle aged man in a suit walking across the car park.

'No, and it's one minute to eleven, so I'll go in.'

'I'll come in too.' In the absence of the solicitor I felt anxious to accompany him as far as I could. In our marriage up to now he'd always been the leading light, the strong one, the motivator, but now he suddenly seemed vulnerable, crushable, like a little mouse walking in the domain of feral cats.

Nick explained to the constable at the desk who he was and that he'd come to see DC Stevens, and was asked to wait. The police station lobby was bare. The walls were painted off-white, and there was a plaque attached to one, enlightening the world to the fact that the station had been opened by Lord Mayor somebody or other twenty years ago, as if anyone was interested. There was a map on the wall which Nick and I surveyed blankly. Looking at it for something to do but not seeing it. After what seemed an eternity the constable reappeared. 'DC Stevens will see you in a minute.' Another interminable wait. Then from a different direction a door opened and I froze momentarily as I recognised the face. There he was standing erect the man who'd come storming into our house two months ago and frightened the living daylights out of us all. He wasn't as tall as I'd remembered and had a pockmarked face, I hadn't noticed that at 6.30 am on the day of Nick's arrest. There he stood as large as life, and I felt terrified. 'Morning Mr Metcalfe, morning Mrs Metcalfe,' he said in a weaselly voice nodding at me. He was intent on appearing friendly but I wondered what evil intentions he had this time, and faintly acknowledged his nod. I grabbed Nick's arm, 'All the best,' I whispered, as I gave him a kiss and turned round. Nothing emotional, stiff upper lip. His whole future was in the hands of that man, but don't betray the emotion, I told myself, hang on in there, be strong for Nick's sake.

I walked out of the station, got into the car and drove to the Darnells', who thankfully lived nearby. I drove slowly, my mind trying desperately to focus on the road, while my insides churned like an old fashioned butter barrel and I kept wondering whether I'd actually throw up. Arriving at my destination I was greeted with a warm hug and how was I? I acknowledged my unsettled state and found that my legs didn't feel as stable as they should either. But coffee was administered and distraction conversation was soon underway. Do you like the way the lounge has been decorated? You haven't seen our latest holiday snaps? What do you think of the new lawn layout, Brian's been working so hard at it? Mental exertions of olympic proportions were required for me to conduct myself in anything even faintly resembling a civilised manner; and during the course of the conversation I was sure there were occasions when an incorrect response was given, but Joyce didn't seem to notice, or if she did, she diplomatically ignored my ineptitudes, which was a tremendous help.

Brian and Joyce were such tremendous friends, I thought as I drifted off into a little world of my own. They'd stood by us from day one, and even now were fighting tooth and nail to clear Nick's name in the church we'd attended in Oxted and in the local vicinity. Where would we have been without them? Remembering the very first Saturday after Nick's arrest, I thought again that it was absolutely wonderful to have had that visit so early on and I realised that we had never appreciated our fellow youth group workers as we should. What amazing friends we had! They were prepared to ignore the 'police instructions' about not visiting us and to come down, reassure us and love us. What more could anyone ask?

Brian and Joyce had helped with the youth group for several years. It was typical of their generous natures that they had seen us (but mainly Nick), trying to run the group Saturday and Sunday night, plus all the preparation involved; watched us building up relationships with the youngsters, welcoming them into our home at any hour of the day and night, and realised that really it was too much for a couple, especially one with a young family. So, despite feeling that they were rather past the ideal age for such work, they had volunteered their services as helpers. Nick remained very much the leader with an excellent rapport with the teenagers, but the Darnells were always there in the wings. They could be telephoned any time for assistance, would help with transport, come on the outings and provide another pair of brains at the planning meetings. I felt again, as I looked across the lounge at them, how unappreciative we had been of all they'd done. How even on occasions we'd criticised them for something or other, and yet here they were, backing us to the hilt, maintaining absolute faith and confidence in us and looking after us in our time of need.

One or two church friends had been invited to the Darnells to pop in and see me. More of Joyce's distraction techniques, no doubt. They were all friendly, concerned, supportive; but the hours ambled tediously on with no news. Lunch came and went, more polite conversation, even a laugh or two; then a figure appeared at the back door and I was almost out of my seat before realising that Joyce had grabbed her purse to pay the milkman. Just at the point when I was thinking it was impossible for time to go any slower, or for my anxiety ever to increase to greater proportions, Nick appeared.

No one beat me to the door that time. I must have made it from the arm chair in almost one huge leap and flung the door wide. He looked more himself, more relaxed, shoulders no longer hunched, with the long absent school boy grin on his face. 'Thank God,' I thought in that split second as the door swung open wide, 'it's all over, they're not pursuing it.' At the same time as that conclusion flitted through my mind, Nick said, 'I've been charged.'

A real criminal now

The nausea resurged, my knees knocked and I grabbed Nick's hand and said, 'Let's go for a walk.' No coat, no explanation to those left in the house, I strode forward, shutting the door behind firmly. If Joyce thought we were rude, it was just too bad, this one had to be sorted before it could be shared. Stuttering slightly and with a lump in my throat, I asked, as soon as we were down the drive:

'I don't understand, why are you so happy? I just don't understand, tell me what has happened.'

For Nick the adrenaline had ceased to flow, the immediate anxiety was over, he knew the next stage; but sensing my turmoil he took me through the events at the police station step by step.

'When I got there,' he explained, 'Mr Dixon was already there and had been talking to DC Stevens. Mr Dixon wanted to see me first before I was interviewed; but the system's crazy, you know. They were all for searching me, taking my belt and shoes and sticking me in a cell again. It was only because the solicitor vouched for me that I was spared that. Anyway Mr Dixon said they were going to charge me with the whole lot. The rape of Anita and sexual assault of the other two. He also told me that the third accuser was Debs.'

'But what had you done to her?' I interrupted in disbelief.

'Tickled her on the back of the leg in our lounge in a room full of young people, in fun.'

'And that's the third accusation?'

'Yup, well when I heard that, to be honest I felt loads better because it was so ridiculous, and it was a relief to know that no one else had concocted anything really foul against me. Oh yes, and now I've been charged I'm a real criminal,' Nick added, with an attempt at a grin.

'Meaning?' I queried .

'I've had my finger prints taken and a swab from my mouth done for DNA. No doubt they'll be desperately trying to match that with forensic evidence from other unsolved rapes.'

Before I could comment, he continued,

'The police asked me a few questions, always playing devil's advocate and on one occasion they said I repeatedly took girls home on their own so that I could molest them. Well! I wasn't having any of that! I explained that the group was mixed, that no one was forced to come, that everyone could make their own transport arrangements and that I only took people home whose parents couldn't or wouldn't pick them up. I also told him that I didn't give lifts all the time, it depended who else was there with a car and available to offer transport; though I did say at one stage Anita used to beg me for lifts 'coz Tony was hotly pursuing her and she wasn't keen. You remember?'

Nick was in full flow, and I listened attentively as we walked along.

'Then after ten minutes or so of questioning DC Stevens asked me if I had anything I wanted to add. After two months of thinking all this through I can assure you I had plenty I wanted to say!'

I squeezed Nick's hand understandingly.

'I told him all about the youth group, the relaxed atmosphere we attempted to create, the fact that we treated all the youngsters like members of our family, and that they'd pop in at all hours of the day and night for chats, coffee or just to doss around. I also told him of the various reasons I'd now thought of that might possibly explain Anita's strange accusations … Not that Stevens was even faintly interested, he was doodling most of the time. But the tape was running so I just ploughed on.'

'Good for you.'

'And that's why I feel a whole load better, I know exactly what the accusations are against me, I've seen their statements now, and I've had a good chance to explain myself. Basically Mr Dixon said, just be myself, that we weren't going to try and play any legal tricks, that my honesty was obvious, so just say whatever. He seemed quite happy with what I'd said and I've got to reappear at Oxted magistrates' court on April 19th.'

'What for exactly?'

'Well, it hasn't been to the Crown Prosecution Service yet, so they'll have a look at it and decide whether to prosecute. Though Mr Dixon says there's only a 50% chance that they'll have looked at it by then. If they haven't, I'll just be told to reappear in another six weeks or so.'

'Good grief.'

'Yes, we could be in for a long stint now, but I do feel a lot more comfortable. At least now, whatever happens, I've had a chance to say my bit having given it due consideration, which is a bit better than when I was interviewed at 6.30 in the morning without a moment's warning.'

Having walked a mini circuit, we were soon back at the Darnells'.

'I assume you want to go in?' I enquired .

'Oh yes, I'm starving. I haven't had anything to eat or drink since I saw you last.'

I was shocked. 'Didn't they even give you a coffee?'

Soon we were ensconced once more with Joyce, who was bustling around in the role she fulfilled so well, that of carer and food provider. Godfrey and Davina Smythe, who'd been there for lunch, had scuttled off upstairs so as not to be in the way when we returned. I went to find them. They were aghast at the turn of events and their horror fuelled my inner distress.

'What I can't understand,' I spluttered in the privacy of the hall, away from Nick, as the tears fell unhindered onto the floor, 'is how anyone can hate Nick so much to tell such horrible lies about him. I'm just overwhelmed by the hate that is being expressed here. Nick bust a gut for the youth group, he only ever tried to be kind, sympathetic, understanding and fun. And this is what's happened. I just don't understand it.'

Even as I spoke the full impact of the situation began to hit home.

'How's Emily going to cope when we tell her? What about my poor girls? It can go public now, now he's been charged. It'll probably be in the papers and goodness knows what Mainwave will say.'

Godfrey and Davina were sympathetic and understanding. Eventually the tears were dried and we all ventured into the lounge where Nick was happily munching away on his ham sandwiches and recounting his adventures.

It was good Nick felt positive. It helped us both respond to the many telephone calls we received that evening. It was a relief that the dreaded session at Oxted was over. But what would the next one involve? How we had hoped that that appearance would have been our last. Our friends had assumed it would, and now we had another one hanging over us, more waiting and, no doubt, considerably more anxiety. Would April 19th hold good? Or would there be a postponement? Would Nick's arrest and charge get into the press? What on earth would Mainwave make of the latest news? Would they want to put him on half pay and ask him to stay away? Nick was due to fly to South Africa for work after the weekend and Mr Dixon had advised him to put the whole mess on one side, to go and try and enjoy the trip. 'After all,' he'd assured him, 'absolutely nothing will happen quickly, it rarely does in the legal world. So just go away and have a breather.'

To a certain degree that is exactly what happened. Nick was worked off his feet whilst away, often tapping away at his P.C. well after midnight, and communicating with me mainly by email. It was an art I struggled to master, but with determination and Jessica at my elbow, I found to my immense satisfaction that the messages were getting through. Nick told me that 'yes' the news of his arrest was out at work, team leaders were being advised and there was no feedback as yet. The next day there was another email. Nick's friend Tom was also working in South Africa and had come to see him in tears, devastated by Nick's news. Tom was baffled by the way Nick seemed to be coping, but then Nick wrote, it was difficult to explain that the shock of it all had dulled somewhat, whereas his colleagues were hearing, experiencing and sharing it for the first time. Also, that whilst the whole thing was devastating, Tom had no faith in God to hang on to; whereas at least he, Nick, knew that the situation was being overseen above.

Then he had a long note from Bella, a warm Italian lady who'd shared his office for five years. She was livid about the allegations, wrote strongly in Nick's defence and said she would trust her teenage daughter to his care tomorrow, she had such faith in him. It was reassuring and encouraging to hear the news, but the question remained, what would Mainwave decide to do with Nick? The uncertainty haunted me as I struggled on in Nick's absence, trying so hard to maintain some semblance of normality for the girls.

He returned safely, and I could tell the change had done him good. Although the trip had been mainly meetings, he had had the evenings free and the weekend. Having a passion for travel Nick had taken full advantage of his location and grabbed the opportunity to visit Soweto, recounting enthusiastically to me the deprivation of the town and the amazingly cheerful attitude that the people there maintained. His grey drained face had a little more colour and his gait had a fraction more of his old jubilance to it. You could still see quite clearly that here was a man under pressure, but it was as if the weight of it had been eased just a little, just a pound or two. As soon as he was back he went in to work to learn his fate. The final verdict, he informed me on his return, was that he'd work from home before Easter, and after Easter work in another office. They were not prepared to let him stay where he had been working as it was an open plan office. One hundred and fifty girls worked there, who might not be too happy if they learnt they were working in the vicinity of a charged rapist. 'There is no justice in this world,' I thought as Nick explained the arrangements. 'The bloke's being punished already before he's even got to court, psychologically he's being worn down, at Mainwave it's as if he's got the plague. Will this nightmare ever end?'

I felt so loyal to my husband and so proud of the way he coped. Yes, he had his irritable moments, but I thought proudly, a lot of other chaps would have cracked up long ago; but here was Nick maintaining a cheerful exterior, philosophical about his desk move at work, and, I thought affectionately, he even remembered to buy the girls gifts in South Africa just as he always does on his travels. Emily and Jessica had been delighted with their animal necklaces, Felicity with her brightly coloured hair band and Esther had thought her elephant pendant the best thing ever. 'He's really someone very special,' I thought, with a half smile, 'and if anyone can cope with this stress, he can.'

Tension

Easter came and went. We continued to feel we were living a dual existence. There was the normal, happy, settled, family life; Dad back from South Africa, delighted girls, thrilled with their gifts, and experiences relayed. 'Daddy, Daddy I was the March hare in my school's performance of Alice.' Felicity excitedly related. 'And Granddad videoed it and you can watch it.'

'I've got my school report, Daddy let me go on your knee, and Mummy says it's really good. Mr Able thinks I'm a good girl Daddy, when will you look at it?' exclaimed Esther, ever anxious not to be left out.

'And Dad we've got our music exam results,' smiles Emily.

'Have you now?'

'And Jessica got …'

'No, no let me tell him.'

'Hold on you two, one at a time, I'm sure you both did brilliantly.'

But just under the surface another picture emerged, that of a couple under strain. I was frequently short with the children, leaving Esther asking curiously; 'Have you got a headache, Mummy?' And Emily in a slightly irritated manner; 'Is there anything wrong, Mum?' as I snapped over the smallest issue. Nick too, tried so hard to be level headed, even tempered, his usual jovial self but the pressure was there. He would bellow at chatty Esther so ferociously that she'd duck, frightened of a thump, and burst into tears; Felicity risked life and limb if she exceeded the mark which she was prone to do being mischievous by nature, and if Jessica dared to remind him again that he'd promised to help her with her clarinet music, an aggressive explosion was nigh on guaranteed. 'We're like a house under siege,' I mused. 'Superficially everything's fine, but it feels so delicate and flimsy that at any moment things could explode and none of us quite know what is happening.'

There were, of course, troughs and peaks. As the next appointment with Mr Dixon approached, both of us felt concerned. Clearly the actual situation wouldn't change by speaking to a solicitor, but it put the whole thing back on the map, back into perspective, back into reality, just where neither of us really wanted it to be.

Nick was fixing a new shower door in the spare room bathroom the day before his next encounter with Mr Dixon, and the girls had decided to go for a walk. Mind you, deciding had taken five arguments and twenty minutes and been a thoroughly trying experience for those involved and those on the side lines. Eventually the four of them set off up the garden.

'Esther, don't forget to shut the door, you're the last one out,' bellowed Emily over her shoulder.

'No, I won't do it,' retorted the megaphone mouth of the little sister. 'It wasn't my fault I couldn't get my wellies on and was last.'

Nick had had enough. Flying to the shower room window, he threw it open wildly and boomed; 'I've had it up to here with you lot today, if you four don't stop bickering ...' But he didn't have a chance to finish, for the unsupported shower door crashed to the ground, chipping the brand new £140 shower tray.

I heard the shouting and the crash as I carried some clean clothes upstairs to the girls' rooms. Did I dare investigate? Or would it be better to leave it? Dumping the clothes on the landing I ventured into the spare room with a tentative, 'Is everything all right?'

'No, it's not,' came the angry retort. 'I've ruined the shower tray because of those wretched children.'

'Ruined?'

'Yes, the door fell and smashed the shower tray when I went to the window to shout at the girls.'

I apprehensively leaned into the shower and looked for the gaping hole I was expecting to see, or else the huge crack. But as far as I could make out the porcelain remained intact, and all that was apparent was a modest chip at the front. Yes, it was noticeable and certainly it was a shame, but not quite as dire as Nick had made out. I made as encouraging noises as I dared and pottered out, hoping that my tense and stressed husband would pick himself up by his shoe laces and manage to get on again. A little later I heard him singing as he worked and was greatly relieved. He still seemed very fed up, but had thought of a way to cover the mark and so rectify the situation somewhat.

The following day Nick set off to Croydon to see Mr Dixon. His mood was resigned but not happy. Once he'd changed into his suit he gave me a hug.

'Are you OK?' I asked; knowing the answer.

'I s'pose so,' he responded despondently, 'But I'm fed up with having to do this.'

'It's too awful,' I thought, 'he's had to use his annual leave from work to go and travel up to Croydon, to talk to a solicitor who costs £150 an hour about a crime he didn't do. He's got to take a list of our finances to see if we're entitled to Legal Aid to defend himself from something completely fabricated. No wonder he's cheesed off. The whole thing is outrageous. Have Anita and Penny any concept of what they're putting us through? I don't suppose so; but I have to assume that even if they had, they wouldn't mind. Good grief, what do they hope to gain? When will this nightmare be over?'

However, I managed to say some encouraging words to Nick as he set off, before I was summoned into the garden to look for a two inch long plastic pig that Felicity had hurled into a fir tree and now couldn't locate. As I pulled aside the branches and shook the eight foot tree as best I could, I couldn't help thinking: 'I'm two people. Two completely different people. The caring mother of four happy girls enjoying their Easter holidays, and the stressed out wife of an innocent man, accused by two girls of outrageous crimes when all he ever did was try to help them through the difficult teenage years, support them, encourage them, offer them an open home. I'm two completely different people, functioning on two completely different levels. It's bizarre. It's crazy. It's insane.' Eventually, thankfully, the pig was found, Felicity was happy and I returned indoors to finish my cooking.

Later the telephone rang. Nick sounded tired but OK. Yes, he'd finished with Mr Dixon and was on his way home. Meanwhile spaghetti bolognaise was dished up and received enthusiastically, followed by chocolate mousse which was also a success, and portions were reserved for Daddy. After tea Jessica was determined to play on the computer, while the other three wanted to watch the video of Beauty and the Beast. The timing couldn't have been better, for as all four girls settled to their respective relaxation, Nick's key turned in the lock. So, after changing out of his suit, he was able to enjoy his dinner in peace and fill me in on the details of his visit.

Although Mr Dixon was himself an experienced solicitor, it seemed he was surprised at the turn of events. He appreciated how strange it was for Nick to find himself in this situation and totally accepted his innocence. All that was good, and I was thankful; but I knew there must be worse to come. What would happen on the 19th?

'Well,' explained Nick, 'there are four options. Mr Dixon, of course, has no more idea than I have which one will be taken. But having said that, he reckons the first is probably the most likely.'

'Which was?'

'Number one: the Crown Prosecution Service (CPS) won't have had a chance to consider our case. In fact there was a lot to write up, so it is highly likely that the police haven't even completed the paper work yet or passed it to the CPS, so then they'll ask to postpone the date, probably for six weeks.

Number two: The CPS will prosecute for everything and I'll go to the magistrates court ready for crown court.

Number three: The CPS will drop the rape charge and go in heavily for sexual assault.

Number four: But the least likely of all four by far, is that they'll drop all charges.'

As Nick ran through the options I felt the lead weight inside me sinking again. Nick continued, 'Whatever I do I mustn't upset the magistrate.'

'Why on earth not?'

'Because, apparently, this sort of case normally precludes bail. Mr Dixon says it's extremely unlikely that anyone charged with rape etc. should receive bail.'

'Can this nightmare get even worse?' I wondered. 'Are they now going to take Nick away? What will this do to our girls?'

Nick continued with the depressing news that legal aid probably wouldn't be forth coming because we had more than £100,000 equity in the house, and as far as the courts were concerned the house could be mortgaged and the 'spare' money used for legal fees.

'Great,' I thought, 'our wonderful legal system are more than happy to force us to re-mortgage the house or sell it to pay for our expenses, probably forcing us to change the girls' school, and disrupt their whole lives. This would be pretty grim if Nick were guilty, but to have to do this to defend a totally innocent man, the world had gone mad! Where in heaven's name was justice? Didn't anyone care about our kids? Could the situation deteriorate even further? Where oh where was all this going to end?'

Mr Dixon had talked to Nick about finances and told him the daunting news that going to court would cost at least £30,000. Where were we to find that sort of money? Short of selling the house. Although the sum overwhelmed and depressed us, clearly Mr Dixon had plenty of experience in that field, and of course, a vested interest in ensuring its production. He told Nick that bearing in mind the amount of support he was already enjoying from friends and family, he should immediately set about establishing a begging fund. The way to do this, he instructed, was to write a clear concise letter explaining our predicament and how much money was required. Then detailing simple methods of payment to a third party (if there was anyone suitable), it could then be distributed to friends and family who'd expressed an interest in being of assistance. Nick was quite confident that his older brother Stephen, who had worked in banking for years, could undertake the task. Mr Dixon was delighted that Nick could handle the matter so objectively, had such support and a brother who would man the funds. He stressed the importance of establishing the account straight away as the first bill was due shortly.

Nick & Melanie Metcalfe
6 Elmtree Avenue
Cranleigh
Surrey

Monday, 10th May, 1999

Dear
As you are aware we find ourselves in very difficult circumstances at the moment with serious allegations being made about Nick. The possibility of a Crown Court case is now becoming more of a reality and we find ourselves in a position where we need to build a defence case to prove innocence. We have unfortunately not been able to secure legal aid, our legal bills at present stand at £5,000 and if the case continues we will need to raise at least £50,000.

In order to produce sums in this region we would need to sell the house which would cause more disruption to the girls on top of the uncertainty of the present situation. Several friends have generously said they would be able to help towards these legal costs and to this end my solicitor has advised the setting up of a 'fighting fund' which has now been done. Nick's brother Stephen has agreed to administer the fund. While Stephen will keep a record of all money donated, he will only supply us with the names and not the amounts. If all moneys donated are not needed or if Nick is found innocent and legal costs are paid, any money left in the fund will be divided proportionally by the administrator and returned to the original contributors.

If you wish to contribute there are three possible ways:—

1 Send a cheque to the fund administrator, together with your name and address. A record of your donation will be made and a receipt issued.

2 Pay directly into the account and send a letter to the administer, advising your name, address and transfer. A record of your donation will be made and a receipt issued.

3 Pay directly to the bank only. In this case the gift would be treated as anonymous , no receipt issued and of course it would not be possible to return any money at a future date.

We are both devastated by the position we find ourselves in, but are grateful beyond words for the support we are being given. We continue to trust God believing that all events are in His hands and knowing we can trust Him for our every provision.

Yours in Christ

I wanted to scream, but glancing across at Nick's face I saw just how much he was going through and what pure purgatory he was experiencing, inflicting all this so unintentionally on his family. I held his hand for a moment, silently communicating; 'We're in this together, hang on in there, we're going to cope, however long and whatever it takes.' Nick appreciated the message, despite being unspoken, jerked himself back to the present from the fearful future and announced he had some computer work to do. I knew that would do him good, and tidied up the dinner things in an uneasy state of mind.

'What did the solicitor say, Mum?' enquired the ever curious and intuitive Emily, grabbing a quiet moment when none of her sisters were around.

'Oh, not much really,' I replied, keen to present the truth but sugar coated without the awful pain of the potential future repercussions. 'He said that there were four things that could happen on the 19th. The most likely is the first, and that is that the case will be deferred to a future date, six weeks or so. The second is that the CPS will charge Dad with everything. The third is that they'll charge him with some of it, and the fourth, which unfortunately is the least likely, is that they'll drop everything.'

'Anything else?'

'No not really, just chat about finances and work.' Emily clearly felt she'd had a reasonable answer and sloped off to read her book.

My response may have left Emily settled and tranquil to a degree, but for us the anxiety was only just beginning. Nick's visit to Mr Dixon was the start of a series of sleepless nights, endless discussion and constant confusion. Nick continued desperately puzzled by the motive of the whole thing. 'Why,' his mind asked constantly, 'why should Anita and Penny concoct such tales? Why did the police pursue the nonsense when there was no substantiating evidence? Why had Anita's boyfriend insisted she go to the police? Presumably he believed her? Presumably she believed herself? But she'd never seemed to be even a faintly malicious character in the past. Why was she out to get me? She'd always liked us, used the computer constantly, not having one at home, frequently popping in for a coffee or to play on the piano. Why had the tables turned? What could induce the girls to be so cruel? Did they hope for financial gain? Because as far as I was aware, there wasn't any in cases like this. Did they even realise the anguish we as a family were going through? Was it a game to them? Were they really prepared to go to court and explain all these fantasies to a jury? Or did they think it wouldn't get that far but it would muddy my reputation?' Why, why, why, resounded through Nick's brain, like a mournful incessant church bell, making no progress but causing ever increasing pain and anguish. Would there ever be any answers to these desperate questions?

My thought patterns took on a different shape. Concerned for the children my mind flew towards the future. 'How will we cope if the invested funds for Emily, Jessica, and perhaps ultimately Felicity and Esther's school fees were used up in legal fees? If we sold the house, that would probably help considerably. We could easily manage in a three bedroom terraced house. But if Nick went to prison what would we live on? I'd have to get a job. But how would I get the girls to school, be there for them when they came home and work and earn enough for us to live on? Perhaps I could get work from home … But that pays badly so it wouldn't help. Part time work, maybe, but what? It's years since I've worked in an office, computers have changed completely, technology's moved on, I'd be starting from scratch at nearly forty. Perhaps shop work? But that doesn't pay much. Cleaning? People always want cleaners. But I hate cleaning! There's plenty of old people's homes, p'raps I could get work in one of them? But I'm not a nurse and hate the messy bits. What on earth could I do? I'd have to be the bread winner and mother and I just don't know how I'd do it. Never in my wildest dreams did I anticipate being in this situation. But perhaps he won't go to prison? Maybe not, but as all the events to date have been totally inexplicable and incomprehensible, what's to say they won't continue so? What is it Dad says? 'Expect the worst, hope for the best.' But if I assume Nick'll go to prison, I ought to plan for it and work out what I'm going to do.'

No wonder the nights were long, filled with tossing and turning with very little rest. Sometimes I would try and read myself to sleep. One night I was devouring *'The Road from Croon'*, a woman's exquisitely clear sighted memoir of growing up in Australia, when I read and reread the paragraph describing life after the loss of her brother.

'After my brother Bob's death, it seemed as though I had lost the capacity for emotional responses. Daily life was in black and white, like a badly made film … Although on the surface I was doing well I was actually going through each day like an automaton … I longed to escape the discomfort of watching the world from the other side of some transparent but impenetrable window … I laughed when people told jokes, but could not really participate.'

How well I could identify with those sentiments, how well I understood the author's distance from the real world. When the brain is overwhelmed with sadness, I realised, it clearly uses so much energy coping with it, that reality, of necessity, distances itself and becomes strangely less significant.

Nevertheless, life had to go on. The children were taken on outings and appreciated the freedom of the Easter holidays. A French girl came to stay and had to be entertained. It was hard; I was irritable, Nick was unpredictable. One minute he was his usual cheerful self and the next, wild with anger and frustration because something minor had gone wrong. A recalcitrant pen was flung across the room, and on one occasion just when the whole family plus the French girl had prepared to go out, the excursion was put on hold. Why? Because, as Nick had been locking up, the conservatory door had stuck, the plastic having expanded in the sun; so the screwdriver had to come out, the door taken off its hinges, fiddled with and shouted at until it was finally fixed. The four girls came to recognise the warning signs of tension and stress and would potter off quietly to do something until the matter was resolved and Dad was calm again.

The pressure forced me to God's word for comfort. I had set myself the challenge of reading the Bible from cover to cover and had reached the psalms. It was as if they were written just for us. Frequently as Nick came into the bedroom I'd say: 'Here, listen to this.' And read him Psalm 3, on another day Psalm 7 and later Psalm 13. Deep down we knew God was with us, close at hand, taking us through each day. Each night our prayers together had an urgency they'd never had before, 'Please help us trust you, help us rely on you, whatever happens.'

After the visit to Mr Dixon, Nick had endless forms to fill in requesting Legal Aid. That, of course, was another irritant. 'All this time wasted,' Nick exclaimed frustratedly as he poured over the paperwork. 'It drives me mad.'

'I know dear,' I soothed. 'But it just has to be done.'

The time he'd spent talking to the police, the solicitor, travelling and filling in forms was like an open wound to Nick. Each time there was more to do, the wound seeped, oozed, frustrated and hurt him. The hours he'd spent in the last three months thinking and dealing with all this hassle were phenomenal; it had completely dominated his existence. The petrol he'd used travelling to Croydon to see Mr Dixon, to go to court, the paperwork he'd had to complete, the prolonged discussions he'd had with his bosses at work; it was all incredible, outrageous, unjust and distressing in the extreme. But there was no escape. It was like being on an unmanned roller coaster, strapped in and out of control. All you could do was sit there and go with the flow. Sometimes there were sudden dips when the pressure was intolerable and there were more gentle parts where the route ran less traumatically. However, normal life was not part of the journey, it was something surveyed from a distance. The sorting out of the new house, buying new furniture, decorating the rooms, tidying the garden, all the sorts of jobs you do in the first years after moving in to a new house, were not even on the itinerary. Quite the opposite. The house took on a different character, we felt as if we didn't quite belong there, as if it wasn't quite ours. It must have been a psychological preservation method, helping us adjust to its possible imminent sale. Just occasionally we were aware that jobs needed doing, but most of the time the outstanding work did not feature at all, we had far too many other things on our minds. Haunting us day and night, rarely giving us more than a few minutes' peace at a time was the awful question which remained; where was all this going to end?

First court appearance

The first court appearance approached. We sensed the tension in each other but tried fervently to maintain normality. My parents came down for the weekend to 'hold the fort' while we went to court. In many ways that worked out well for it forced us to focus on things around us, entertaining the grandparents, minding our P's and Q's for the older generation and ensuring there was something vaguely edible on the table at each meal. The Saturday was happily spent showing Grandma and Grandpa the girls' new schools and in the evening they kindly offered to baby-sit thus allowing us to go out for a meal. It was an opportunity not to be missed, a little oasis of peace and quiet, and appreciated by both of us. It was marvellous to escape the superficialities and just be ourselves. But as we sat and ate, chatting happily and casually about films, the in-laws, the girls, it again went through my mind, the complete insanity of the whole situation. It was a combination of romance, no responsibility, and basking in being quietly with each other, together with something resembling the last meal before an execution. After all, if Nick was not granted a continuation of bail, it would be a long time before the pair of us could enjoy another meal out together. A very long time, months to the court case and then, please God, no, the prison sentence after that.

The day inevitably came at last. Nick had calculated that we needed to leave at 6.30 am to guarantee punctuality, so we were out of bed as soon as the alarm had rung. Tea was made for the grandparents—together with a number of instructions clearly left for them on a sheet of paper, a flask of coffee made for us to take and we were off. I recalled previously feeling a sense of relief and resignation that the next hurdle had been reached and I sensed Nick felt the same. He was calm, almost chirpy, relaxed but resolute. In some ways this wasn't a big hurdle. The solicitor had indicated that there was no point applying for legal aid because of the mortgage on the house, so the two remaining issues were whether bail would be maintained and whether the CPS had had a chance to read the statements and what they intended doing with them. Mr Dixon had been adamant that they wouldn't have had a chance to look at them, and consequently was pretty sure that

that aspect of things would be postponed. Although it prolonged the agony, I felt relieved that no decision was likely. We weren't ready for the next onslaught yet. Mr Dixon had informed us of the harsh realities we were facing, but we couldn't take more blows yet. Going to court would be bad enough.

The drive was uneventful. I was so relieved that we were not having to appear at Oxted. Mr Dixon, just at the last minute, had managed to switch courts on the grounds that he had another case the same day at Sevenoaks. This meant that none of our friends, or enemies, had a clue where the case was being heard and so wouldn't be able to attend. Also, as Nick was not a resident of the Sevenoaks area, the press were unlikely to pick up his case. At least that was Mr Dixon's plan and how Nick and I hoped it worked.

A good hour before we were due, we reached Sevenoaks' magistrates court, parked and surveyed the surroundings. 'Not a particularly attractive place,' I thought as I looked up at the tall grey building. As there was plenty of time we went for a walk round the shops. There was a strange silence about the place. It was only 8.30 in the morning and we were accustomed to the hustle and bustle of busy shopping centres, not the half dormant atmosphere of this one. We saw a road cleaner and a couple of suited young men scurrying off to work. We looked aimlessly in shop windows and talked about nothing in particular. Then it was time to find a cup of coffee. After a futile hunt and the discovery that neither the Wimpy nor McDonalds were open at that time in the morning, we wandered back to the car to drink from our thermos. 'Are you nervous?' I asked, and after a pause, 'Yes, I suppose so, a bit,' Nick replied. 'I just hope they don't take me in on remand.' We then prayed together, as we had done at Oxted. I felt it was already becoming a routine, but it was so necessary and gave us enough confidence to climb out of the car.

Nine o'clock. 'Time to move, I guess.' Clearly Nick was anxious not to be late. We tentatively walked up the concrete steps of the imposing Magistrates court. It was a squarish construction, grey and very stereotypical of such a building: it looked dour and unforgiving. I wondered what was in store for us. Just outside was a young man with short cropped hair, puffing apprehensively at a cigarette. Waiting for his solicitor perhaps? Or waiting to go into court? I could empathise with his tension and suddenly in this crazy topsy turvy world I felt sympathy oozing out of me towards those charged. Perhaps not everyone there were villains? Perhaps not any one there was a criminal? Perhaps the majority were totally innocent like Nick? Perhaps they'd been set up, arrested unjustly or by mistake?

Mr Dixon had told Nick that it was good the case had been moved from Oxted to Sevenoaks, not only for the sake of publicity but also because the waiting room was so much more pleasant. As we entered I surveyed the 'much more hospitable' waiting room. It was an area the size of that at a doctor's surgery, but far less inviting. The walls were painted white, or off white, it was difficult to discern which, as they were so grubby. There were rows of plastic chairs fixed to the dirty linoleum floor which might once have been red; the usher of the court was behind a glass screen, just like a ticket seller at a station, an 'Out of Order' drinks machine, a grafitteed sign to the 'Ladies' and a television screen with pictures of some educational children's school programme intruding into the room with no sound. 'If this is a good waiting room,' I thought, 'I don't ever want to see a bad one.'

Again, like a railway station, there was a large sign in flashing neon lettering requesting everyone on arrival to report to the usher of the court. Nick duly did. The usher was an elderly man wearing a black gown, with a hard expression, who asked Nick's name and then said, 'Why are you here?' 'This is untrue,' I thought. 'They don't want him to have to pronounce the charges in front of all these unknown people, do they? It's outrageous.' But Nick, who seemed totally under control replied calmly, 'I've come to answer bail at 9.30 am. Next ridiculous question; 'What are you pleading?' 'He's not pleading anything,' I mused. 'At least not to you, you horrible interfering person.' Again Nick simply responded; 'Not guilty.' And N/G was written next to Nick's name on the list.

We then took a seat at the back of the room, and perused our setting whilst waiting for Mr Dixon. The room was definitely shabby and the people in it a remarkable contrast. There was an interesting range of legal types, conspicuous by their smart suits and the sheaves of files they were carrying. On the other hand the variety of 'villains' was enormous and intriguing. To our right sat a middle aged man in tweed jacket and trousers sitting with his wife. They both looked anxious and I speculated that they were not regular attendees at the court but perhaps had been caught for drink driving. In front of them sat a whole family crowd. There was a young man in scruffy jeans, big black boots and black T-shirt sporting a skull on it. He had broad shoulders and tattooed arms. With him sat a girl with bleached hair, a wide variety of ear rings, skimpy top, tight leather skirt and long black boots. She was clutching a miserable looking infant that apparently hadn't had a bath for quite a while, with mess all down its front, determined to make its mother's life as difficult as possible. It wriggled incessantly, thrashed around violently and occasionally let out such blood curdling yells that the hubbub of the waiting room came to an instant stop. At this point the mother would swear profusely and 'gran' would grab him from her muttering an interminable stream of profanities. 'Granddad', disturbed by the racket then got to his feet muttering, and fishing his cigarettes out of his jacket pocket, disappeared outside.

It was interesting to be in the court waiting room, watching people. The solicitors were easily identifiable, the complainants too were pretty obvious by their nervousness and uncertainty. Then, of course, there were other folk, the support teams, like myself. I overheard one older lady clearly explaining to a solicitor, 'My son wasn't driving, definitely not. It was Ian, the chap who got out and ran off, you do understand that, don't you?' 'If I sat here day after day,' I thought, 'I'd hear such a variety of tales, it'd be so interesting. I should have gone into the legal world, it's fascinating. Then I could have explored its niceties properly, and not like this.'

There was also a young chap, only about seventeen years of age looking very worried, with his parents in tow, and a whole crowd of teenage lads with a group of miscellaneous adults accompanying them. All in all it was an intriguing bunch of people who, I thought, in other circumstances it would be fascinating to watch, and try and work out why they were here and what they'd been up to. However before my meditations could continue further, they were interrupted by Nick saying, 'Here he is,' and I looked up to see a tall gentleman, mouse brown hair and moustache, wearing a suit and carrying the all important papers, come striding in. He immediately came over to us, introduced himself to me with a slightly ingratiating grin, and then bustled off with his case and sheaf of papers in a brusque manner which seemed to say: 'I'm a busy man, loads to do, people to see, arrangements to check etc.' We sat down again and waited. Five to ten minutes later he reappeared. 'I've had a word with the clerk of the court,' he said. 'Unfortunately he hasn't the authority to prolong bail, so we'll have to see the magistrate at 10 am The case'll be adjourned, because the police only got the papers to the CPS last Friday and they've not considered them at all. So just before 10 am I'll come down and fetch you and you come up to court one,' he said looking at Nick.

'Can I come too?' I asked anxiously. This world was so new to me, I had no idea where I could or couldn't go, what I should or shouldn't do.

'Yes, yes, of course', said Mr Dixon. 'You go in the public gallery.' As he turned away, his better nature obviously overruled, compassion prevailed. He was hectically busy, but he would take five minutes out to show pity on this bewildered, inexperienced couple. He swivelled on his heels and looking us both in the eyes, asked; 'Shall I show you now where to go?' I was most relieved.

As it turned out, it couldn't possibly have been simpler. Up the stairs, straight ahead of us, turn left and there was the court room: about the size of a small classroom with a raised platform at the far side opposite the door. It was full of chairs and desks and people bustling around appearing incredibly busy. None of them took any notice whatsoever of us. A small proportion of the room was partially partitioned off with a glass screen about three quarters the height of the room. That area had a separate door, Mr Dixon explained, and was the public gallery. With a few parting words of wisdom to Nick about standing up straight, not putting his hands in his pockets and not sitting down until told to do so, Mr Dixon was off and we retreated downstairs to wait.

Moments later Mr Dixon reappeared and beckoned to us. No fuss, no one shouting out Nick's name or the charges, and before we knew it we were upstairs again in Court 1. The people were still bustling around, conferring, looking out documents and again took absolutely no notice of Nick whatsoever. Mr Dixon led him into the centre of the room where there was a raised square with a waist high barrier. I went into the public gallery and sat down. I could feel the tension in my body, the perspiration building up and my head ache as I performed mental gymnastics, praying frantically that Nick wouldn't upset the magistrate and bail would be renewed. The paper shuffling and hushed conversations of the previous business went on for what seemed an age. Twice Mr Dixon walked over to Nick, presumably to reassure him and explain that this waiting was all part of the course. Nick had his back to me, but I could sense even from that perspective that he was nervous and tense.

'Will the court please rise,' said a smart suited young man at the front of the room just below the platform; and at that, a door at the back of the room opened and in walked a shortish grey haired gentleman wearing a gown. Everyone had sprung to their feet at the instruction, including me, I was somewhat bewildered as to whether or not the 'rising' included me; but felt that on the whole it was better to be safe than sorry. Everyone was then allowed to sit, apart from Nick, and there were various conferrings between the magistrate, the clerk, Mr Dixon and one or two others. Nick then had to give his name and address and the charges were read out.

'You are charged with the rape of Anita Carol Simpson of Hurst Green, the sexual assault of Anita Carol Simpson of Hurst Green, the sexual assault of Penny Esther Finch of Oxted, and the sexual assault of Deborah Katy Islington of Oxted.'

I writhed. Nick sounded like a complete maniac with charges like that against him, he wouldn't have a hope. He'd go down for this, he'd be put on remand, he'd definitely not be coming home that night.

More mutterings and the prosecution explained that they'd only just received the papers from the police, so the case was to be adjourned. There was some query as to where it would be adjourned to and then just when I was hoping it was all over I caught the sound of the magistrate saying, 'It's not normal for bail to be granted in a case like this.' I froze and saw Nick do likewise. The magistrate looked to the prosecution to comment, but he, not having read the case, was somewhat caught out and muttered something about the police having been happy to bail him so he assumed it could still stand. At which point Mr Dixon stood up and explained lucidly that the police had been quite satisfied with bailing Mr Metcalfe and the only conditions were that he had no contact whatsoever with the three girls in question; which, of course, had been adhered to and would continue to be so.

There were a few more mumblings during which I held my breath, but it appeared that bail would be granted and I nearly collapsed with relief. God had heard our desperate prayers. What I only realised months later was that he'd actually heard the prayers of dozens, if not hundreds, of Christian friends who'd been on their knees on our behalf. The court was told to rise, the magistrate went out of his door and Mr Dixon and Nick reappeared outside the court room where I promptly joined them. Nick was a free man, at least for the time being. It was a huge relief that it was all over; the whole event had lasted five to seven minutes, but it felt like a lifetime. The three of us descended the stairs and went outside to discuss the situation to date.

Mr Dixon took control of the conversation: 'So you're released on bail to reappear here in a month when, with a bit of luck, the CPS might know what they're doing. Assuming this goes to Crown Court, we're going to have to do a lot of work and it'll unfortunately cost a lot of money. So, as I said in my letter, I really do need £5,000 now. I've received copies of all the statements the CPS have got which I'll photocopy and send on to you; and in a week or so I'll ring the CPS and see how they're doing, try to build a bit of rapport. Then, of course, I think you'll have to come and have another word before the 17th.' We both nodded, and within seconds hands were shaken and Mr Dixon was back through the doors for his next case.

One of the hundreds of character references sent by friends to Mr Dixon:

Mr P. Dixon,
Dixon, Dixon and Partners,
115 London Road,
Croydon
Dear Mr Dixon,
Nicholas Metcalfe
I learned recently from some friends of Nick and Melanie Metcalfe about the sexual assault charges brought against Nick and I felt that I must write to you to express my extreme surprise that this could possibly have happened.
I have known Nick and his family since 1986 when they started to attend the Maidstone Evangelical Free Church where I was involved in the leadership. They were members of the church until 1989 when due to the location of his employment, they moved to Oxted. While he was with us Nick became a Deacon and helped with a number of

youth camps and was considered as a great asset at that time, both spiritually and socially.

In my view, and in the view, I am sure of other people involved in the work of the church at that time, Nick is a man of high integrity, completely honest and trustworthy and conscientious in any work he is engaged in. Also, the way in which he and Melanie conducted their family life with their young daughters was a fine example to other young families in the church. He certainly is not in any way inclined towards the kind of action he is being charged with. I find it incomprehensible that these charges have been made, and I am certain that they cannot have any foundation.

If I can be of any further help, please let me know.

Yours sincerely

S. Brown M.B.,Ch.B., M.R.C.G.P., D.R.C.O.G., D.C.H., F.P.Cert.

Evidence arrives

'That was pretty scary,' I volunteered. 'But at least it went according to plan. You looked petrified, were you scared?'

'Yes, I suppose I was a bit. And I don't think much of all this kow towing to the magistrate as if he's God. He didn't look me in the eye once during the whole thing.'

We were both relieved that that stint was over, and knew that we could at last relax a bit. We drove to Brian and Joyce's house, having promised them an update before returning home. There we were given coffee and cake and loving listening ears. Nick was his usual happy, relaxed self and I found myself wondering what Brian and Joyce were thinking. Did they appreciate the stress of it all? Or seeing the normal happy go lucky Nick, did they mistakenly assume he was handling all this in the merry light hearted way he approached the rest of his life?

There was a ring at Brian and Joyce's front door, and Tim Warrington, the minister from the Oxted church popped in for an update. His questions were precise, and he seemed genuinely shocked by the answers. 'What exactly were you charged with? There's definitely three girls involved? And four charges? Does your solicitor really think this will be pursued?' As Nick filled Tim in on all the details a silence fell over the room. It was as if the reality of the whole thing was only just penetrating. After what seemed an age Tim ran his hand over his face and exclaimed; 'This is a nightmare.' Frustrated and exasperated breaths escaped from both of us as we saw the penny was only just dropping. Yes, yes, it was a nightmare. One we'd been living with for the last three months and one we were going to have to go on living with for months, if not years, to come.

The journey home was quiet. The grandparents were pleased to see us, and listened carefully to the account of the day. The following day they left, and we sensed that we were beginning to surface again after the strain. However it was only twenty four hours later when another bomb exploded full in my face in the form of a wad of papers equivalent to the thickness of a telephone directory. These were the statements from Anita, Penny, Debs and various other people from the church. The post arrived early in the morning, after Nick and the eldest three had left for school and work, but Esther was still around. Without giving it much thought I opened the package and began to scan the contents. Within seconds my stomach was knotted and tears fell. This was worse than anything I'd even begun to imagine. Explicit sexual details about what Nick was supposed to have done. Account after account by Anita of how Nick would give her lifts home, say he loved her, say he needed her, cry, tell her about his problems at work and at home and then take her inside, up to her own room … I just couldn't bear it. Grabbing the telephone, I rang Angie. Inarticulately I explained to their lodger that I'd appreciate some help, she had a quick word with Angie, and assured me that Angie would be round by the time I returned from taking Esther to school. It was several years later that I learnt that Angie had actually been putting her shoes on and getting ready to go to an important meeting when I rang. This had been promptly cancelled and she appeared a short while later giving me the impression she had all the time in the world.

'Why are you crying, Mummy?', Esther's little voice penetrated the black foul fog I was in. I brushed my hand across my eyes and said, as lightly as I possibly could, 'Oh, it's only this trouble Daddy's in with the police.'

'Is there something new?' enquired Esther.

'No, no darling, now you get ready for school and I'll wash my face and be with you in two ticks.'

I retreated to the bathroom where I feared I might be sick.

'Mind over matter,' I told myself. 'Get Esther to school before you let it get you. Come on, hold up. Rebekah told you early on you were strong, so for goodness sake, get a grip of yourself and be strong.'

A cold flannel helped reduce the evidence of upset; I took a deep breath and went downstairs with only a mildly distorted face. 'Ready for school, then? Good. Right, let's go and get the bikes out.' To my relief, Esther seemed convinced that Mummy's tears were now over, made no further reference to it and, in her usual way, talked non-stop all the way to school.

Returning home I managed a smile to the lollipop man, put my bike away, key in the door, coat off, before collapsing in an armchair and audibly groaning. How would Nick handle this? How would he cope with the pain?

What would he think of the lies? Clearly Anita had had a crush on him and dreamt up all this, but would a court be able to understand it? It all sounded so graphic, as if it really had happened. And then as if Anita's account wasn't bad enough there was Penny saying similar things. 'He rang me up and said he loved me.' 'He begged me to go with him.' 'For goodness sake,' I screamed inwardly, 'he's not like that, he doesn't say that sort of thing. He never could express himself in words, but who will believe me?' It was so clear to me that the accusations were obviously false. The statements from the girls about what Nick was alleged to have said and done were totally out of character. This was not the way Nick had ever spoken to me, it just didn't ring true. At that point in my musings Angie arrived, coffee was made and we sat down together to look through the paperwork.

There it was in cruel black and white. First Anita's statement, page after page detailing how Nick had given her lifts home after the youth group and on several occasions gone up to her room, undressed her and raped her. She explained how she didn't know what was going on, she was only young, she didn't feel it was right but didn't know what to do, etc. On these occasions Nick had jumped up afterwards, pulled up his trousers and behaved as if nothing had happened. There'd been other times when he'd hugged her, explaining how much he needed her, how life was a strain for him and how he needed her support.

Penny's comments weren't quite so disgusting, but there too Nick had brushed her breast, stroked her bottom or cuddled her, and also told her he loved her and needed her.

The more I read, the more I despaired. Black waves of grief swept over me and I noticed how my hands shook as I turned the pages. It was a conspiracy of the grossest proportions. Anita's family and sister substantiated her statements, no comments from Penny's family, but Deb's family too seemed to substantiate Nick's villainy. In total, I calculated that it meant there were ten people all either stating categorically or implying subtly that Nick had committed every single one of these horrendous sexual offences. 'It might make a good novel,' I pondered, 'but this is real life, this is my husband, whose only aim ever in running that group was to help and encourage young people and provide them with loads of fun. What has he done to deserve this? Can no-one see the nonsense of it? The gossipy nature of three friends alleging crimes against him. Can't anyone see even a hint of a potential miscarriage of justice? Is my poor husband going to be put in prison, his name slandered for life for foul crimes he didn't commit? But it seems inevitable that that will be the case with so much information given against him and so many people lying about him.' My mind raced on, the tears flowing the whole time as I skimmed sheet after sheet. Angie wept and prayed with me and it was an inexpressible comfort.

By midday I was totally exhausted, resigned to a prison sentence for Nick; my stomach was knotted with stress and anxiety and now my chief concern was how Nick would handle the ghastly documents. In many ways it was a relief when the telephone rang about 12.30 and I heard Nick's voice reminding me to send off the cheque for £5,000 to the solicitors to cover the initial fees. After all, to date we'd had appointments, letters, not to mention Nick's visits and the appearance at the magistrates court from the solicitor and no payment had been made. We felt that by using our savings we could probably rustle up that much, but where the £40,000 for defence in a Crown court was to come from, that we didn't know. That was another big problem. But yes, meanwhile, I had forgotten to dispatch the cheque and promised to do it straight away.

Wiping my tears and clearing my throat I endeavoured to sound composed as I informed Nick that the statements had arrived. 'All the papers arrived today,' I said, in as objective a voice as possible, and before Nick could comment I added: 'They're pretty foul.'

'Yes, I thought they would be,' he replied. 'Remember I've had bits of them thrown at me already by the police.'

'Yes, I guess so,' I said. 'But I just thought I'd warn you.'

'Thanks.' Retorted Nick in his usual cheeky tone. I was relieved. I'd been careful to stress how graphic and unpleasant they were to begin to prepare him for what was to come. In his usual coping manner he didn't seem too worried which helped lift me from the depths of despondency I'd descended into. 'Surely,' I felt, 'if he can cope with all this relatively philosophically, it's my duty to do the same and support him.'

I'd warned him. I couldn't do much to soften the pain, but at least I'd warned him. I then hid the insidious papers in the back of my wardrobe under some clothes, hoping and praying that Emily, even in her most curious moments, might never ever locate them. 'Never', I thought, 'not ever, must the girls get hold of them. The sexual details are too graphic and the lies are too awful. How could a fourteen year old read such things about her dad and cope? I'm not sure I'm going to survive, but the girls must never get even a glimpse of them.' Having done that I washed my face and aggressively attacked the bathroom cleaning. 'That was today's quota of tears,' I resolved. 'Now I'll get something done to show I've not wasted the day.'

It wasn't until several days later that Nick actually had a chance to look at the statements. We'd had an endless stream of well meaning visitors and I wouldn't even divulge the papers' whereabouts after 10pm knowing full well that once Nick saw them, he'd need to read the lot and subsequently wouldn't sleep a wink. The tension built as he struggled to make time from work to get to grips with them. It was three days after their arrival that he planned to take the girls to school and then work from home and start the dreaded job of ploughing through the statements.

But he didn't appear back at the house at about nine, his usual time, and I began to wonder what was up. Perhaps he'd popped in to a shop or garage for something? 9.15 and 9.30 came and went and I was getting worried. Eventually the telephone rang.

'Hello, it's me. You won't believe this; but after I'd dropped Felicity off I walked back to the car and my car keys had gone.'

'What?'

'It's true. They must have pinged off my key ring and I've been looking for them for the last hour or so. Can you bring your keys round?'

I took a deep breath. At least he was OK. Yes of course I'd take the spare keys round, but this would have to happen the morning he wanted to start the statements. I jumped into the car and eventually met up with a bedraggled looking Nick. Together we retraced his steps from Felicity's school back to the car and half heartedly searched the undergrowth. There was absolutely no sign, as Nick didn't hesitate to point out. After all he had spent the last hour and a half or so looking. This was the stupid sort of thing that happened when you were stressed I told myself: keep calm, it's nothing compared to what is happening in the rest of our lives.

'Just before we go, I'll pull the car forward in case the keys are well underneath, though I have looked,' said Nick. I peered down amongst the puddles and the odd sodden sweet wrapper, and there I caught sight of a gleam of metal. There it was. 'I've got it.' I squeaked triumphantly. 'I don't believe it,' exclaimed Nick emerging from the driver's seat, with a mixture of frustration and delight in his voice.

Once home Mainwave gave him no respite. He hardly had a second to think and the tension was obvious as he felt the need to get to grips with the legal paper work more and more, without the slightest opportunity of doing so. That same evening Mrs Banbury rang.

'Melanie?'

'Yes.'

'Is everything all right?'

'Yes, of course.' I paused and with an alarming sinking feeling realised that for the first time ever I'd forgotten to take Jessica to her piano lesson. 'Oh, it's Jessica's lesson, isn't it? I'm so sorry. I can't believe I've done this. Oh, I'm such an idiot … I'm really extremely sorry.' I went on to explain the morning's adventure and hoped that was sufficient explanation for my inadequacies. How could I begin to explain what I was going through? Of course, I couldn't. My mind struggled to focus on what to have for the next meal, let alone piano lessons.

At last, Nick had a free day. He reckoned he was as clear as he could ever hope to be at work and left a message on his answer phone requesting that he was only contacted if it was very urgent. Using his computer, he scanned in first Anita's statement, then Penny's, then Deb's. It was his aim to work through them, typing his comments in red alongside the statements to help Mr Dixon get a picture of what had been going on. After all, the statements covered a vast period of time, about seven years in total, the chronology of events was important and many of the girls' details just didn't add up. I tried to get on with the housework, but found it impossible to concentrate. I continually popped in to Nick; how was he doing? Did he want a coffee? He'd spelt this wrong. Predictably Nick didn't like it, and after a couple of jibes, he exploded: 'Let me get on, will you? Just let me get through this. Then I'll print it out and you can change the whole thing to your heart's content.'

I backed hastily out of the study with a mumbled apology. I must, I told myself, remember my dire reaction when I'd initially read the statements, and I'd only scanned them. What it must be like for Nick, reading the horrendous lies in the form of intimate sexual details in Anita's statements, and rather more passionate declarations he'd allegedly made to Penny, I really couldn't begin to anticipate. 'All I know', I thought, 'is that it's going to be very gruesome, that the next few days will be tough with a big T, and somehow we've got to get through it.'

I was absolutely right. The subsequent days were grim. Nick hardly slept at all, and looked increasingly tense and drawn. I tried not to cross him, but you could sense the tension all over the house. 'It's like walking along a knife edge together,' I mused. 'If I slip I crack up, destroy myself and am no use to anybody, if Nick slips the same thing happens; but we could, if we're not careful, try so hard to keep the other one safe, that we actually both lose our balance and both go down.'

Crown court anticipated

Finally Nick began to emerge from the depths. He'd dealt with the first three statements as far as he was able, and didn't anticipate commenting much on the others, which at least superficially seemed genuine enough, and not full of creative fantasy as the others were. 'In some ways,' he said, 'I feel better having gone through them, because they're so ridiculous.' I wondered whether the CPS would see it that way. 'I mean as if I'd tell Penny how much I loved her and that I didn't love you and the girls. Anyone at the church in Oxted will verify that that's a load of nonsense.' I so hoped that would be the case. 'As for telling Anita I needed her hugs, "they were so special etc." for goodness sake, what have these girls been conjuring up in their minds?'

'I've no idea,' I replied. 'But it seems so obvious to me that they've got together, conferred and then come up with these balmy stories. Though I'm still totally baffled as to why, I s'pose they had a tremendous crush on you and when it wasn't reciprocated, they just wanted to get you?'

'I guess so,' sighed Nick, clearly exhausted from the unpleasant job he'd been doing and emotionally drained.

'It's really good he's dealt with that,' I thought. 'But it doesn't really change anything. We're still on that frightful legal roller coaster rushing forward, out of control, with no obvious end or even assistance in sight. Three and a half months this has been going on and I'm shattered, absolutely exhausted. So's Nick. How on earth are we to keep going? What is going to happen? Are the CPS going to plough on regardless of the contradictions in the statements? Is anyone going to speak up for us? You'd never have thought the British justice system maintained people were innocent until proved guilty; we're guilty unless we can possibly prove we're innocent.' Such thoughts circulated in my brain in a vicious figure of eight, sometimes going along one track, sometimes another, but never stopping, never giving me respite from the oppression we were under.

Nick on the whole, coped well. Work was hard and demanding but at least it kept his mind occupied, though he yearned for time off to complete working through the statements. He knew he'd never get it all done before his next visit to Mr Dixon, but he'd try. He'd sit up late at night, after all he couldn't start until Emily had gone to bed, for fear that curiosity got the better of her and she was tempted to peruse the comments over her Dad's shoulder. So he rarely was underway until 9.30 pm. Then after a few minutes readjusting to where he was on the document, which point he'd reached, he'd write his comments next to the girls' statements. There were huge chunks of print he'd put in red brackets with, 'This did not happen, this is fantasy,' by it in red. There were sentences that were chronologically idiotic, there were phrases that he knew could be contradicted by friends who'd been there on the occasion, there were the emails that proved Nick had never said how much he'd loved Penny and his irritation and exasperation increased as he read again how he'd said he didn't love Melanie and the girls. As if!

The night he completed working through the three statements, I had been to a school concert with Emily. On returning late I immediately enquired how he'd got on, and if there'd been any phone calls.

'Yes, George wants you to ring him back.'

'What, at this hour of night?'

'Yup, and Michael Brookwood rang and he wants the family to go round for an hour or so to meet Lydia—you know, his handicapped wife. I've agreed we will go round this Saturday.'

'Oh, for goodness sake,' I exclaimed. 'There'll be nothing in it for the girls, they'll be bored out of their minds, it's ridiculous'. I was tired and intolerant, but Nick too was tense. Totally unexpectedly, the pan he'd been scouring was thrown into the washing up bowl with venomous force. There was an almighty splash and crash, and broken glass and water were distributed instantly all over the kitchen.

'Why is it,' he erupted, 'that I can do nothing right? Absolutely nothing? Everything I do is wrong.'

With that he wrenched open the kitchen door almost pulling it off its hinges, stormed up the hall out of the front door and slammed it behind him.

I stood frozen in the kitchen. To my surprise I didn't feel like crying, I was stunned. Poor Nick, I'd not meant to upset him. But what would be the best thing to do now? Ring George? Clear up the mess? Go after Nick or prepare the girls' lunch boxes for tomorrow? I paused. Surely Nick was the most important? So grabbing my keys, I hurried to the front door and went out. The evening was misty and murky, the nearby street lamp wasn't working and I could only see a few yards up the road. No sign of Nick. I took a couple of irresolute steps up the road. 'This is ridiculous,' I thought. 'He could be anywhere. I can't just abandon the girls. I must hold steady here, stay put and hope Nick returns safe and sound. It's awful, the strain he's under.'

I let myself in again, went back to the kitchen and started collecting up the pieces of broken glass in a newspaper. Although the event had been quite spectacular, only one glass had been in the sink and therefore the damage wasn't serious. As I was mopping the floor, the back door opened.

'I'm sorry,' said a haggard looking Nick.

'It's OK,' I replied, flinging my arms round his shoulders. 'I didn't mean to irritate you'.

'I know,' said Nick. 'I'll finish mopping up while you get on with the lunch boxes.'

Quietly the evening resumed a degree of normality, and when the chores were complete we retreated for another night of unsettled sleep.

'It's strange,' I thought, several days afterwards, 'You think you're coping so well, holding things together, keeping calm and level headed, but the tension's still there, very much so. It's like a firework that only needs a spark to get it going. It's like that for both of us. The girls only have to step out of line and we're short tempered and irritable; and now and again things get out of control, like they did the other night. Poor old Nick. I think it gets worse near a particular event like the next visit to Mr Dixon or a court appearance.' We were only a couple of days off Nick's next visit to Mr Dixon, so I was probably right.

The day he went was a busy one for both of us. Nick had to go into work in the morning and on to the solicitors in the afternoon, while I had a friend to lunch, another to dinner who was planning to stay overnight and a couple of lads from Oxted popping in for the evening. It was probably a good thing for me that I was so busy, for it stopped me dwelling too much on how Nick was getting on. But as the day passed I wondered more and more how he was doing; whether Mr Dixon was all doom and gloom again, and whether there were any glimmers of light. How much we had to disprove before anyone listened to us, and whether the hours Nick had spent on the computer were going to be relevant. 'Oh, please,' I murmured to no one in particular, 'don't let him emerge too despondent from all this.' It was hard to concentrate on the guests, and I knew I should be thinking about preparing the evening meal but I couldn't even decide what to eat, let alone get it ready.

The telephone rang. I snatched at it with understandable violence.

'Hi it's me.'

'Oh hi, have you finished? How did you get on?'

'Yes, I'm just setting off home now.' Nick was aware we had a very sociable evening ahead so, despite the cost, took the time to fill me in on the events of the afternoon from his mobile phone.

'There's sort of good news and bad,' he explained.

'Nick doesn't sound too down,' I thought. Out loud I said, 'Go on.'

'It looks as if the rape charge is going to be dropped. It's very confusing, but apparently they can't prove it or prove it was without consent so it's going to be dropped.'

'Oh?'

'Well, in the worst scenario, that brings the prison sentence instantly down from a maximum of life to a few years.'

'Oh.'

'Which might mean you and the girls could stay put while I'm in prison and we could think what to do about the house afterwards.'

'Right.' My head was spinning. There was so much to take on board all at once.

'Mr Dixon says it'll definitely go to Crown Court, probably around Christmas time and last at least a fortnight 'coz of all the witnesses that'll be called.'

'I see.' Crown Court for a fortnight, it didn't bear thinking of. Why should he be subjected to that? My stomach seized again at the injustice.

'And what they'll do, is dissect the girls' statements and make each one into a separate charge, working on the basis that if they sling enough mud, some'll be sure to stick.'

'Really? Oh no!' I was shocked. All too recently I'd ploughed through the documents and there were innumerable, horrific, graphic occasions of sexual assault described. If they were going to separate each incident, there'd be loads. Surely a jury would never believe he was innocent? It was logical, wasn't it? That if the person being tried was accused of twenty alleged crimes, he must have done some of them, mustn't he? I could feel my heart pounding and my brain on fire.

'Mr Dixon was pleased with my work on the statements and all the supportive letters from our friends I took, and he's already told the CPS there's a groundswell of support for me.'

'Good, what did the CPS say?'

'I don't think it phased them, their approach is that someone is lying in our case, and it's the job of the jury to find out who.'

'Oh, I see.'

'Anyway, that's it in a nutshell. I'll go through it again with you later, if we get a chance. I'll be on my way now, home about 6.30. OK?'

'Yea, fine, I'm just off to take Felicity and Esther to their piano lessons.'

'Right, I'll see you later then, 'bye.'

I put the telephone down, my head was reeling. 'Come on,' I said out loud to the two little girls, 'we must be off quickly or we'll be late for your piano lessons. Sorry about the long phone call, but we must rush now. Have you both got your music books? Your coats? Right, into the car then.'

I made an effort to sound business like and capable. Inside, my stomach griped and my mind was spinning. 'Drive carefully,' I told myself. 'Don't let it get to you, keep calm. Get the girls to their lessons first, take a deep breath.' I parked the car, escorted Felicity and Esther to Mrs Banbury, managed a polite smile and 'See you later', then retreated hurriedly to the safety of the vehicle. 'Don't let yourself go,' I told myself firmly. 'Not here, drive to Tesco and for goodness sake drive carefully.'

As I pulled into the car park the first tears fell, but I concentrated hard on parking before switching off the ignition, putting my face in my hands and crying uncontrollably. The news I'd just been told bubbled through my head in a fermenting froth. Crown Court for two weeks? All that publicity, the strain on our girls, the pressure on Nick. But he was innocent. He shouldn't have to suffer like this. Each allegation a separate charge. How many of those would there be? Oh why did this have to happen? Why did

Anita, Penny and Debs have to conjure up such insanity? Would everyone believe them? Wasn't there any hope? Would it definitely be prison? I continued to sob. My sleeve and the steering wheel were wet, but I didn't care? I thumped the wheel angrily. This was all too much, it was too unfair, it was too tortuous; Nick shouldn't have to suffer like this. Why was it that once on the legal roller coaster there was absolutely no getting off? Because no one had the courage and confidence to say what complete nonsense this case was, because no one really cared at all about Nick Metcalfe, because the police, the CPS, were just trying to achieve a result, make their books look good, regardless of what the real truth was or how much suffering was involved in the process.

I sighed miserably, wiped my face, and went into Tesco to get the eggs and milk I needed for the evening meal. 'I wonder if anyone'll notice my face?' I pondered. 'Does anyone see the anguish in it? The pain we're going through? Probably not. It doesn't affect them, they've got their own problems.' I paid for the goods, took half a dozen deep breaths once outside, then climbed into the car and returned to collect the girls. The outburst was over, I was calmer and knew that now I could concentrate on the evening meal, the children, welcoming Nick when he got in, and the lads from Oxted. 'It's good, you can only cry for so long.' I thought. 'It means you can let at least some of the anguish flow out, have a really good howl and then pull in the reins, get under control and be strong. Quite clever really the way we're made.'

Second court appearance

Predictably the pendulum swung after the visit to the solicitor. Another hurdle had been crossed, though many, many more lay ahead. We were able to enjoy life a bit for the next few days. The sun shone and Nick worked hard in the garden erecting the mini swimming pool. It was only 12 feet across, and 3 feet deep but the girls loved it and were thrilled that Daddy had found the time to put it up. Now the weather was brighter, they were outside a lot enjoying the sunshine. The flowers in our new garden bloomed in abundance and it all looked most attractive. 'And would be wonderful,' I thought, 'if we knew we'd be staying here to enjoy it. If we could be sure we wouldn't have to sell up shortly, if we didn't have the executioner's axe hanging over our heads, if the sun wasn't always darkened by a big black cloud.' But despite the pressures, to a certain degree we were able to appreciate the good weather, being together and the stunning beauty of spring. Blackbirds were busily collecting worms for their young ones, a pair of jays, not seen before, picked up snippets of garden clippings for a nest, and a bright eyed, brilliantly breasted robin kept a close eye on all proceedings; often chirruping away with his head on one side without a care in the world.

After church one Sunday, Nick and I sat together in the conservatory looking at the garden. It needed loads of work done on it, having been left without any attention for years; but it had a tranquil rugged beauty about it nevertheless. We talked about this and that, keeping away for once from topics of law and wrongful accusations. It was pleasant now and again to almost forget the mess we were in, to sit back and live a 'normal' day: to enjoy the outdoors, laugh at the girls' antics and put our anxieties aside for a while. Perhaps the Almighty had made Sunday with that in mind? It was supposed to be a day of rest, perhaps even rest for the poor old over worked, over stressed, over anxious brain? I smiled unconsciously. It was a nice thought anyway and certainly seemed true to an extent.

Court day came round like the inevitable hands of a clock. We felt philosophical. We were hoping that it wouldn't be a long session and having done it once, knew the route to Sevenoaks, our way round and what to expect. The girls were primed that Angie was coming at 6.45 am to have breakfast with them and then to take Emily, Jessica and Felicity to school, followed a little later by Esther to her school. They were under instruction to be good and I had every confidence. It was rare for them to let the side down and certainly since Nick's arrest there had been conscious efforts by all four to be 'extra good' and co-operative.

It was inevitable that the conversation in the car turned to the case. What else was there to talk about? What had we discussed before these events had taken place? If and when it was all over, what would we talk about then? The matter dominated every aspect of our existence, our thoughts, our actions, our reactions, even, I thought, our sleep patterns. Nick hadn't slept well since his arrest, waking every morning about 4 am and getting little sleep subsequently. Whereas I, well only last night I had that terrible dream about Nick in prison. I was being incredibly calm and coping well but I wonder if I really will, if it comes to that? Why, oh why can't the girls take back their lies? If only they'd admit it was all completely fabricated. But, I pondered philosophically, that is unlikely. If they'd settled on going to the police, signed their statements saying they were prepared to stand up in court and testify, then no doubt they would want to go the whole way.

We arrived in good time for our appearance, and went for the familiar stretch leg round Sevenoaks shopping centre. As before, the shops were still closed and I was aware for a second time that everyone out there was busy getting on with their lives while Nick and I were on a huge black roller coaster going goodness only knows where. Back to the car for coffee and a quick prayer and then we returned to the magistrates court, registered at the familiar little desk reminding me again of a station ticket office. The usher was a lady this time, much more genial and less officious. Then we discreetly sat down in the back row of seats. 'What made me think you'd be here already?' Mr Dixon bounded in with a smile. He looked happy and confident which was reassuring for both of us. He shot off up the stairs two at a time and returned a few minutes later. Leaning forward he said: 'I think we're on course. As I told you the rape charge has been dropped and it's simply a question of giving your name and address and fixing the next appearance. Are you busy any time in the next few weeks?' The question threw us and for a brief second we looked blankly into each others faces. I wished I'd brought our calendar but had had no idea that we would have had any say in anything. Up to now the dates had all been dictated from above with absolutely no recourse to us. However putting my wits together speedily I said; 'We're away for half term, at least we hope to be; we could come back of course.' Mr Dixon whipped out a pocket electronic calendar and tapped at it with efficiency. 'No problems, we'll go for the week after that,' he said, and with that he turned his back and was gone.

After a couple of minutes Nick disappeared off to the toilets. 'The excitement's too much for me,' he muttered with a grin, though I knew quite well that anxiety was taking its toll. Predictably as he vanished Mr Dixon reappeared to say he was needed. I hastily explained that he'd be back shortly and to my relief he rounded the corner. The three of us climbed the same flight of stairs as before, same court room, same row of seats in the public gallery, far fewer people bustling around though. The clerk of the court looked little more than a school boy with shortish ginger hair cut in the latest fashion. He seemed genial and smiled at Nick. Whether the atmosphere was really less intimidating than previously or whether it was because we'd been through it once already, I didn't know; but all Nick had to do was state his name, address and date of birth. He was allowed to sit down. There were a few comments about the rape charge being dropped, bail being confirmed and then Mr Dixon and the CPS man were looking at diaries and June 7th was mentioned. Nick was asked to sign a piece of paper and they'd finished.

Once outside the magistrates court Mr Dixon looked like a Cheshire cat. 'There now,' he said proudly. 'That was quick and efficient, wasn't it? As I said, the rape charge has gone, so now, we've got to get to grips with the rest. You'll want to make an appointment to come and see me next week. Great, good. That's all sorted then. Good. You can be on your way.' We muttered our appreciation and ambled back to the car in a bit of a daze. So the rape charge had really gone? Admittedly there were numerous counts of sexual assault remaining: but rape, that foul and terrifying crime had somehow been wiped off the slate. That really was wonderful, less stigma, shorter sentence, but still many, many unpleasant and untrue allegations which would have to be worked through thoroughly in order to stand the faintest chance of refuting them.

We sat in the car holding hands. It was strange how we felt. A sort of emptiness pervaded us, mental strain perhaps? Fatigue? But tinged with a minute ray of light. It was all far from over but the very worst charge had gone which was a huge relief. We drove to Brian and Joyce's for a coffee, shared the news and were soon on our way home. The whole episode had been a non event in many ways, I thought, but one we could so well do without.

For the first time since Nick's arrest, when meeting the girls from school and being plied with a string of questions, largely from Emily, we were able to give more positive news. It was veiled in loose terms while the two younger ones were around, but once they'd gone to bed, I was able to sit down with Emily and Jessica and take them through it. The reaction wasn't one I had anticipated. Emily seemed nonplussed. I had hoped the news would cheer them noticeably, but Emily was too canny for that. 'So Dad's going to be tried for everything else?' she asked.

'Yes, that's right.'

'Well, I suppose it's good in a way, but to be honest Mum, it doesn't seem to make a huge difference to me. They're still saying Dad did a load of horrible things he didn't do, and somehow or other Dad's still got to try and prove he didn't do them.'

'Yes, you're right, of course.'

'Well,' Emily said with a slight teenage gesture of 'I've got life sussed' and a toss of her shoulders, 'Thanks for telling me anyway.'

The hurt went on. She wasn't impressed. Lies were still there, against her father. Lies that were totally fabricated but had shaken her whole family's existence to its very core.

Nick's next appointment with Mr Dixon was the following week. I noticed how, as with the court appearance, knowing his solicitor a little now, where to go and what to do eased some of the stress. Nick was getting to know his solicitor quite well now. Mr Dixon believed in him which gave him confidence and helped him find the sessions more acceptable. It was as if they were planning a battle. But at least they were both very much on the same side, it was just the technicalities of strategy that had to be discussed. Nick was confident of his route to Croydon and was settled in his own mind that there was no more mud to be unearthed and slung at him. While the police had been rooting around looking for further proof against him there was a continual fear that someone else would allege something gross. But that stage seemed to be behind them, so it was now a question of dealing with the mud that had already been slung. The session was briefer than anticipated, as a partner was sick and Mr Dixon was having to do two people's work. However Mr Dixon's main aim was to have a brain storming session with Nick, firing question after question at him, desperately trying to piece together the puzzle, to make coherence out of chaos and logic out of a situation that seemed to be completely lacking sense. What he needed, more than ever was a psychological profile of Anita and Penny. 'If I can work out what's driving them, then I'll know how to defend this.' He said. An hour and a half later, Nick really wasn't sure he'd been of much assistance. After all he was a computer man not a psychologist. Mr Dixon was still struggling to sort this one. Nick had commented that both girls seemed to have gone off church, but Mr Dixon felt that was largely irrelevant, explaining that this was a specific venomous attack on an individual and his family rather than an institution.

The only other important detail Mr Dixon had sorted was the appointment of a barrister. He explained how the sooner this was done the better, as the barrister could then get to know the defendant and build up a rapport. 'I've contacted Chambers,' he explained. 'And we've been allocated Mr Stephano, an excellent choice in my opinion. First rate. He's an experienced lawyer, a solid family man and should do a most satisfactory job. You'll need to meet him in due course, my secretary'll contact you once it's all sorted out.' Nick speculated that even more money would be involved, but didn't comment. He knew he'd be told at an appropriate time. He drove home feeling relatively calm. He'd done his very best to assist Mr Dixon and his understanding of the two girls, and there'd been no further worrying revelations.

It wasn't until a couple of evenings later when Andy came down for a meal, that I began to wonder if we were beginning to make some headway. Andy was a good friend from Oxted, who'd gone to Italy with Nick on both occasions, had done a psychology degree and was interested in the whole bizarre situation not only as a friend of ours but because it intrigued him greatly. Motive was probably the paramount question. As the three of us discussed events, the girls' characters from every possible perspective, I said thoughtfully, 'You know, I'm wondering whether it's Penny who's the chief instigator in all this, not Anita, though I know Anita's allegation is by far the more serious.'

'Why?' Demanded the two men together.

'Well, I'm just thinking back to that time I upset Penny on Guy Fawkes night, you remember, Nick?'

He did of course, but Andy had to be filled in. I had been shopping and bumped into Penny who was back for the weekend from university. Penny informed me that although Anita, who was by then a junior leader, was committed to going to the display at Guildford with the young people that night, she'd arranged to go out with Penny instead. I had been unimpressed. I was already taking our four girls to a local display in Oxted and so was unavailable, so if Anita didn't go it left Nick without a female leader, a situation we made every effort to avoid. It was essential that a lady should be in attendance and Anita had been quite happy to come. Nick, who'd had a variety of pressures at work had been most relieved.

'So what did you say to Penny?' enquired the curious Andy.

'I'm not sure exactly, but assuming Penny would understand, I remember saying that Anita couldn't just let Nick down like that, it was so unreasonable. I was hopping mad actually, but I don't think I came across as too irate, it's not in my nature.'

'So what happened then?'

'Before Melanie was even back from the shops,' filled in Nick, 'the pair of them were both on our doorstep demanding to see me. We went into the study, Anita seemed overwrought at my disappointment in her, and said she needed a social life as well as helping in the youth group and I think it was from that point on that she stopped assisting. And in the end I had to go to the fireworks without a female leader, because I tried several other ladies in the church and none of them could do it.'

'Yes,' I interrupted impatiently. 'but the point I'm making is, that if Penny hadn't gone and wound Anita up nothing much would have come of the event. Anita would never even have known how cheesed off I was.'

'So what you're saying is,' said Andy as the light began to dawn, 'that Penny could well have instigated the whole allegations in much the same way?'

'Exactly,' I said emphatically. 'Anita's always been a weak and easily influenced character. Alice, Deb's sister, was told off at school by her form tutor for dominating her. I've been so baffled thinking that she would have taken the initiative to set this whole thing up, but perhaps under Penny's influence it could well have happened?'

'You do have a point,' remarked Nick. Meanwhile Andy had grabbed a pen and paper, determined to jot down some of the latest ideas and suggestions. We all felt how essential it was to try and unravel the mysterious knot of intrigue that we found ourselves tied up in; whether we were actually making any headway was not very apparent.

'I'll try and draw up a psychological profile of each of the girls for you to give to Mr Dixon,' said Andy. 'This evening's certainly been most interesting, but we must keep working on it. We've got to try and sort this mess out.' Nick and I so appreciated Andy's support and commitment. So many of our friends were living through this with us. Concerned, anxious, puzzled friends were offering assistance at every twist and turn and we couldn't have managed without them.

It was only a fortnight later when Andy visited again. This time with Andrew, who'd grown up through the youth group and was quietly firm in his support and had visited several times since Nick's arrest. Andrew was at university, but on every possible occasion had come down with Andy to express support and go over the thorny issues, offering assistance wherever possible. They'd arranged to meet us in time for our church service, and then return with us for lunch.

As we walked into the building we saw Andrew and Andy already there and greeted them briefly. They sat diagonally opposite us and the service commenced. Throughout our ordeal Nick and I had found the services comforting and soothing, but the hymns always proved an emotional experience. We knew God cared and the other people at church cared, but it was so good to be altogether in one building worshipping and praising him; putting aside other issues and being reminded that he was sovereign.

On this occasion as we stood up for the third hymn I looked across at the back of the two Andrews and it occurred to me, not for the first time, how exceptionally lucky we were to have these two young men offering their wholehearted support. They telephoned regularly, visited as often as they could, and even amused themselves keeping an eye open for Anita, Penny and Debs in Oxted. Appreciation and emotion swept over me and to my immense surprise tears fell. I hoped no one noticed, but continued to be grateful for the exceptional support Nick and I were receiving.

It was rather embarrassing when Andy, over Sunday lunch, ever astute, enquired as to why I had been looking at them during the third hymn. I blushed like a beetroot and acknowledged that due to the strange circumstances in which we found ourselves I'd been overcome with appreciation for all that he and Andrew had done for us. Andy grinned wryly, knowing full well he'd embarrassed me, and left it at that.

A welcome holiday

The day after Andy's evening visit, whilst busying myself with a duster, I couldn't get the thoughts of the previous night off my mind. 'I wonder if there's anything at all in the girls' statements,' I thought, 'that would confirm our suspicions?' Abandoning the housework, I pulled out the well hidden brown envelopes and poured over its contents. As always the intimate sexual details caused me to feel nauseous, but I was determined to track down a clue if there was so much as a hint of one to be found. What do they say in detective games and novels? The clues are always there, it's simply a matter of finding them. I read through both Penny's and Anita's statements twice, and felt quite sure on the second reading I'd unearthed just a snippet of information. Anita stated that 'when Penny told me she had been touched by Nick as well, I realised I wasn't the only one and knew something had to be done.' Penny stated; 'I told Anita what Nick had done to me and she then told me all he had done to her.' 'Yes,' I thought, 'Yes, it's nothing amazing, but the way I read it, Penny instigated this mess and Anita's gone along with it for some unknown reason. I wonder what Nick'll think? I wonder if Andy will read this as I do?'

A few days later Andy's psychological profile arrived neatly typed up on A4 paper. We poured over it with interest. After outlining Anita, Penny and Debs' characters, he then suggested two possible motives, putting his backing on the first one. The first suggestion was that Anita's boyfriend had been of great influence. Perhaps their physical relationship hadn't worked and Anita had blamed Nick. Then perhaps the boyfriend feeling there was mileage to be made and/or feeling protective of Anita had persuaded her to pursue it and Penny had jumped on the bandwagon. The second idea was more along the lines that I had been thinking; that Penny had felt peeved with Nick for interfering with her night out with Anita, had wound Anita up and together they'd come up with their amazing concoction of sexual abuse.

While both versions had hints of veracity about them, we felt they were really no nearer the true motive or getting to the bottom of the mess than we had been before. We were, of course, grateful to Andy for his logical thinking and help, but were frustrated that after all this time and consideration we were no nearer the truth. Was there any getting into the machinations of two teenage girls' minds? Would we ever have a clear picture of how they'd arrived at the dire stories they'd told the police?

It was so baffling, and continued to irritate and frustrate us as the weeks progressed. One telephone call from Joyce Darnell went over the same material again. Anita's boyfriend was mentioned and Joyce reminded me: 'You do know he's a medical doctor, don't you?'

'Yes, yes, of course.' I knew, but I replied sceptically: 'He says he is, I wonder if there's any way we can find out?' Once I'd finished the call I pondered the matter and felt it was worth pursuing. I rang Ann Wilson, whose husband was a GP and explained my predicament. Ann kindly said she'd talk to Ian about it. About midday Ian rang back. He'd rung the General Medical Council and they had no Tim Long registered on their books. After a brief conversation with Ian, I established that the way to find out more was to write to the G.M.C. myself. Ian kindly provided the address.

Grabbing pen and paper I jotted down the query in as brief and polite a manner possible. I felt the information I could give about him was scanty to say the least, name and address and approximate age. Had Tim Long ever been a medical practitioner? If so when, and why was he struck off? I enclosed an S.A.E. to encourage them to reply.

Great was my surprise and delight when two days later a response came. A delightfully civil letter from the G.M.C. explaining how they'd checked their records and could find no one of that name, however if any more information was forthcoming they'd be only too pleased to be of further assistance. I wasn't sure how to react. Should I be glad to have discovered that this chap was lying? Or did he simply practise under a different name? Did it matter anyway? And would it be of any assistance whatsoever in helping to clear Nick's name? Once again I felt baffled and confused, but decided to forward the letter on to Mr Dixon with a brief explanation just in case it ever was of any help.

The school summer half term came as a blessed oasis amidst the cares and concerns of the case. I was forced to turn my mind to packing and preparing for a visit to Herefordshire to see my parents. Nick too had to give it some consideration even though he'd only be there for the weekend while the girls and I were to stay for the full week.

My parents, hidden away in their tiny three bedroom thatched cottage provided a perfect escape from the anxieties that haunted the pair of us. The accusations somehow seemed less real and less threatening there in the peace and tranquillity of the quiet countryside. Instead of a fear of the telephone ringing and the letterbox clanking bringing more ominous news, the only background noise was of the sheep bleating and the house martins chattering. Life at Ivy Cottage was like living alongside the world. Remote in the extreme, the old low ceilinged Tudor home had a tranquil atmosphere and a time scale unlike anywhere else. The grandparents had tea in bed about nine and breakfast was rarely before ten. The meal was casual and relaxed, the children leaving the table while the adults lingered to chat. By the time breakfast was washed up it was coffee time and then there'd be a trip down the road to play in the stream, or to see new born lambs on the nearby farm, before lunch.

In the afternoon some sort of gentle activity was usually devised, a walk over the hills, or along the lanes a mile and a half to the next village, or even a little further to the friendly little coffee shop. There was never any rush, no keeping to timetables, no rigid routine or regime; but each day drifted by in a pleasant and relaxing way. The pressure was off, Grandma did the cooking, Grandpa sorted out the Aga, and Nick and I were free to sit, stroll, read, or play with the children as the mood took us.

We both slept long eleven and twelve hour nights and felt a lot better for it. There was no rowdy television, the telephone never rang and the post was negligible and didn't concern us. It was good to go for a stroll over the hills and discuss the rolling landscape, how far you can see, the flora and fauna and how it had been affected by a particularly dry spring; and to let the more pressing issues fade away, not into total oblivion, absolutely no chance of that, but at least into the background, to assume a less dominant position, more of a dreamlike quality. Nick returned home after the weekend to resume work, but the girls and I stayed on.

The girls had a wonderful week. The weather was far from spectacular, one bright day and the rest pretty damp. Nevertheless, they too benefited from the relaxed atmosphere, the calm surroundings, the slower pace of life, good food, plenty of sleep and the enchanting countryside. Grandma and Grandpa didn't hesitate to spoil them, as they did every visit. Riding mornings were arranged at the local stables, also a trip to a Victorian working farm and to a beautiful medieval castle where the girls romped around playing imaginary games of knights and ladies, servants and scullery maids until nearly closing time. Nothing eventful happened that week. It was a blissful insert of almost magical quality that the whole family so desperately needed. None of us really wanted to come home. Back to the housework, washing, cooking and cleaning for me; the girls back to school exams and SATS, and of course, why could it not go away? Back to yet another court appearance.

Thankfully in the car on the four hour trek down south the girls seemed cheery enough; after all they were going to see Nick again and their beloved cats. 'At least we won't have to be polite now,' stated the cheeky Felicity, having found the etiquette of the older generation a bit of a struggle as she always did on every visit. 'And I can say 'Me and Felicity' now without Grandma always correcting it to 'Felicity and I!' piped up Esther, with such a perfect imitation of Grandma's disapproving tone that there were howls of laughter from the back seat. 'Yes,' I thought, 'it's good to go away and it's good to come back too; if only the executioner's axe weren't hanging over our heads.'

Nick was pleased to see us all again and while the girls were busily unpacking he sat with me over a coffee and related all he'd been up to. It was mainly work, work and more work with an hour or two gardening thrown in for good measure.

'But you won't believe what happened this morning,' he said with his mischievous schoolboy grin. 'What?' I asked.

'There was a knock at the front door at about 10 o'clock and when I answered it there was a smartish looking chap, who appeared vaguely official.'

'Yes?' My heart beat faster, what on earth was coming next?

'He said, 'Good morning, I'm from the Cranleigh News ...'

An audible gasp escaped me as my mouth dropped open, but seeing my alarm Nick continued quickly; '... and I'm doing a survey to see whether or not you take it regularly.'

'I don't believe it,' I exclaimed. 'I just don't believe it. I bet your face was a picture. Oh, wow! I'd've slammed the door in his face, or died or something. Do you think he realised how panic stricken you were?'

'I've no idea,' said Nick. Then added with a wry smile, 'He probably rushed back to his office and said 'there must be something very fishy going on at 6 Elmtree Avenue. The bloke who opened the door to me didn't half act strange when I told him who I was!'

'Oh don't,' I muttered. 'It's too awful.'

Our great fear was that the story of Nick's arrest and subsequent court appearances would be splashed all over the papers. So far nothing had been printed. It was only much later that we realised that this was the result of the fervent prayer of our friends at Oxted who made it a matter of daily concern.

Third court appearance

We had Sunday to find our feet after the break and then Monday was yet another court appearance, with the added complication of an Inset day for Felicity. After a lot of consideration Nick and I decided to take Felicity up to Oxted with us, leave her with Brian and Joyce and drive on to court. The routine was as before. Angie kindly came and had breakfast with Emily, Jessica and Esther and ensured they got off to school, while Nick, Felicity and I set off at seven to drive up to Oxted. The journey felt different as the usual subjects of conversation were out of bounds with Felicity's little ears ever alert. The school summer fete was discussed; what she'd do at Brian and Joyce's and what colour guinea pig she was hoping to have for her birthday. Joyce welcomed the three of us with open arms and had nobly brought all Rick's old Lego downstairs for Felicity's entertainment. It was clear that Felicity was quite tickled with all the individual attention she was going to get, as she was offered first fizzy lemonade and then chocolate biscuits. I felt relieved. At least I didn't need to worry about her, she was obviously in for a good time and blissfully unconcerned about her parents' antics. After coffee and a chat we drove on to Sevenoaks. Neither of us knew quite what to expect but were sure it would not be such a brief session as previously, that more details of the case would be voiced and very possibly the press would get hold of it too.

Mr Dixon arrived minutes after us with his reassuring smile and handshake. 'Our aim,' he said decisively, 'is to get the CPS to agree to Crown Court with as little fuss and bother as possible and to get you out of here and on your way as soon as we can.' We nodded in agreement. Mr Dixon then darted off up the stairs to organise the hopefully slick operation. He'd previously explained to Nick how essential it was to go to Crown Court and be judged by a jury. The alternative was a magistrates court which admittedly was much less intimidating and the procedure probably quicker, but it tended to deal with lesser crimes and the majority of those were clearly guilty. The magistrate therefore, had the right to sentence and nine tenths of the time he did so for anything up to the maximum of one year in prison. Whilst Crown Court was far more of an upheaval, one had far greater chance of having the whole case heard in every detail and consequently being assessed totally fairly. Mr Dixon had been adamant from the start that, bearing in mind the gravity of the accusations, the complexity of the case, and Nick's total innocence, Crown Court was definitely the place to have the case tried.

At just after ten he appeared again and beckoned to us both. Although this was Nick's third session at Sevenoaks it didn't really help much. It was nerve wracking each time and I loathed seeing my innocent husband standing so apparently helplessly in the dock. I sat in the Public Gallery once again, hoping and praying it would all go according to plan. Nick confirmed his name, address and date of birth and then the clerk of the court explained to the magistrate what was going on. The CPS lady, a young woman with a large blond pony tail, then stood up and outlined their case. She requested that the identity of the 'victims' might be protected throughout the trial having been under age at the time of the assaults. She also explained that in view of the serious nature of the offences and the huge disparity in age, the CPS requested the case be taken to Crown Court. The accused being forty and the 'victims' merely twelve years of age. She then detailed one or two of the gross sexual acts Nick was alleged to have committed to emphasise the gravity of the whole affair.

At this point Mr Dixon popped up and explained that whilst the defendant was pleading 'Not Guilty' to all the charges, he too felt that Crown Court was the appropriate place as the accusations were so serious. After a moment's pause the magistrate seemed quite happy with that suggestion. Looking round the court she announced: 'If there are any members of the press present will they please note the required anonymity of the victims.' There were more shufflings and looking at diaries before July 5th was settled on for Mr Metcalfe to appear at Guildford Crown Court. Nick signed a couple of pieces of paper and the trauma was over.

Outside court Nick, Mr Dixon and I congregated. I was seething. 'Victims!' The only person who was a victim was standing in the dock. It was outrageous. As for the disparity of age, Nick was forty one now so how could he have been forty, six or seven years ago? And how could Anita have been twelve when these dreadful assaults took place when she only came to the youth group when she was fourteen? And what on earth was all this business about protecting their identity? *They* bring these ridiculous accusations and *they* get protected. They were nineteen or twenty now, so why did they need to remain anonymous? It didn't make sense. 'We've got a twelve year old daughter, but I bet there's no protecting her identity, is there?' Mr Dixon shrewdly let me vent my frustration and wrath before responding to the various questions I'd raised. They can, of course, be called victims, he explained, because if the alleged offences had been committed then they most certainly would have been victims. Yes, the law did protect their identity throughout and regardless of the outcome; and no, there was absolutely no protection whatsoever for Nick, me or any of our children. He went on to discuss other aspects of the case and reminded me that 'This is clearly an attack on the whole family, not just Nick but the whole unit. It'll probably help you cope with the onslaught if you bear that in mind.'

To us the case was an outrage, the law an ass and justice non-existent. But we fully accepted that there was no other course of action than to continue the ride along the tortuous legal roller coaster we were already on. We were both wildly frustrated with the situation but resigned as we drove back to Oxted. We agreed with each other completely about the ludicrous untrue comments of the prosecution, and hoped to goodness that when it finally came up at Guildford, someone somewhere would speak up for us and get across the reality and truth of the matter.

It was reassuring, arriving at Joyce's, to discover what a good time Felicity had had. Not only had she built an amazing Lego house, stuck in many of the stamps in her collection but she'd listened to *'The Secret Garden'* on a cassette and seemed very pleased with herself. Joyce unexpectedly offered lunch which was appreciated by all of us, before our not too disconsolate trio set off home. Nick had decided to stop off at a garden centre and buy some equipment with which to build a barbecue. I wondered whether that would interest Felicity much, after all it was her day off school and Mum and Dad hadn't exactly entertained her royally.

The situation was soon resolved as Nick bought his barbecue bits speedily and then eyed up the packets of seeds. 'I thought I might buy some runner beans,' he said. 'My Dad always grew them with great success and he's no gardener, so I thought I might have a go.' He considered the assorted varieties and Felicity idly eyed them too. 'Look, look, Dad,' she exclaimed excitedly. 'There's 'Seeds 4 Kids' here, runner beans. Can I have these, please?' 'That's an idea.' I interjected, 'You can have the big bean bonanza. Daddy growing his and you yours, and we'll see who produces the most beans!' Both packets were duly bought and the conversation for the rest of the journey revolved round bean growing; happy banter between Nick and Felicity on whose would win and why. As I listened quietly, I couldn't but notice the amazing contrast of the day. In the morning Nick was in the dock at Sevenoaks court being accused of abominable sexual misconduct and in the afternoon he was joking with Felicity about planting beans. 'He really does cope well with the situation,' I thought. 'Incredibly well.'

A couple of days later after work Nick was digging in the garden. I was tidying up the usual post bath time chaos upstairs when he called me with a note of urgency in his voice. Wondering what was the cause and with a little apprehension I dropped the towel I'd been folding and hurtled down the stairs two at a time and out through the kitchen into the garden. Nick's voice called again from beyond the garden gate, 'Has he put a spade through his foot?' I wondered as I darted across the lawn like a frightened rabbit. 'Come quietly,' muttered a very healthy sounding voice, 'and look over there.' I stepped gently forward through the bracken and brambles and looked. There, not a hundred yards away, stood a young deer. It seemed to be looking at us and was standing stock still. The sheen on its coat in the setting summer sun was stunning, its ears were pricked up and the chestnut brown on its side against the fresh green foliage was spectacular. We both stood there, not daring to move, hardly daring to breathe. The sight was strangely comforting, amidst our nightmarish existence it was reassuring and peaceful seeing the beautiful creature standing there so gracefully and poised as if just for us. It was a moment you wanted to capture in a time capsule and keep for ever.

Then, in a split second it turned and vanished into the bushes, the spell was broken and we looked at each other with relaxed contented expressions on our faces. 'That was fantastic,' I said quietly.

'Yes,' agreed Nick, 'I thought you'd like to see it.'

Nature once again had spoken to us, calmed us down and given us some valued temporary respite.

Nick's next hurdle was meeting Mr Stephano, the barrister Mr Dixon had located for him. The date was arranged, then rearranged, then rearranged again. Apparently barristers are hard people to pin down but Nick found the situation frustrating in the extreme.

'First I moved my meetings to Friday morning because I was meant to meet this bloke in an afternoon,' he spluttered in a slightly raised, exasperated voice. 'Then the appointment was changed to the morning, so I moved some of my meetings to Friday afternoon and some to Monday afternoon, and now it's gone back to being in the afternoon. It's hopeless. How on earth can I carry on at work when this sort of thing happens?'

I was oozing with sympathy and knew how essential it was to remain calm while he was so tense. 'I know,' I said. 'It's really tough, but as all this progresses, work'll have to let you off some of your duties, otherwise things'll be impossible.'

'They'd better,' he muttered between his teeth.

The following morning he set off to work as usual and was then going on to see Mr Stephano. 'Unusual name,' I thought as I waved him off. 'I wonder what nationality he is? I do so hope Nick takes to him. I hope he's sympathetic. I wonder what line he'll want to take on our defence? It's so important that Nick trusts him and feels he'll fight our corner well. I trust there won't be a character clash.'

The day crawled along for me, and Nick was never far from my thoughts. Eventually the telephone rang and Nick's cheery voice announced the interview was over.

'How did it go?' I enquired anxiously.

'Oh fine.'

'Did you like him?'

'Yes, yes, he seemed really clued up. He's about fifty, reminds me of that cousin of yours, you know the one with specs?'

'Mike Hammond?'

'Yes, that's the one. Very similar in many ways.'

'What did he say?'

'I'll tell you about it when I get home, it'll be at least a couple of hours, the traffic's dire and I am sitting doing absolutely nothing in a traffic jam at the moment.'

'OK don't worry. I'll serve up dinner for the rest of us and you can microwave yours. I'm so glad you liked him, I'll see you later then; take care.'

I put the telephone down with a huge sense of relief. At least that hurdle had been crossed satisfactorily. Of course, my mind was buzzing with questions, but I was so delighted that Mr Stephano had proved satisfactory. 'Good old Mr Dixon, he's really chosen the right man by the sounds of things,' I thought. 'And he'll definitely be the right man if he can get Nick out of this hole.'

Turning my mind to the children, I made a concentrated effort to prepare the meal, communicate genially with the girls, take an interest in the fact that Esther had been chosen to sing at the wedding of one of her teachers in the summer, and to share the concern of Emily and Jessica at their imminent school exams. The three younger ones were in bed by the time Nick finally arrived and Emily was practising the piano. So he was able to come in and have his meal and chat straight away. I half expected him to be tired, jaded and looking rather drawn; after all, some of his visits to Mr Dixon had left him very much in that condition. But he seemed cheery and chatty and clearly pleased with the meeting.

Over his chilli con carne he told me all about it. 'Mr Stephano is English, about fifty, glasses, a little tubby, very very much like your cousin as I said. He's obviously incredibly clever, absorbs facts like a sponge and is already getting everything sussed. The solicitors have a lady called Janice who acts as go between. She's bright too, well clued up and I had a good chat with her after I'd finished with Mr Stephano. She works for Dixon and liaises with Stephano, and says that by the time of the trial, he'll be eating and sleeping our case and know everything there is to know about it.'

'Good,' I interjected. I liked what I was hearing and was eager for him to carry on.

'The good news is he says it should only take a week in court. The bad news is that he'll probably want you as a witness.'

'Why is that bad news?' I asked. 'It's about time someone wanted to speak to me. No one's even asked me a thing and I am ever so slightly involved,' I said with indignation and a note of sarcasm in my voice.

'Yes, I know, but if you're a witness you can't sit in the public gallery and listen to what is going on. So you won't hear all the prosecution witnesses statements or them being questioned; you won't hear a thing until you've been called.'

'So I'll miss the worst bit, when I really wanted to be there for you?' I asked in dismay.

'Looks like it,' replied Nick. 'Janice explained it all to me afterwards. Apparently all those really concerned with the case, like Brian and Joyce, are sure to be called as witnesses, so I'm all on my lonesome ownsome when the prosecution are going for the jugular.'

'That's awful.'

'That's the way it is.'

'Oh well, we'll just have to do whatever Mr Stephano says; he's the boss and knows, I hope, what he's up to. But what a pain.'

'Yup, and there's another thing.'

'What?'

'You won't be allowed to meet Mr Stephano if you're a witness. 'Coz it mustn't look as if he's been influencing the witnesses at all.'

'Oh great!' I paused. 'If that's the way it is, so be it. What else did he say?'

'Well, he hasn't had long to read through everything yet. Apparently he's off to Lewes tomorrow for a fortnight's murder trial and he'll take all my papers and read them in his hotel. But he asked me loads of questions, jotted down the answers and says that one way of tackling this might be to bring in all the girls from the youth group, one after the other who are so adamant that nothing dodgy was going on. That's just one possible approach. He wants to have a longer session with me after the next court appearance in July.'

'Did he say what would happen at court then?'

'Yes. Apparently it's another one of these formalities and should only take about five minutes. All I have to do is say my name, date of birth and address again. The prosecution will then state their case and Mr Stephano will state ours and roughly how many witnesses he intends calling and then the judge, I think it's the judge, allocates an amount of time, like three days or a week, to the case and the clerk of the court looks in the diary and says when there's next that length of time in court free. Oh yes, and you have to say if you need video evidence etc. Because then you have to have a court room with a video machine. 'Though,' Nick added, 'if there's any documentation or whatever missing, the whole thing's adjourned and we go through the same loop a month or six weeks later.'

'Great,' I said sarcastically, fully appreciating that the agony was set to continue for many a month yet, if not into next year. 'Did Mr Stephano say much else?' I enquired, anxious to glean every bit of information. But Nick was getting tired and felt he'd done a more than adequate job relaying information.

'Oh don't go on at me, I've told you all I can remember. How's your day been anyway?'

The barrister conversation was clearly over and I took the hint and told Nick how the girls' school days had gone. I related how Esther had been chosen by the head mistress to go to the local Church of England church with three other children from the school to dedicate the new church hall, also how she was to sing at Mr Orbell's wedding. Then I went on to explain how Felicity had fallen off her bike, cycling round after school; no serious damage done but a nasty grazed knee and a slightly bent pedal and that Emily and Jessica had been busy revising hard upstairs for their forthcoming exams.

Meeting the barrister

There was no written confirmation of Nick's meeting with Mr Stephano and soon it faded somewhat into the background; we were able to put the case on the back burner and get on with living. It was still a bizarre existence, trying to live 'normally' when in reality everything was so abnormal. Great Aunt Grace came to stay and spoilt us rotten, paying the weekly bill in Tesco and insisting on 'little treats' for us on every possible occasion. It was very sweet of her I felt, and certainly I was more than grateful for any financial aid that was offered, but it was still such a strain having to act out the farce of everyday living when in reality life was one big chaotic query.

Once she'd gone, absentmindedly leaving her wash bag behind, the young people from Oxted descended on us. Mary Darlington, one of the current youth group leaders, had rung up previously and explained that the group were coming down to the area for a camping weekend and could they possibly pay us a visit? I was touched but a little apprehensive. Was Mary sure that it was OK to bring the young people to our house, bearing in mind the charges levelled at Nick? Mary's reply was encouraging; 'Oh, nobody believes those, or is the least little bit worried. We thought we might come to your church Sunday morning and then back to lunch at your house? Not that we want you to have to cook, of course, we'll bring something we can just heat through.'

'That really would be great,' I exclaimed. 'It would be good to see you all again, and it'll encourage Nick to feel he's not such an outcast when it comes to young people after all. It'll be good for our girls too, after all they've had the house full of young people for so many years that it'll make life seem normal again. That's a really lovely idea as long as it fits in with all your plans?'

'Of course, otherwise we wouldn't have suggested it.'

'Well, leave the puddings to me,' I said enthusiastically, then remembering the busy weekend I had ahead of me, I added, 'actually, I'll probably not have time to do anything epic, is ice cream from Tesco OK?'

It was a hectic weekend. Felicity had a party in Oxted so she had to be driven over there and collected a couple of hours later, Emily had a friend to stay for the night so beds had to be made up and rooms tidied, and Esther went for a sleep over with Katy, her little chum from school, necessitating me to organise some comprehensive packing: otherwise some essential item for the sleepover such as a night-shirt, or even worse her teddy, was sure to have been forgotten. Nick and I seemed to be rushing around like lunatics, and then there was the prospect of twenty two youngsters descending on us for Sunday lunch. Nevertheless, it all went off uneventfully and gave us plenty to think about other than the forthcoming court appearance. The young people all appeared at church and then followed us back to our house in an assortment of vehicles. Coffee and casual chat ensued and it was lovely to have the house alive and vibrant once again. Teenage banter, humour and antics had been so noticeably absent over the recent months and it helped all six of us to have the house full of lively conversation and laughter once again.

The following Monday disaster struck. We were all tired and not up as promptly as we should have been. Nick and the girls were already running five minutes late when Nick rushed into the kitchen with a concerned look on his face. 'You haven't seen my wallet have you?' I hadn't, but instantly went into hunt mode. 'I had it when I popped into B & Q on Saturday,' explained Nick, 'but where has it gone since?' The tension was tangible as we both scurried around looking on surfaces, in drawers, behind curtains and down the sides of armchairs. 'It's no good,' announced Nick, his face drawn with anxiety, 'if I don't leave now the girls are going to be really late for school.' He leapt into the car where the girls were sitting like statues, only too aware of the severe stress and determined not to exasperate the situation, slammed the door and shot off.

I felt totally despondent. 'I really can't handle any more hassle,' I thought. 'I just can't. Living with this burden is almost more than I can bear, anyway. Yet I have to bear it for everyone's sake. I have to be strong for the girls, for Nick, for normality, for routine. But it's such a strain and I just can't take any more.' I sank into an armchair and the tears cascaded down. Then remembering that Esther was still around I rubbed my eyes aggressively, blew my nose and resumed the hunt. The garage, perhaps? The car, the kitchen drawers, or had it been picked up in a pile of clothes?

Soon it was time to take Esther to school and on returning I was so tempted to sit down and howl. But I didn't. Forcing myself to do the washing up, I stood, my mind in neutral due to emotional exhaustion, and wondered what would be thrown at us next. Nick had lost all his credit cards, £100 in cash and would be completely stranded. Several coffees later and bed covers changed, I felt more composed. 'After all,' I reasoned with myself, 'Monday mornings never were my speciality, so it's not surprising that this one in particular got me down so much.' I'd now rung the police and asked if it had been handed in, unfortunately not; and rung the stores Nick had visited on Saturday, but they'd seen no sign of it. Nick had then contacted me from work to say he was having the most awful morning with a key member of his staff threatening to walk out because he was getting too many work calls on his weekends. Despite this he had managed to cancel his credit cards. So all the necessary action had taken place and all was not lost. It was just one more of life's many frustrations hurled at us at this time and one more that had to be overcome in order to maintain our sanity and remain intact.

When Nick's Dad rang, and was told the whole story, he oozed sympathy and understanding. 'You need a break,' he said. 'A weekend away or something, just the pair of you.'

'Fat chance of that,' I thought, 'with four kids.'

'I'll tell you what,' he continued. 'We're coming down on Wednesday, let me treat you to a meal out, we'll baby-sit.' I could hardly refuse and the thought of a bit of time out was attractive.

By the time Wednesday arrived I wondered whether it was such a good idea after all. I had to cook dinner for the children and the grandparents before we went and felt totally exhausted from a busy day. But I dutifully changed and accompanied Nick for a meal out. Once there, the evening took on a new appearance. Fresh surroundings, new faces, exciting menu, I was glad I'd come. We had a fantastic meal, ate far too much but thoroughly enjoyed ourselves. Surrounded by young people and families with babies, it reminded us of our courting days when we were footloose and fancy free without a care in the world. It may have been a totally fanciful feeling, but it was very pleasant. 'This is the sort of moment it would be good to freeze, and dip into on occasions to experience the pleasure over and over again,' I mused.

The dream sadly had to come to an end, the grandparents had to make tracks and lunch boxes had to be prepared for school the next day. Nevertheless, the switch off time had been useful and beneficial, and perhaps had even helped equip us for the events which were to follow. Firstly there was the concert at Felicity's school, where Felicity sang her little heart out and Nick and I, Emily and Jessica sat back and relaxed and enjoyed it. Then a weekend, long since booked up with my sister Rebekah. Although I was looking forward to it, it meant even more business than our normal hectic routine. The children had to be helped with their packing and someone asked to feed the cats.

'On reflection,' I realised, 'that weekend had been a good distraction. Frantically busy but giving Nick and me no time to fret about Monday. The girls had enjoyed it, the travelling had gone well, Nick had helped Chris in the garden, I had pottered around assisting Rebekah and the girls had rushed off with their cousins, had had a whale of a time and had only re-appeared, as is the wont of children, at mealtimes! Yes, it was definitely a good weekend, even though I hadn't really been looking forward to it at all.' I concluded.

Then came Monday. The court appearances came round with monotonous regularity and Nick relished this one no more than he'd relished any of the others. Thankfully we'd both slept well the night before. Probably not having slept particularly well in strange beds at Rebekah's and Chris' we were so shattered on Sunday night, we crashed out. This time it was Guildford Crown court, not Sevenoaks, so we could afford to leave a little later. Esther was dropped off at her friend's house and the other three were left at the bus stop. 'What exactly's going to happen today?' I enquired once we were on our own and en route at last.

'I don't know exactly,' retorted Nick with one of his cheeky grins which I loved so much. 'But according to Mr Stephano I've just got to do the usual trick, name, address, date of birth and not guilty.'

'You should be able to manage that,' I said wryly. 'Anything else?'

'Apparently they set a date for the trial.'

'And that's all?'

'Yes, it'll only last about ten minutes so Mr Stephano says. But then, of course, he wants to see me.'

'I know. Well once the court thing's all over I'll hop on the train.'

'They're half hourly all through the day to Cranleigh.'

'How did you know that?'

'Looked on the Internet last night.'

'Oh, you're such a sweetie.' I gave Nick's hand a quick affectionate squeeze as he changed gear.

The traffic was slow but kept moving. After all it was the rush hour on a Monday morning and eventually after getting considerably confused in the Guildford one way system we found Riverside car park. We quickly located the law courts, prayed as urgently as ever and then nipped off to McDonalds for a coffee.

'You nervous?' I asked.

'Not particularly,' Nick replied. 'I'm getting used to it by now. And it's not as if anything particularly momentous is going to happen today. Knowing my luck, it'll probably be adjourned, and we'll be doing an action replay in a month or six weeks time. Anyway, drink up, it's time we were there.'

We marched resolutely back up to the law courts. An impressive, tall modern building constructed in light stone towered above us. There was a large open area in front of it giving it a spacious almost Italian appearance, reminding me briefly of a happy relaxed weekend I'd spent with Nick in Rome, years ago. The square in front of us was clean and fresh, not nearly as daunting and hostile as I had expected. Inside, it reminded me slightly of an airport. Spacious, clean, considerable security and various official people in uniform. There was a central desk marked 'Reception' which Nick strode to.

'Hello,' he said briskly. 'My name's Nick Metcalfe, I've a hearing today.'

'Right, Sir,' replied the efficient looking lady behind the desk; youngish, blond, in uniform, a cross between a police officer and a parking attendant. 'If you'd just show us what's in your pockets and walk through the security doorway, and,' she added, noticing that I was with him, 'could we check your bag too please, ma'am?'

Having passed through security, there was another desk marked 'Information' towards which Nick headed. There were also flights of stairs off to the left and right and a couple of lifts, a variety of destinations such as courts, robing rooms and restaurants were indicated. Nick repeated his speech and this older lady peered down her list of names. 'Oh yes,' she said after a moment. 'Court 6, that's along to the left and up the stairs.' We proceeded as directed. We were in good time and climbed the flight in a leisurely fashion. The first landing was spacious and had an assortment of signs but no obvious ones to courtrooms; so we continued and on the second floor there was a notice pointing through double doors indicating that the court rooms were that way. We entered and were immediately aware of being at one end of a very wide landing or corridor lined down either side with upholstered chairs in a crushed raspberry colour with a carpet to match. There were gaps in the lines of chairs with doorways in and these were to courts, robing rooms and interview rooms. We quickly established where court number six was, where a typed list of names was pinned up outside it and the fifth name down was Nick's.

'Do we wait here for Mr Stephano?' I asked.

'Yes, I guess so, they didn't exactly say where to meet them, but here's as good as any.'

It was at least as interesting as an airport or railway station, and considerably more luxurious than Sevenoaks magistrates court. A vast assortment of people wandered up and down the wide corridor. Some were obviously professional, wearing gowns or wigs, with piles of papers and thick briefcases. Though even these differed immensely. There were older men, grey haired who gave the impression that the place belonged to them, plummy voices and very laid back. There were younger women, smart suits, short skirts looking efficiently busy and one or two of these pulled their cases along on wheels, no doubt because of the weight. There were older women of the roundish variety, permed hair, crimplene flowered dresses and wearing name tags. They seemed to be looking after those completely new to the set up. Also, I could see people who were clearly there to be tried, looking nervous, smoking anxiously or subconsciously chewing their nails. The activity never ceased for a moment: and as each person passed Nick, he glanced up to check for Mr Stephano or Janice.

After a short while Nick said; 'There's Janice.' I looked up and saw at the far end of the corridor a smart lady approaching, early thirties, short cropped hair, dark suit, demurely dressed. We were introduced and then

Janice said she'd go and see if she could find Mr Stephano. There was a good half hour's wait, inevitably meaning the tension rose and Nick had to make a couple of trips to the gents. I began to wonder what on earth would happen if Nick was called in and Mr Stephano was nowhere in sight. However, after that panicky thought Janice reappeared with an exceedingly tall bespectacled gentleman beside her, who was, of course, the barrister himself. He looked in his forties, a young, round cheery face, gold edged spectacles, slightly plummy voice but definitely approachable and acceptable. I was grateful that he seemed so human. Introductions made, 'I'll just go and get my monkey outfit on,' he said with a smile, and disappeared into the 'Robing Room'.

Moments later he was back wearing a gown and carrying a wig, disappearing almost instantly 'Just to see how things are going.' When he returned he'd clearly assessed the set up, felt under control and started to take command of the situation. 'Pleasant enough judge,' he said. 'Slow though, very slow. It'll be ages before we're seen; so Nick and I can talk now, it'll save time later. Let's go into one of the interview rooms, if they're free.' Nick jumped up, Janice joined him and all three disappeared behind closed doors. Remembering what Nick had said about the possibility of being a witness, I made no attempt to follow, but calmly got out my book and began to read. To my astonishment I was soon engrossed and wasn't aware that an hour and a half had ticked by, when the three of them emerged .

Again Mr Stephano was at the helm. 'Now we've had our chat, I'll go and see how things are going.' He strode through the doors labelled Court 6. A moment later I nearly froze, for along the corridor I saw Penny, considerably changed, but Penny even so. She'd always had a distinctive appearance, being petite with long dark hair and slightly oriental looking. Of course, I hadn't seen her since we'd moved from Oxted over six months ago; she'd dyed and permed her hair and looked very different, but nevertheless it was definitely Penny. My heart was beating so loudly I felt sure the others would be aware of it as I tugged at Nick's sleeve and muttered: 'There's Penny.' She was still some distance away and whether Nick's eyesight was worse than mine or whether he was too shocked he obviously couldn't identify her immediately. 'It's not, is it?'

'Yes, yes it is,' I replied insistently.

'What on earth is she doing here?'

'Absolutely no idea.' Penny was holding a young man's hand and an older lady was with them. Whether this was one of the 'usher' ladies or a friend I couldn't tell, but it certainly wasn't Penny's mother who I knew quite well.

The startling trio walked up to the door of court number six, peered at the list and walked away again. My heart was still pounding fit to burst when Janice, who'd briefly vanished, reappeared, and we pointed Penny out to her. 'What's she doing here?' enquired Janice. 'We've not a clue,' said Nick. 'Thought you might have some idea.' One hundred and one possibilities went through my mind. Was she here to crow over the fact that she'd got Nick just where she wanted? Did she doubt the police had taken her seriously and wanted to make sure? Was she apprehensive that her name might be mentioned and wanted to check it out? Or did she just want to get a glimpse of Nick before the trial to ensure she could handle it? What was going on?

Mr Stephano reappeared and said in a composed manner, 'We've still a long while to wait I fear. This judge is very slow. Pleasant and efficient, I believe, but very, very slow.' By now it was past 11.30 am and I faintly queried whether we'd be done in time for me to retreat and collect Esther from school at 3.10 pm? After consolatory reassurances, the four of us settled down to wait. We talked about this and that but little directly to do with the case. Mr Stephano did ask which dates wouldn't suit Nick for the trial and I was gratified to hear him mention half term. We were expecting three French girls for the October half term and how we could possibly manage that and the trial at the same time was beyond even my wildest imaginings.

At last, at twelve-ish we were summoned in. The court room was about the same size as that at Sevenoaks, but it seemed slightly less intimidating and the public gallery was just two rows of chairs at the back of the room at right angles to where Nick sat and not behind a screen. It was good to be near Nick and smile at him, I appreciated that. Previously he'd had his back to me which made us feel very distant. To my horror already seated in the court room was Penny and the young man. They were at the far end of the public gallery farthest from Nick. At least it made it easy for me to know that I should sit as near to Nick as possible and as far from those unwelcome faces as I could.

The judge was on a raised dais with an impressive coat of arms hanging on the wall above him looking on as people came into court. Below him sat two ladies, clearly court officials, likewise surveying the action, as one group of people left and another came in. Nick sat on one side with a burly black haired fellow beside him. Was that in case he tried to escape or got violent, I wondered? Mr Stephano and the prosecution barrister faced the judge at desks and there were various other people seated. They were not bustling around, as they had been at Sevenoaks, but all seated quietly. There was an air of calm authority over the place.

Glancing up at Penny, I once again found my heart thumping; was it fear, anger, frustration, confusion? Probably a combination of all four. Before I had a chance to analyse my inner emotions the proceedings began. Nick gave his name as usual and then one of the court officials began. 'Nicholas Metcalfe you are charged with the sexual assault of Anita Carol Simpson between July 1990 and June 1991, how do you plead?' Nick said, 'Not guilty,' loud and clear. This was repeated by the lady at the front and no doubt written down. As the list of charges had grown to twelve the court proceedings took on a surreal quality. 'Nicholas Metcalfe' was charged again and again and replied persistently with 'Not Guilty.' At the mention of Penny's name and the 'not guilty' plea, Penny got up, tossed her head, and left the courtroom which provided a brief diversion to the monotonous proceedings. I saw it all in slow motion; her wavy dark hair, now with a distinctive red tinge, swung from side to side as she shuffled along the row of empty seats and walked out of the door. The man friend, however, remained.

The judge then commented that having read the papers through, he was somewhat puzzled as to why the event on page three hadn't been taken into account. Both of us froze. Although we had no papers in front of us, we both knew exactly what page three contained. The alleged rape incident. My mind somersaulted; 'Oh no, not the rape charge again, please. If the judge gets really agitated, bail might be withdrawn and Nick put on remand.' The muscles of my face tensed and my head pounded with anxiety.

The prosecution barrister either hadn't read the papers or hadn't taken them in, for he was flicking forwards and backwards through the file, obviously embarrassed until Mr Stephano leaned across and whispered something. He then arose and said, 'My learned friend informs me it could have been omitted because of page six.' The judge turned over a few pages and perused his papers. 'I see. It doesn't seem entirely to follow to me.' He said. 'Could you make contact with the CPS and check this out?' He paused. 'Mr Stephano, would you and your client be willing to remain in the building until this is sorted?' Mr Stephano agreed. Meanwhile I was trying frantically to imagine what page six involved and finally came to the conclusion that it must be where Anita said that Nick hadn't raped her three times, only once; and that the CPS felt the whole thing was all too precarious to try and push through, and attempt to gain a conviction on such tenuous statements.

The judge and barristers were talking again about the number of witnesses required, and when Mr Stephano said 'about thirty' the judge's eyes nearly popped out of his head.

'Did you say thirty, Mr Stephano?'

'I did, sir.'

'Are these just character references or factual evidence as well?'

'Both, sir, but most have some factual details of assistance.'

'I see.'

'Do you have any video evidence?' enquired the judge.

'At this point I'm not exactly sure,' replied Mr Stephano. 'But that could well be the case.'

'Let's say it is the case.' responded the judge with a touch of humour. 'We'll get a much better court room that way.'

The judge paused. He looked at Nick again, and whether or not it was wishful thinking I could not be sure, but I felt he warmed to Nick and perhaps even saw him more as a victim and less as a criminal, with that latest piece of information. After all, thirty witnesses who were all prepared to stand up in court and speak up for Nick was quite an impressive number. He glanced through a book which must have been the court timetable, and after a moment said, 'Would October 11th for a week be satisfactory?' Mr Stephano and the prosecution barrister both acquiesced, and then the judge added with a slight twinkle in his eye, 'Or perhaps we'd better say a week to ten days bearing in mind the number of witnesses!'

He then turned to Nick, confirmed his bail conditions in a very gentle and humane manner and said he was free to go. One or two people were talking, and Nick and I were momentarily confused as to whether or not we could leave. But it seemed as if we were allowed to and we left the courtroom noticing Penny sitting in the chairs just outside, waiting, no doubt, for her boyfriend. We moved to the end of the corridor and sat down with Mr Stephano and Janice to await the CPS barrister's comments on the item on page three.

Trial date set

Although I had received the impression from Nick that Mr Stephano wouldn't discuss the case in front of me, he now chatted away in a relaxed manner. As yet he wasn't a hundred per cent 'au fait' with all the details; no doubt he hadn't had time to read the mountain of paperwork that had accumulated, but he talked in general terms about motives for these wild accusations and he gave us the distinct impression he'd dealt with other such cases before. It was reassuring to hear Mr Stephano holding forth in an authoritative way on the subjects of jealousy, being unable to back down, believing one's own fabrications and so on. 'Perhaps,' I thought, 'just perhaps, there might be a chance he can vindicate poor old Nick.'

After an hour or so, the prosecuting barrister appeared and called Mr Stephano away. A minute later he was back with the news 'The CPS are adamant there is no rape charge, which is a very good thing.' Rapidly hands were shaken, farewells said and Janice assured Nick that she'd put all that he needed to do, which was a considerable amount, onto paper and in the post. We walked down the stairs together, hardly daring to believe that another mountain had been peaked, the rape charge hadn't been reintroduced, Nick's bail hadn't been withdrawn and the next time we'd be coming to Guildford crown court would be for the trial itself. We were tired and hungry. It was nearly two o'clock and we'd had nothing to eat. So wandering back to the car, we decided to stop at the next garage and buy some sandwiches.

'What did you think of Stephano?' asked Nick between munches.

'I liked him,' I replied, swallowing down my cheese and pickle mouthful. 'Yes, I liked him. He seemed human, intelligent, and on your side and we can't ask for more. Though I didn't feel he'd read all the papers, to be honest, which was frustrating.'

'No he hadn't. He admitted that to me when I was with him on my own. I told him he had to read the statements which I'd put my comments on in red, because that would give him a much better picture.'

'Oh, right, I guess he's got loads of cases and hasn't really got to grips with yours yet.'

'I reckon you're right. It would be good if we could employ him just to do us, but imagine how much that would cost!'

'I don't like to think. What did he say to you when you saw him alone?'

'Oh, we went over things quite a bit. It's all more complicated than he initially thought, I think. There's so many people involved and it stretches over such a long period of time; but he says the time line I prepared is useful.'

'Good.'

'Then we discussed witnesses. He's got loads of people he wants to call because of all the fantastic letters we've had. Oh and he's impressed with you and says you'll definitely be a witness now he's met you.'

'Great,' I retorted flippantly. 'What was it that appealed, my pretty dress or my stunning personality?'

'Both, I expect.' said Nick laughing quietly and the conversation turned to other topics.

As on the other court appearance days the evening adopted a now familiar routine. We told the older two girls what was happening, Felicity and Esther being blissfully ignorant and disinterested, and this was followed by a succession of telephone calls informing close family and friends of the situation to date. It was an exhausting business and we were glad when the last call had been made, the house locked up and we could retire to bed. 'We've a lot to be thankful for,' I said as we prepared for bed.

'How do you mean?' queried Nick.

'Well, we didn't exactly get much choice as to the date for the trial but it's not in the summer holidays, it's not in half term when we've got those three French girls coming, it's not on Emily's birthday in November and it's not next year, so at least it'll all be well over by Christmas.' Nick grinned.

'I'll be locked up by then.'

'Rubbish!' I replied indignantly, flinging myself into bed; 'We're going to fight this one, remember?' I hoped I sounded considerably more optimistic than I felt.

I had been encouraged by the number of letters friends and relatives had written; some to us and some sent direct to Mr Dixon. He'd carefully perused them and passed on those that he felt were relevant to Mr Stephano. All those that interested Mr Stephano were potential witnesses and it was most heart warming to see the number of our contacts, both recent acquaintances and from previous years, who were so willing to stand by us.

As the system of choosing witnesses became clear to me, I too had written as factual an account as possible of my years as Nick's wife and as a youth leader. Emily, who'd been monitoring these affairs most conscientiously, said to me one night, 'Would it be all right if I wrote to Mr Dixon?'

'Why, yes, of course,' I replied.

'Only I can say how often Anita baby-sat and how she was our favourite baby-sitter, and I want to have my say to stand up for Dad.'

'Yes, that's fine dear,' I said, moved by my eldest daughter's astute, caring approach.

'Would you like me to read it through before you send it?'

'Yes please, but I know what I'm going to say.'

I was mildly amused at Emily's approach. No doubt she'd been mulling it over for days and having decided to involve herself, knew exactly what she intended saying. 'You realise that if you write, you might be asked to be a witness?' I checked. 'Of course,' came the response. 'I can cope!'

Sure enough, the following day Emily presented me with a neatly written letter covering two sides of A4 explaining all she knew of Anita, Penny and Debs. I checked it through and it was duly posted.

I had been banking on an emotional let up after the last court appearance, but nothing could have been further from the truth. My mind was continually besieged with questions to which there seemed to be no answers. 'Why are Anita and Penny doing this? Do they realise what they are doing to us as a family? Do they know they're lying or have they convinced themselves it's all true? Will Mr Stephano be able to make a good case for Nick? There are so many details and facts that he can use, but will he take in the complexities? How can we get across to him the happy relaxed atmosphere at our house when we were running the youth group? Will he take into account the fact that Anita and Penny were two of the most regular attendees? What are we going to do if Nick goes to prison? He'll get a criminal record, Mainwave won't want him, we'll have to sell the house, Felicity and Esther will have no chance of joining Emily and Jessica at the High school. What about the Press? What if our four girls' school friends read about Nick in the paper? Mr Stephano seemed quite convinced the trial would get into the press. Perhaps parents won't want their daughters coming to our house any more. Perhaps they'll lose their friends and become outcasts? How will they cope? They're being fantastic at the moment, but what if Nick really does get done?' I groaned out loud. 'It doesn't bear thinking of.'

'Why was Penny at court yesterday, what is going on? How did she know where to go? Why did she want to attend? Was it to spy on Nick and relay information back to the others? Why did she fly out after she'd heard her name? Was she genuinely troubled? Perhaps she'd never meant things to get so far? And what about Anita? Was she mad? Or vindictive? She'd always been so sweet at the youth group, good with our girls and their favourite baby-sitter. So what was going on? Would she be able to maintain her stance in a court situation? Surely one of them would crack? If only that could happen and they'd admit it was a load of lies, fabrication and fantasy. If only Nick could be spared the ordeal of going through court. It would be such a strain, how would he cope? What if he were locked up, the strain on him would be intolerable. If we appealed, no doubt, it would cost even more money.' And so the spiral of miserable thoughts continued to make my mind spin relentlessly. There was no let up and the tears fell profusely once I'd taken Esther to school each day and was on my own.

Nick seemed quite cheery, he had a date to aim at, he'd seen his manager at work and told him he'd complete the project he was on and then he required a backwater job until after the trial. Something undemanding, unstressful and a job which could be put down and picked up as and when, depending on when he had to go and see Mr Stephano and how much preparatory work he had to do at home. At last his boss had taken on board the gravity of his situation and agreed to Nick's proposals. So on the work front the pressure was easing and Nick could at last see ahead of him the chance of getting to grips with looking through his videos and photos in case he could locate anything of any use in the case.

News continued to drift down from Oxted; sometimes encouraging, quite often not. 'Deb's sister, Alice is definitely supporting Anita,' I was told on one telephone call. It made my heart sink and I didn't altogether believe it, because it seemed singularly unsubstantiated. Being such depressing news I chose not to pass it on to Nick. He had more than enough pressures and hassles to cope with. One night he came home from work and explained how Karen, a young lady of twenty six from work whom he'd known for years and who was a loyal supporter in the current crisis, had informed him that another girl in the office had asked her what exactly the case against Nick was? Karen had, of course, kept quiet, but felt obliged to inform Nick that the gossip had started.

A few days later came more demoralising news from work. Nick's boss had been chatting to him. 'This case then, it's still going on?'

'Yes.'

'But I thought you said the girls' allegations were all a load of nonsense with no substance to them?'

'That's right.'

'Well, hang it all, it strikes me there must be something to it, dragging on like this, otherwise the CPS would have thrown it out long ago.'

Nick had apparently kept his cool and replied with a despondent. 'Well there isn't,' and left the room. 'But,' I thought, 'how many people were thinking along those lines? As time ticked on, did it somehow give credence to the allegations? Did no one understand that the law was such an ass that it followed such things through to their conclusion however misfounded they were? No, I sadly concluded, people didn't understand. I probably wouldn't have had a clue if I'd not been in the current situation. People were going to assume guilt, that was something I'd have to live with; especially if Nick went to prison. We would cope, somehow, I was determined. It wouldn't be much fun, no, be realistic, it would be a horrendous experience during the trial having it plastered all over the tabloids. Mr Stephano reckoned it would make the National Papers. But we'd cope. I bit my lip with grim determination. If the worst came to the worst and Nick went down for this, the girls and I would hold our heads high and fight tooth and nail for justice ... Justice ... What a joke ... Where was the justice in the present condition? Nick had given his heart and soul for the youth group, depriving himself of free time, recreation, family time, socialising and this was the result. The biggest kick in the teeth imaginable by three of the keenest supporters. What had happened? Where were they coming from? Why, oh why, were they making poor Nick's life such purgatory?'

Building our case

The end of the summer term was rapidly approaching and the girls were getting excited about the various plans for the school holidays. Life was busy for us, the weather was good and, as we attended sports days and summer fairs, the pain eased a little. Jessica was anxious to celebrate her birthday before the end of term as she knew once the holidays had begun there'd be little or no chance of rounding up all her friends. What exactly did she want to do for her 13th birthday? Silly games in the garden and a barbecue came the answer. I was quite happy with that; it only left me with the food to prepare which wasn't a problem, but I felt concerned for Nick. Being regarded as 'Super Dad' by one of his most doting fans he was expected to come up with unusual and entertaining garden games despite the many pressures on him. Being totally unable to say 'no' he'd agreed to all Jessica's ideas. Yes, he'd organise a variety of silly games, yes, he'd do an obstacle race round the garden and yes, of course, he'd cook a barbecue.

He returned home from work early on Jessica's birthday in order to get the games under control. I was impressed with how organised he seemed and hoped to goodness it would remain that way. He'd bought doughnuts to eat off strings tied to the washing line, apples for apple bobbing, sweets to unearth from piles of flour and potatoes to be located blind folded, picked up in the mouth and then returned to an awaiting bucket. He filled balloons with water by the dozen to toss over the badminton net and to be caught by a pair of girls each holding the end of a towel, and balloons were filled with water and frozen ready for some complicated juggling act to be performed in teams. Jessica was most impressed.

The friends arrived, a dozen in total, presents were given, opened and appreciated and then out into the garden for games. Within a minute of starting the balloon volley ball, Philippa had trodden on a wasp in her bare feet and began to cry. 'Don't worry,' I reassured her, 'Nick's trained in first aid, come and sit down a moment and he'll sort you out.' Nick appeared promptly with some antihistamine, checked the sting, cleaned it and applied the cream. Philippa put on a brave face and a pair of shoes and returned to the game. But I was unhappy. 'Of all the times and places for a wretched wasp to get trodden on it had to be at Jessica's party. I mean, we're bare footed all the time in the garden in this hot weather and none of us have ever, ever trodden on a wasp. It's ridiculous.'

However the wild games were in full swing and everyone was participating well, so I dampened down my outrage and saw to the final preparation of the food. After the obstacle race Nick lit the barbecue and the girls took time out to admire Jessica's gifts and chat.

I drifted out to assist Nick, only to discover that predictably the pressure and responsibility were getting to him. He was working like a mad thing, criticising the sausages for being too fatty, the bacon too thick, the chicken legs too chunky and the burgers too frozen. 'I'll never get this lot cooked in time,' he exploded, 'it's ridiculous, I couldn't do the games and cook the food all at once. Look, I mean, just look at it, there's far too much food; it'll take forever to cook. The parents'll be here before they've even started to eat; everything keeps falling off the rack, there's no way I can fit the bacon on, look at the way the fat falls on the coal and makes it flare up, that's why everything's so black, but nothing's getting cooked inside.' I was familiar with the 'Nick in a tiz' scenario, and offered soothing platitudes which fell on deaf ears. I returned to the lounge to see how the girls were doing; they seemed quite happy, chatting and admiring the birthday cake. For some strange reason Jessica had chosen an igloo cake which seemed singularly inappropriate for a midsummer birthday party and barbecue, but Jessica had been insistent.

A little apprehensively I went back out to Nick. The food was looking good and Nick had calmed down. All was now cooked apart from the bacon, so the vultures were summoned and tackled the food with gusto. Nick spent the first five minutes of the meal apologising profusely for the black sausages, greasy chicken etc. But the girls were so insistent that everything was fine that he was eventually convinced and finally subsided. Comments such as 'This is great!' 'Brilliant food,' and 'Wow, what a feast' cheered me and I too began to relax a little and realise that to an onlooker all had gone incredibly smoothly. Only I was aware quite what an heroic effort Nick had put in to make it all work, and only I appreciated the mammoth achievement he'd had in quelling his anxieties enough to produce amusing antics in the garden and a delicious barbecue.

Once the parents had arrived, the social niceties carried out, the birthday cake distributed and the front door shut for the final time, we flopped into arm chairs and looked at each other.

'Well, that went OK,' I said. 'You did really well with both the games and food.'

'Sorry, I got a bit ratty,' said Nick with a grin.

'That's OK,' was the reply. 'It was mission impossible really being in charge of the games and the barbecue but I think everyone enjoyed it, don't you?'

'Yes, I think so. Was Jessica happy with it?'

'Oh yes, hugely. I've just tucked her down and she was beaming all over her face and said "I'm glad I chose to do that, it was brilliant".'

'Good,' said Nick with a note of relief in his voice. 'Now to the tidying up. I'll do the garden.'

'Yup, and I'll attack the food.'

'You can leave the dishwasher to me, if you like.'

'That's sweet, but you've probably got enough to do, I'll see how it goes.' I enjoyed a quiet smile. 'Dear old Nick, always willing to help, Jessica, me, anyone, and it was so sweet of him to apologise.' I then turned my mind to the chaos in the kitchen. The surfaces were piled high with plates of half eaten food, and plates, bowls and cutlery were all over the place. The room closely resembled a bomb site.

In the first week of Emily and Jessica's holiday, while Felicity and Esther were most indignantly at school, it fell to me to organise a day in Oxted for Mr Dixon and Janice to come and interview as many of the potential witnesses as possible. It was an administrative nightmare and took hours and hours of time. I had a list of all twenty eight names, most of whom lived in Oxted. First I systematically rang them up to work out which of the three days the solicitors had offered was most convenient to the majority. Having ascertained that, I then again telephoned those available on that day, to inform them of the date and check what time of day would suit them best. The results, of course, were widely diverse. Some, like the students, could do any time. Others, like those at work, could only manage their lunch hour, and others had dentists appointments, physiotherapy sessions and other responsibilities, and consequently requested a specific time. At last all the requisite information was accumulated and I drew up a provisional timetable. Mr Dixon and Janice hoped to see people simultaneously with half hourly appointments. Naturally some would take longer and others shorter, but it gave them something to work to. Various friends had offered the use of their houses for these interviews and the solicitors were choosy. Nothing, but nothing must be done to upset the prosecution; so anyone who'd offered their house and had already been interviewed by the police was automatically dismissed. Eventually location and timetable were finalised and then, of course, the alterations commenced. 'I'm really sorry, Melanie, but I've got to be in Birmingham by 2 pm so can I be early in the morning instead of the afternoon?' 'You won't believe this, but my great aunt's funeral is that day, so I definitely won't make 11 am. But if you stick me on at the end I'll try and get back for it.' By the day before the interviews were due to take place, I had a mutilated dog-eared timetable sitting by the telephone which I hoped was the final copy. I rang Janice and told her I'd fax it through to the house where the sessions would take place.

It was with a sense of relief that Emily and I drove off up to Oxted for our appointments as potential witnesses. The whole thing was at last underway and if there were any further hiccoughs they were hardly my problem. We arrived safely and Emily went a little apprehensively to Mr Dixon while I sat down with Janice. I was relieved to discover that it wasn't a gruelling question and answer session, but Janice casually chatted over the contents of the letter I had written previously to the solicitors. I couldn't really offer any further information so then took the opportunity of asking Janice several questions. 'We've got an old calendar showing Anita baby sitting, might that be useful? Nick kept a register for about a year which shows the three girls regular attendance, would that be any help? We have most of the youth group programmes that we ran, would you like to see them, to get a bit of a feel for the sort of things we got up to?' Janice was keen to get hold of all possible material and so she instructed me to send everything I'd mentioned to the solicitors as soon as I could.

As I emerged I found Emily was already out and waiting.

'How did it go, love?' I enquired.

'Fine I think,' Emily replied calmly. 'He didn't ask me much, but he did ask whether I'd be happy to go to court if it was required.'

'What did you say?' I quizzed anxiously, wondering whether at fourteen she was really up to it and how she'd cope.

'Yes, of course,' retorted Emily with a condescending teenage glare.

That evening it became evident that the day of interviewing had run smoothly and more or less according to schedule. Mr Dixon and Janice had been encouraged by their sessions and wanted to see one or two people again to have a longer chat. It was a relief for us to hear positive news for a change. A couple of days later Mr Dixon rang me and confirmed that they'd had an excellent day and one or two possible motives were beginning to emerge. To my frustration he did not enlighten me further as to what they were, but nevertheless it was pleasant to hear that Mr Dixon at least was starting to get on top of things. He'd had a trying weekend as Mr Stephano had been summoned to another case on October 11th and Mr Dixon had had to go back to Chambers for someone else. Apparently he'd expressed his displeasure at being let down relatively late in the day when Mr Stephano had already read the paperwork and formed a relationship with his client; and after some wrangling and haggling Mr Dixon had been offered a QC for no extra charge and without needing a junior. Mr Dixon sounded delighted with himself, like a dog with two tails as he recounted his success to me. Just before the conversation closed he popped in, 'I'm afraid I'll have to ask you for another cheque for £10,000.' I gulped, assured him that would be fine, thanked him for all he'd done and put the telephone down.

'£10,000 … What an amazing amount of money all this is costing,' I thought. I remembered with gratitude how the money and pledges of finance had flooded in to Stephen, and how to date there had always been sufficient to pay the solicitor's bills. The fighting fund had £10,000, I knew, but very little else, and that was before the actual trial had even begun, which no doubt would be horribly expensive. I wondered if the three girls had any idea what they were doing to us? Did they have the faintest clue of the vast expense their lies were incurring? Probably not, I assumed. All they'd done was walk into a police station, suggest they were poor victims of assault and the whole thing had just rolled on from there. 'It's completely insane,' I muttered. 'We live in a mad, mad world.'

In due course the money was sent to the solicitors and Stephen, Nick's brother in charge of the begging fund, assured me that whilst only £2,500 remained, more had been promised. I was amazed at the amount raised, how money had not ceased to be sent in large and small amounts; whatever the size of the legal fees they'd always been covered. Stephen explained that he wouldn't pursue additional funds over the summer, but if more was needed by early autumn he could track it down. It was a great relief, of course, but the feeling of indebtedness to friends and family grew and grew. Where would we be without them? I made a mental note, 'When this is all over and friends or relatives are in dire straits, don't be afraid to fork out for them and be really generous too!'

I found myself wondering what on earth would have happened to us without all the support we were receiving. It illustrated more powerfully than words, the firm belief our friends and family had in Nick's innocence and the high esteem in which he was held. The future would have been far, far bleaker. If the money hadn't come in we would have had to sell the house to raise the legal fees and with no friends backing Nick, the case of ten people all substantiating each other and maintaining that Nick was a serious sex criminal would have sounded very convincing. He'd have had no chance, no chance whatsoever. 'Thank God,' I thought, 'for good, solid, supportive friends and for at least the slight chance of fighting this with a degree of justice. How many people are in prison wrongfully,' I pondered, 'because they haven't had the benefits Nick and I have enjoyed?'

It wasn't long after I had gone through this thought process that we invited Tom and Faith Holt to coffee one evening after church. Tom was an engineer in the fire service, but in his spare time he visited prisoners. It was a noble selfless work, and one which he was committed to and dedicated hours to, encouraging and supporting those locked up. 'He was,' I thought, 'an excellent person to inform us a little more about prison life, visiting hours etc.' And so over coffee and cake my concerns poured out. Tentatively at first, but then as Tom, ever understanding, gave frank and honest answers the questions popped out like rapid gunfire.

'If the worst came to the worst and Nick goes down, would I be able to see him before he's whisked off to prison?'

'It depends very much on who's in charge, but most likely no.'

'Would I be told where he was being taken to?'

'Yes, most probably.'

'How often would I be able to visit him?'

'Once a month.'

'What?' I was aghast, I had envisaged a daily visit, perhaps with a meal, a note from the girls, clean socks.

'Yes, really, visitors only once a month and that only on certain conditions, good behaviour etc.'

I gulped. I was visibly shaken. How naive I'd been, simplistic. Of course, if you were in prison as a criminal, luxuries like visits wouldn't be two a penny. I managed one more question before changing the conversation; 'and what's life like inside?'

'Tough' replied Tom. 'Very, very tough, particularly for sex offenders.'

A surge of nausea swept over me as I tried to take the information on board. It was hard to maintain my composure. I wanted to scream about injustice, about how cruel the world was and to dissolve into tears all at the same time. But outwardly, I tried to put a brave face on it and enquire about Tom and Faith's daughter at university.

Nick now had to meet another barrister, a QC in fact, who was to take on the case. Although I hadn't fully appreciated what this signified when told of the change by Mr Dixon, I gradually ascertained that a QC was higher ranking, more experienced and consequently would help our cause even more. But I was still slightly apprehensive knowing how much regard Nick had had for Mr Stephano. An appointment was duly made and Nick travelled on the train to London 'Chambers' to meet Mr Bassett. 'Chambers', Nick informed me, was the name of the building where anyone of high legal esteem worked in the city. To my shame I'd never even heard of it. According to the report that came back from Nick, Mr Bassett was middle aged, short, plumpish, very genial, had a plummy English accent and 'if you thought Mr Stephano was quick on the uptake, you should meet Mr Bassett,' Nick added with relish. He had an extraordinarily quick mind, had grasped all the intricacies of the case and had quizzed Nick on some of the finer details. He seemed totally together and clearly Nick was delighted with the substitute. I was relieved beyond measure: neither of us had had any doubts as to Mr Stephano's ability, but if Mr Bassett was that much better it could only be to Nick's advantage. Although so much of the recent months had been overwhelmingly depressing, the employment of Mr Bassett for no extra charge, seemed very much in our favour.

A summer break

Amidst much excitement, the term broke up and all four girls were delighted to be able to enjoy a late breakfast and relaxed schedules. The first weekend ran uneventfully until Sunday tea time. Nick was just getting ready for evening church when he looked out of the window and noticed clouds of smoke rising from the fields behind the house. The rest of us all peered anxiously out, then we rushed downstairs in a whirlwind of curiosity and no little concern, and out of the back gate to investigate. Vast clouds of grey smoke billowed up in ever increasing volume from the dry scrubland and Nick tore back inside and dialled 999. Worried looks spread over the family's faces and Esther was inclined to cry. 'What are we going to do?' I enquired. 'Well, I've got to go,' replied Nick matter of factly, 'in fact if I don't go in the next minute I'll be late. You and the girls can go or not whatever you think best.' With that indecisive comment, he grabbed his bag of music, his car keys and shot off; thinking primarily about the new tunes he had to play at evening church, the fire just being an additional irritation.

'What about the cats, Mum?' asked Emily anxiously. One was asleep inside, the other, nowhere to be seen. 'I think it's best if we leave them outside,' I replied. 'If the fire does come towards the house they're free to run, whereas if we shut them in, and the worst happens,' (a loud sniff emerged from Esther's frightened face), 'they'd get roasted.' So Sooty was thrown out and the cat flap securely locked. The sound of the doorbell broke the tense atmosphere and all five of us went to answer it. It was Janet from next door. 'Did you know there's a fire out the back?' she asked.

'Yes, we saw it a few minutes ago.'

'There's always been a problem out there with the dry grass and everything,' she explained. 'Last year there was an enormous blaze and the fire engines came here and used the water points in the drives and had hoses running through our gardens.'

'Wow! I hope it doesn't come to that,' I exclaimed. 'We were just on our way out to church but wonder whether it's OK to go?'

'Oh,' said Janet confidently. 'I don't think it'll blow this way, the wind's in a totally different direction.'

'Why don't we take Dad's mobile?' interrupted Emily, 'and Janet could ring us if there was a problem?'

'Would you mind, Janet?' I asked. 'It seems an awful cheek.'

'No, no. That's absolutely fine. I think you'll be OK but if it'll put your minds at rest, of course I'll give you a ring if it comes any nearer.'

'That's really kind of you.'

The number was promptly given, I snatched up the mobile and the five of us jumped into the car and shot off to church.

Concentrating was quite a challenge while wondering what was going on at home. Had the Fire Service arrived? And if so had the fire been put out? However the last hymn was soon sung and the final prayer said with no interruptions on the telephone. Our family were prompt to leave, parked in the drive and then walked out of the garden through the back gate to inspect the damage. The first thing that hit us was the smell. The harsh, pungent, though not totally unpleasant smell, of a country bonfire or burning stubble. Then we saw a blue flashing light and realised that the Fire Service were still in attendance. Blackened grass and bushes betrayed the fact that the fire had spread extensively, and on enquiring of the firemen, we were informed that there had been seven fire engines and a couple of land rovers involved in controlling the blaze. We strolled round the blackened area, intrigued, fascinated and very thankful that no damage had occurred to our property, or anyone else's.

It was certainly an unexpected beginning to the summer holidays and one we wouldn't forget in a hurry. But then 1999 was a year that would be etched on our memories for life anyway. However much we might wish to, it was a year that we'd never forget.

The holidays were uneventful, tranquil and in many ways an oasis in a turbulent year. The girls went off to various camps, had no traumas, accidents or alarms and before I knew it the whole family were on the Portsmouth ferry heading for Bilbao, Spain. Once the boat had left the dock a period of respite and relief commenced for all six of us. There was no telephone, no post arriving with upsetting information and demanding our immediate attention, no over anxious friends, no police, no courts, no solicitors and no finance to worry about. It almost felt as if normal life had returned. Indeed, as the holiday progressed, Nick began to let his hair down and clowned around as he'd always done. It was such a relief to me to see Nick's old self back again and I desperately hoped that his old ebullient personality would be back for good after October.

It was one of those unique holidays when everything went right. The campsites we found were welcoming, the views we saw panoramic, the people we met friendly and the food we ate delicious. Up in the Pyrenees in Spain we were on a remote site three quarters of the way up a mountain after twenty seven (Felicity counted them) hairpin bends. It was quiet, peaceful and extremely relaxing. The hassles of home seemed remote and we both felt safe for a while. Down on the Costa Brava several days later, the sun beat down, the sea was warm and the highlight was the snorkelling. The one set of snorkel and goggles was shared among each member of the family in turn and we floated around in the luxurious, tepid sea water mesmerised by the shoals of beautiful fish swimming through the water. The variety of colours and shapes was breath taking, the greys and greens of the rocks, and their exotic shapes all made for an experience which none of us had enjoyed previously. When we weren't in the water, there were sandcastles to be built, books to be read, post cards to be written and ice creams to be eaten.

Heading back up the west coast of France we managed to locate a campsite Nick had visited as a teenager with his family a mere twenty one years ago. It was on the side of a lake with pine trees all around and very attractive. We spent another five blissful days canoeing, swimming, going to the Atlantic coast and braving the rollers, reading, collecting the enormous pine cones there and eating 'gauffres' at the lake side cafe. These huge delicious hot waffles became a feature of the last few days of the holiday and were greedily devoured by all of us as we surveyed the lake in a state of contentment and serenity. It was quite an experience and we all inevitably ended up well doused in chocolate and cream, the smaller you were the messier the business; but it was a hilarious and enjoyable messiness which was caught repeatedly on camera. However as J.R.R. Tolkien writes in *The Hobbit*, of the travellers sojourn at Rivendell, 'Now it is a strange thing, but things that are good to have and days that are good to spend are soon told about, and not much to listen to; while things that are uncomfortable palpitating, and even gruesome, may make a good tale, and take a deal of telling anyway.'

All too quickly the going home day came and the tent had to be dismantled for the last time, bags packed and we headed back towards England. It had been a memorable holiday, not, as is so often the case, for the hiccoughs but for the tranquillity. Both of us had been able to put our anxieties aside, relax and unwind. The imminent court case had been mentioned in passing on several occasions but hadn't been the dominant theme of the period. Neither of us had made a conscious effort not to talk about it, but, what was there to say? There was no stopping the injustice, so the best approach was to put it on hold and enjoy ourselves, something we all succeeded in doing extremely well.

It was good returning home again and greeting Sooty and Sweep. The post was not mountainous and contained nothing from the solicitors. That fact somehow prolonged the holiday feeling and the washing machine worked steadily for several days non-stop while Nick sorted out the tent, cleaned it and left it in a manageable state for a holiday next year ... If, of course, we were all together to have a holiday next year.

After a few days of sorting out, Emily, Jessica, Felicity and Esther were all back at school. They were pleased to see their friends again and discover what their new teachers were like. Emily, quiet and resolute, was determined on keeping up with her work and achieving great things as she embarked on her GCSE course, despite all that was happening at home. Jessica, as laid back as ever, didn't quite manage to get her room tidy and under control after the holiday, before she returned to school, and I was not impressed. Felicity discovered to her horror, that now she'd reached the dizzy heights of year six, she had homework every night and claimed to be devastated, while Esther went back chirpy and chatty as ever to enjoy every minute of every day.

When there was no news from the solicitors for several days Nick gave them a ring. They'd been on holiday too, but no they hadn't forgotten him and would be putting together witness statements for the potential witnesses to sign in the near future. 'Yes,' said Janice, 'I'll make a list of all the jobs Nick has to do and put it in the post.' It duly arrived and Nick groaned. 'There's sixty or seventy hours' work here at least,' he said.

'Oh, it can't be as bad as that, can it?' I questioned. 'Are all the jobs monstrous?'

'No,' came the irritated reply, 'but the main one is. I've got to go through my life detailing all I can about the youth work, my contact with Anita, Penny and Debs and write it as a witness statement chronologically. It'll take forever!'

'Oh well,' I responded, 'if it's got to be done, it's got to be done. Is there anything I can help you with?'

'You can't help me with that and the other things are not too major and probably best if I do them, like a chronology of the youth group, who came and who left when, for the jurors, on A4 paper. I've done one already, but it covers twelve sheets and has various details Mr Bassett, the Q.C., says aren't required. So I'm to remove those and shrink it somewhat. Actually,' Nick continued after a brief pause, 'you could research this one for me, though I can't remember anything.'

'What's that?'

'Any physical contact with boys, such as hugging, that can be recalled,' read out Nick.

'Great, thanks,' I exclaimed. 'You're not exactly the sort of person who goes around hugging boys! And if you were, people would probably get the wrong idea, but I'll give it some thought and p'raps ask one or two people.'

'Thanks.'

I thought that I could see the way Mr Bassett's mind was working. By demonstrating that Nick had physical contact with boys as well as girls he could explain that any hugging, tickling etc. which had involved Anita, Penny and Debs was just part of his normal behaviour and nothing out of the ordinary at all.

A couple of evenings later Andy North telephoned. He'd been so supportive and so involved that I ventured to ask him if he could recall any 'hugging' or the like. Slightly bemused by the concept and reasonably convinced that he couldn't, he assured me he'd give it some thought, for he could appreciate where the solicitors were coming from. Before Nick had an opportunity to get to grips with any paper work, Janice rang him. Something important needed to be discussed and could he come to

Croydon tomorrow? The appointment was made leaving both of us totally in the dark. What was so important? Janice had said it could be very relevant to Nick's defence, but that was all. What had they unearthed and would it really help?

That night reminded me of the night after Nick's arrest. It was a restless one for both of us. Questions haunted us with not a single answer and consequently we tossed and turned and couldn't settle. I irritated Nick at about 1 am by asking, 'You really haven't a clue what all this is about?' And he retorted with justifiable indignation, 'If I did, I'd've told you by now, wouldn't I?' I knew he would have done so and felt suitably subdued. But what had Janice found out that was so crucial? Something about Anita's past? Penny's? Something that showed they'd lied about other things? Something that would prove convincingly that Nick was telling the truth? The night dragged on. At one point I thought I heard steady breathing the other side of the bed, and didn't dare move a muscle hoping beyond hope that Nick was at least getting a little rest before the revelations of the next day, whatever they might be.

Chapter 21

Assistance?

As normal, Nick's appointment at the solicitors was in the afternoon at 2pm. So he went to work and then on to the solicitors. At about 4 pm the telephone rang. It startled me out of the reverie I tended to drift into whilst preparing the evening meal, on the odd occasion when no children were around. I answered the telephone and heard an unknown male voice. 'Hello, Mrs Metcalfe?'

'Yes.'

'Is Mr Metcalfe there please?'

'No, I'm afraid not, can I help you at all?'

'No, I think not.' It sounded as if the call was at an end when the caller changed his mind and enlightened me a little as to the purpose of calling.

'I do hope you'll forgive my intrusion like this,' he said, 'but it's Trevor Westward here.'

'Oh?' I queried wondering what on earth our old friend from years back wanted with Nick.

'I think I might have found something that might be of interest to Nick.' My heart began to race as I remembered that Trevor worked in the police force, some administrative job or other, and I wondered frantically if he might be able to help us. I recalled faintly that early on after Nick's arrest, he'd rung Trevor for advice but had received the impression that it wasn't really his field and that he wanted to keep his distance. Perhaps things had changed?

'Might he be able to pop in and see me on his way home? You know I've moved to Godalming now, so it wouldn't be much out of his way.' I didn't like to enlighten him that Nick wasn't actually at work but seeing the solicitors so I cautiously replied, 'No, I don't think he would.'

'Well,' resumed the slightly frustrated voice, 'it's just that I've been concerned about his case and I have discovered something which might interest him.' I was stunned. So was I right in my speculation, there was a connection between this telephone call and that of Nick's to him months previously? If he had any information that might help Nick I had to be careful to be encouraging and appreciative, so I replied, 'That's good of you, I know he'd be interested. Could you tell me your new address please and phone number and I'll try and contact him on his mobile and see if he could meet you for a chat. Assuming I make contact I'll ring you straight back.'

With that I put the telephone down in complete bewilderment. Things seemed to be getting out of control. First the solicitors wanting to see Nick so urgently and now this, unless the two were somehow connected? But having promised Trevor that I'd try and locate Nick I duly, in a state of absolute bewilderment, picked up the telephone and dialled his mobile.

Still completely mystified I explained what Trevor had told me. 'Yes, I see,' was Nick's response, 'This was what Mr Dixon wanted to see me for, too. I do need to talk to him but I'm nearly home now so it's probably best if we meet up later tonight, give him my mobile number and I'll fix something up.'

'Are you sure it's all right?' I asked curiously. 'You've not told him much about the case, apart from that initial phone call, have you? And what's it all about anyway?'

'I'll tell you when I get home.'

'But everything's all right?' I was anxious and insistent.

'Yes, yes, but I'll not discuss it on the 'phone. See you later, bye.' Nick clearly didn't want the matter pursued and I was left playing a very bewildered middle man.

'What's all that about, Mum?' demanded an inquisitive Emily, who'd been listening to one side of the conversation and found herself singularly ill informed.

'I've no idea.'

'What do you mean?'

'Well, that was Trevor Westward, a man we knew years ago when we lived in Maidstone (he used to go to the church there). I think you've met him a few times, do you remember him at all?' Emily looked blank. 'Anyway he wants to talk to Dad about something to do with the case, but he didn't tell me what, nor did Dad, so I'm none the wiser. Now go and do your homework, I've got to ring him back and give him Dad's mobile number.'

When Nick arrived home I was consumed with curiosity and a degree of anxiety as to what was going on, and it seemed an age that he spent cuddling Esther, listening to Emily's latest piano piece and hearing about a mishap at school from Jessica. At long last he came into the kitchen with his mug of coffee, shut the door firmly and began his explanation. Twice we were interrupted by girls wanting this or that but he was eventually able to pass on the essential information.

Trevor worked for the police administration department in Maidstone, he was a middle-aged man with a degree, and had been concerned when Nick had contacted him with the news of his arrest. Working for the police he'd found his interest aroused and his curiosity growing. He'd asked Nick for the names of the three girls and had jotted them down immediately after the telephone call. He may not have sounded very interested to Nick but he was intrigued. Although he'd not had a lot of contact with us over recent years he knew our standing and was confident of Nick's innocence; thus he was particularly fascinated to try and work out what was going on.

After thinking it over for a while and finding the subject wouldn't leave him, he resolved to take further action and the following day Trevor had gone into work as a man on a mission. What he planned to do was against all the work codes of practice, of that he was well aware; but he was eaten up with curiosity; determined to see if he could find out any information of relevance. Consequently, as soon as he had a free, unobserved moment he typed 'Anita Simpson', 'Penny Finch' and 'Deborah Islington' into the computer and searched for any records. Under 'Finch' and 'Islington' there were none, not even under other first names; but when 'Anita Simpson' was entered an instant match for the surname was found. The first name was not the same, but it gave Trevor something to go on. He jotted down the file number 12443990 and resolved at the next possible opportunity to have a thorough look at it, feeling more and more hopeful that his speculations were correct and could possibly help Nick in his defence.

At lunch time, when a good half of the staff were absent, he wandered nonchalantly to the basement room where the files were kept, located 12443990, whipped it out, put it in his brief case and disappeared into a cubicle in the toilets, firmly locking the door behind him. At leisure he scanned the file and found exactly what he'd suspected and been looking for. A few years ago Jasmine Simpson, Anita's twin sister, had gone to the police and reported sexual abuse by her father. As far as Trevor was concerned this information might well be of considerable interest and assistance to Nick and his solicitor. It was highly likely that something had initiated Jasmine's visit to the police, a small something maybe, but a young teenager, as she would have been then, would not have gone for no reason whatsoever. Consequently if someone, friend or relation, had abused or attempted to abuse Jasmine, the same thing might well have happened to Anita. If it hadn't happened to Anita herself, but had to her twin, it was highly probable that Jasmine would have confided in her sister. This information, either imparted or experienced, might just be the grounds on which Anita was basing her allegations. So at last Trevor felt he might have unlocked the door providing a possible motive for Anita's accusations. He was anxious and excited and had determined to contact Mr Dixon. He obtained the solicitor's address from the Darnells with whom he was very friendly and, having surreptitiously photocopied the requisite documents and returned the file, then proceeded to ring Mr Dixon with his discovery: which had resulted in Nick being summoned to Mr Dixon's office so urgently.

What had happened subsequently was that Trevor had put the documents in the post and Mr Dixon had read them, shown them to Mr Bassett who had felt they were singularly relevant and that the originals should be obtained. While we had been away on holiday the solicitors had tried desperately to obtain this information from the Child Protection Unit (CPU), who, not surprisingly, had refused to co-operate. Mr Dixon had requested anything on their files relating to any of the three girls and had been assured there were no records. He'd pursued it further and specifically asked for details of Anita Simpson's background, but had again hit a brick wall. The CPU were adamant that they could divulge no information whatsoever because of client confidentiality. So the only possible way of obtaining it, having exhausted all other processes, was to demand it specifically.

'How do you mean?' I asked, my head was reeling from these tails of intrigue and mystery of which I'd been so totally unaware.

'What I mean is, that the solicitors have to admit they know of the documents existence. Because up to now they've only asked about it in loose terms. Now they have to request document 123 or whatever ...' He paused. 'Consequently the CPU will realise that someone's leaked something and Trevor could be sacked with very few future prospects as he's broken his oath of confidentiality or whatever they swear to in the police.'

'Oh gulp.' I ran my hand through my hair in an exasperated gesture.

'So,' Nick continued, 'the solicitors felt I should know all this before they proceeded any further, in case I didn't want them to follow it up.'

'But it could save your bacon?'

'I know that, but there's Trevor Westward to think about. Anyway I've said I'll ring tomorrow with my answer and meanwhile I've arranged to meet him at the Horse and Groom for a chat.'

'Wow!' I said. 'This thing's a huge mess. It's awful to think of all Jasmine's allegations coming out into the open and specially if members of the family hear who hadn't a clue. But then if Anita's generously ascribing to you things that someone in her family did either to her or to Jasmine you could end up in prison which isn't the answer at all. Oh dear, this is really gruesome. Still, I s'pose we should be thankful that Trevor happened to be so intrigued by it all that he decided to take it on himself to investigate.'

'Absolutely. It's an amazing sequence of events; but the problem is, what happens now? Anyway I must be off to meet him and we'll see what happens then.'

Nick returned about 10.30 pm, reasonably cheerful to my great relief, and he duly related all that had happened.

'Well, when I got there the place was deserted apart from a tall middle aged chappy sitting at the bar with a beer. So I went up to him and as soon as he turned round I recognised instantly it was Trevor. He hasn't changed a bit, he looked just the same. Anyway he bought me a drink and then we went and sat in an alcove, which was just as well 'coz just then a whole crowd of giggly women came in. A hen party I imagine, making a right racket. But in some ways that was good because it meant no one was in the least bit interested in anything we said and even if they had been they'd never have heard anything above the noise of that crowd.'

'Go on,' I said, not in the slightest bit interested in the hen party and very keen to know what Trevor had had to say.

'Basically he told me the story Mr Dixon had related about how he had discovered the information and then asked what we were going to do with it. I told him that that was where the problem lay, because as the CPU wouldn't release it, the only way we could get hold of it was to request it specifically which might well end up incriminating him.'

'And?'

'Oh this is the funny bit,' said Nick with one of his mischievous grins. 'He grabbed my arm and said in a terribly upper crusty voice, "My dear boy, don't think I haven't thought about that, what do you take me for?" I was pretty startled but he went on, "I can assure you that the moment I discovered the file I realised I could be in the soup. As I sat scanning that folder in the gents I thought that it might be more sensible to pop the file back in its place and leave well alone. But then I thought of you, old son and the scrape you were in and my conscience wouldn't let me. Oh no. I've long since decided that this information must come out and your name cleared; and if I end up getting the sack, well so be it. I'm nearly at retiring age any way, and I've a few savings. So don't you worry my boy, you just go for it, otherwise all that effort and subterfuge will have been in vain and we can't have that now, can we?" Wasn't that sweet of him? I tell you he's a really great guy, I can't quite believe he's putting his job, reputation and future on the line all for me, it's incredible. Trevor is adamant there's no turning back. He's committed the crime whether we use the information or not, so it's only a matter of when and if it's discovered. Apparently there are other ways the information could have got out. Social services have details of the case on file, so it could be through them that the leak occurred and apparently the thing wasn't handled very well at the time so when the authorities realise that they might not want to investigate the situation further in case they end up with egg on their faces. So,' Nick concluded, 'he's absolutely adamant that the information must be requested direct. He says I mustn't hold back because it's more important that I'm proved innocent than anything else. He's thought and thought about the consequences and he's quite resigned to them.'

'What an incredible man,' I said with feeling.

'Yes, he is. I wish you could have met him again. You know, he says he's absolutely convinced God wanted him to find that file because normally he's a hundred per cent useless with computers and has to enlist help.'

'That's incredible,' I commented, then went on, 'so you'll ring the solicitors tomorrow and give them the go ahead?'

'Yup,' replied Nick. 'I've not really any choice. Trevor's risked life and limb for me, I'd be a nutter to say "no thank you, not today" wouldn't I?'

'I suppose so,' I sighed, 'but what a mess.'

The trial approaches

S oon our friends began to receive their witness statements, which had to be signed and returned to the solicitor in case Mr Bassett wanted to use them in person or their statement. Emily received hers which clearly agitated her somewhat.

'Mum,' she said, 'can you read this through slowly and make sure I haven't said anything wonky. I'm so frightened something I say might be taken out of context and used against Dad.'

'I know, dear. It's scary stuff. But we just have to hope that the prosecuting barrister's not too vicious. Anyway,' I added reassuringly, 'they'll probably be pretty gentle with you seeing as you're the youngest person appearing at court, that is, if they want you. Just because you've signed a statement it doesn't mean you'll necessarily have to go to court.'

'I know, I know,' responded Emily. 'But I just wanted to be absolutely sure this is right.'

After checking and double checking the statement it was put in its envelope and returned first class when I took Esther to school. Emily had been too young to attend the youth group in Oxted but spoke about knowing the girls involved, that they were regularly in the house and often baby-sat. She stated that there'd been absolutely no problem with any of the girls and so she logically enquired at the end of her statement, 'If there had been, why did the girls continue to come so often to our house?'

'That's such a reasonable question,' I contemplated. 'Why on earth didn't the police at least consider it?'

A couple of weeks after this our social life suddenly livened up no end. It was as if all the friends from Oxted had realised that the autumn term was underway and consequently Nick's trial was rapidly approaching, so they wanted to visit us before the dreaded event. Visitor after visitor drove down, and I found myself running a permanent restaurant. Thankfully food had regained a certain amount of interest since the early days, so cooking a meal for them was not a problem. Some, the more discerning and compassionate perhaps, declined the offer of food, while others brought 'goodies' to be popped in the freezer, or 'for the girls' lunch boxes' or 'just a little something to cheer you up', all of which were hugely appreciated being of both practical and psychological assistance. People did still love us, did still believe in us, we had to hang on to that. Most of the guests had no new information as to the whereabouts and attitudes of the three girls. But one particular evening just as Nick was tucking Felicity down, Tom, a close friend of all three girls and contemporary at school and college, mentioned to me; 'I saw Anita the other day.'

I felt my heart stop momentarily, but tried to maintain my composure. 'Did you? Where?'

'At the Kings Head. I think she goes there quite a lot. I was there with Pete and she was with Jasmine.'

'What did you do?' I enquired. 'Did you speak to her?'

'Well, I pointed them out to Pete but wasn't going to go over to them particularly. But when I got up to go and get some drinks I had to go right past her. She said "Hello," and I didn't like to be rude so I stopped to chat.' I inhaled deeply.

'What did you talk about?' I asked as casually as I possibly could.

'First of all about university, and then I told her I'd split up with Emma and then we went on to discuss church. She said she couldn't understand why everyone was ignoring them and being so nasty to her, Penny and Debs. She said she knew what Nick had done to her, and Nick knew what he'd done and even if he didn't get justice on this earth he'd get it in the future. She was really convincing, and cried, and I think she believes every word she said. I asked her if she was worried about going to court and she said she wasn't looking forward to relating everything Nick had done to her, but it was the right thing to do and she had to do it. Mind you she didn't seem particularly anxious.'

'Did she say anything else?' I asked, my pulse racing and, I felt sure an audible thump resounding from my chest.

'Not really. Oh, she said she'd seen Debs and was going on holiday with Penny down to Cornwall next week.'

'This is awful,' I muttered, 'The fact that she really believes this nonsense.'

'I know,' agreed Tom sympathetically, putting an arm round my shoulders. 'If it weren't for the fact that I know you both so well and the dates are all wrong I'd've believed her.'

'I think I'd better write down what you said,' I said. 'It could be useful to our barrister to know Anita's approach, especially that her story sounds so plausible and that she seems totally convinced of its veracity.'

So I grabbed a pen and paper and with Tom's assistance wrote down a brief summary of what had taken place at the Kings Head. All that I heard disconcerted me considerably and I had visions of jurors oozing with sympathy for this poor damaged girl as she wept in the witness box. I didn't sleep well that night, though I'd been encouraged that the news hadn't worried Nick as I'd feared it might. He was philosophical, knowing that so many of Anita's statements could be disproved however convincing she was, and so remained tolerably optimistic. The following morning, after delivering Esther to school, the tears fell again and brought back vivid memories of the days after Nick's arrest. 'But I'll not let this defeat me,' I muttered. 'It could be just as well we've heard it now, so we can pass it on to Mr Dixon.' With an effort I blew my nose, turned the radio on loud for distraction and proceeded vigorously with the housework.

The following evening a friend from Oxted telephoned with the news that he'd written a letter to the head of the police commission, protesting at the way DC Stevens had misused information given to him in interviewing other members of the youth group and threatening a possible complaint. As we listened, we felt our hearts racing. What had been going on? A well meaning friend interfering with the case could result in disaster. The trial could be postponed or we could get into even more trouble. We were horrified. But a prompt reply had been received which informed him that as the case was imminent Mr Burrows couldn't comment on it because of the laws of sub judice. But the letter had been forwarded to Stevens DC. No. 3748 along with a copy of this reply, and the correspondence had also been copied to the CPS Mr Burrows hoped the answer had been of some assistance and he enclosed a leaflet about how to proceed with a police complaint. I wondered apprehensively, as I listened to it all, what Mr Dixon would say if he knew what had been going on. But as we had had absolutely nothing to do with it, I certainly hoped it was OK. I also hoped it made Stevens sweat a little, feeling that he'd done nothing to further our cause, or even to take note of anything Nick had to say; but had been solely concerned with 'proving' the girls' statements to be true. It was an anxious time and the gesture of our well meaning friend worried us more than we liked to admit.

As time crept inexorably on, the nausea and headaches returned to me with a vengeance, and I woke each day thinking I might be pregnant because of the sickness that swept over me as soon I opened my eyes; knowing I wasn't, and almost wishing I was. That at least would give me a legitimate reason for feeling so foul. I found myself continually, futilely, pinning my hopes on the post coming or the telephone ringing. Might this be the letter or telephone call from the solicitors saying the whole thing had been cancelled, the CPS had realised it didn't add up and had therefore decided not to proceed? Could it be Nick on the telephone informing me it was all over, Mr Dixon having just rung and told him? How I longed for that to be so! I pounced on the telephone every time it rang, but it invariably turned out to be a well meaning friend ringing to find out how I was or the dentist confirming an appointment for the girls. Life reminded me so much of that at Longbourne in *'Pride and Prejudice'*, when Elizabeth is awaiting news of Lydia, 'Every day … was now a day of anxiety; but the most anxious part of each was when the post was expected. The arrival of letters was the first grand object of every morning's impatience. Through letters, whatever of good or bad was to be told, would be communicated, and every succeeding day was expected to bring some news of importance.'

About three weeks before the trial, the telephone did ring with unexpected news, but not the sort that either of us eagerly anticipated; in fact not the sort I would have conceived of in my wildest dreams. My father told me in gentle terms that my cousin Mark had died of a brain haemorrhage the day before. It was horrific news and I struggled to get my mind round the shock and tried to think about sending flowers and a letter of condolence. Uncle Patrick, Mark's father, totally unaware of Nick's situation, rang a couple of days later to ask him to play the organ at the funeral in a few days' time. Nick immediately complied, 'You can hardly say "no", can you to a request like that?' he said with a grin to me, once the call was over.

So arrangements had to be made for Monday 4th October. Flowers ordered, clothes checked and of course, someone to look after the children. Thankfully Angie who'd stood in so nobly for all the court appearances was quite willing to collect them from school and cook them a meal.

During the long drive to Over Wallop, where my Uncle and Aunt lived, and where Mark had spent his formative years, Nick seemed calm and relaxed. The sun was shining and the miles flew by. Despite the great tragedy of the occasion it provided us with a distraction from our own traumas, and of necessity we would have to converse civilly with a variety of distant relatives, forcing our minds away from ourselves, at least temporarily. As we entered the village I read out the instructions dictated over the telephone by Uncle Patrick and we quickly located the church. It was a typical Anglican building in grey stone with an impressive square tower. On one side was a modern extension which housed a church hall and several other useful looking rooms. We had arrived an hour and a half early to enable Nick to familiarise himself with the organ, establishing exactly which knobs were required and the volume and tempo of the music. Thankfully, the building was unlocked and as we entered the church itself, we were met by a round faced, smiling lady who introduced herself as the minister's wife. She explained that she'd known of our early arrival, we were welcome to play the organ straight away, or would we rather have a cuppa first? We declined a drink and smiling politely left her to the finishing touches on the flowers while Nick settled down at the organ. It was a modern instrument, only a few years old, with computerised settings and an amazing range of sounds. Nick was in his element, changing the buttons here and there and producing all sorts of tones. He experimented enthusiastically with the multitude of different ranges and computerised combinations to try and achieve a significant sound, but sufficiently sombre. Once he was happy with the result he practised assiduously, asking me to stand at different places in the church to check the music could be heard, but wasn't deafening. We then sat in the car drinking our thermos coffee and eating our sandwiches. Returning to the church, Nick seated himself at the organ and as friends and relatives drifted in he played gentle, quiet music.

At last the congregation was requested to stand and the coffin was brought in. It was an orderly service; in true British stiff upper lip fashion there were few overt demonstrations of grief, the scriptures were read, the prayers said and a summary of Mark's life presented in a calm unemotional manner. The last hymn was sung and everyone gradually made their way out. Then on to the graveside for the committal and back to Auntie and Uncle's house for a cup of tea and chat. That was the bit I found the hardest, seeing relatives one only ever sees at weddings and funerals, searching desperately for intelligent conversation topics and when asked politely how we were, replying, lying through my teeth, that we were just fine thank you. And the girls? Yes, yes, they were fine too, yes thoroughly enjoying their new schools, yes settled down very well, yes lovely new house, you must come down and see it sometime.

'What a load of total and utter rubbish,' I thought even as I replied. 'We're not fine, the girls are not OK and whatever you do, don't even think of visiting us. Anyway if you do come down in a few months' time we'll probably not be there, the house'll be sold, Nick'll be in prison and goodness knows what'll be going on.'

'Oh, thank you,' I exclaimed out loud, disturbed from my unsettling reverie. 'Yes, I'd love another cup of tea.'

As we drove home I mulled over the bizarre situation I'd found myself in. One Monday at the graveside of my cousin and a family gathering in distinctly sombre circumstances; the next Monday another family get together, not at a graveside but at Crown Court. Could be quite gripping in a woman's magazine or a soap, but in real life it was far from fun. I returned with a cracking headache but glad to see the children and hear their news from school. 'What will my home coming be like next Monday?' I wondered.

Countdown

The week was busy with the Monday jobs to catch up on, meals to be planned for the duration of the trial and the freezer to be filled. On Wednesday a substantial package arrived from the solicitors. Nick (who happened to be working from home that morning,) and I fell on it like a couple of vultures. Once again, I felt the all too familiar signs of a racing heart beat as we ploughed through the 'additional' evidence from the prosecution. What on earth could they have dragged up now? To our relief the additional evidence proved to be singularly unalarming. Photocopies of the *One Minute Bible* and John Blanchard's *Ultimate Questions*, proof that Nick had lent Anita books. Actually we'd given her those, but it didn't make any odds, Nick wasn't even thinking of denying that he'd lent her books. The only other evidential documents were photocopies of the girls' birth certificates and completed forms about the three girls' medical history. They all claimed to be in sound mind and never to have suffered abuse of any description. The paperwork also contained a list of witnesses that Nick's solicitors were planning to use, including Emily and myself. Though I had the option to support Nick in court in the public gallery rather than act as a witness if I preferred. We'd already discussed that point long and hard; and as Nick's Dad, my parents, Rebekah's husband Chris, plus Nick's brother from Australia were all going to be there, we felt it was probably better for me to be a witness and show that as his wife I was with him all the way.

Having ploughed through the paperwork, I then rang Janice to discuss one or two niceties of the case and to confirm that I would stand as a witness rather than go into court to support Nick. I asked if Janice had had any luck extracting Trevor Westward's information from the Child Protection Unit. A few weeks ago the situation had appeared absolutely hopeless as first the CPU had denied such a file existed, and then when the number was given to them they'd refused to hand it over.

To my delight Janice affirmed that the file was sitting on her desk at that precise moment and that she was checking it through ensuring it was complete. Janice then proceeded to elaborate on the difficulty they'd had in obtaining the file, and as I listened to all that had gone on I was so thankful that we had solicitors working for us and weren't trying to go it alone. Apparently, after the CPU had admitted the existence of the file Trevor had unearthed, Mr Dixon had then instructed Janice to set in motion the process of forcing them to hand it over by obtaining a legal injunction.

Consequently a few days previously Janice had been at Guildford court with a judge in attendance and a representative from the CPU. The judge had listened to Janice's explanation as to why the file was required, that allegations of sexual abuse by a family member at an earlier date might be relevant to the allegations made about Nick, and asked the lady from the CPU if she had the requisite file with her. She'd replied positively and the consequence had been that the judge had concluded with: 'Well, I don't see much of a problem here. You, (pointing at Janice) require the file which you (pointing at the lady from CPU) have. I therefore instruct you, the CPU, to hand over to Janice Everett, representing Dixon, Dixon and partners, the file; and', he finished with a wry smile, 'we're all done and dusted.'

Janice had been completely baffled by the simplicity of the whole set up until she'd returned to the office and found an urgent message on her answer phone. It was Mr English, head of the CPU, requesting that she contact him immediately. This she duly did.

Initially Mr English came across as extremely friendly and anxious to please as he carefully explained how Miss Greenhowe, the lady who'd been at court, was new to the department and of course rather young and had naively misunderstood the situation with regard to Dixon, Dixon and Partners. She just read the note requesting the file, retrieved it from the filing room and took it to court without consulting anyone. On her return she'd detailed all that had taken place and it had been pointed out to her that no one was allowed to remove files without the permission of a supervisor, and no one was allowed to take them from the building without the authorisation of Mr English himself. Miss Greenhowe had been devastated and very apologetic, so now Mr English was left to make one quick telephone call to rectify the situation.

'What exactly are you saying?' enquired Janice cannily.

'I'd have thought it was obvious,' responded Mr English, clearly beginning to feel under pressure. 'Miss Greenhowe is young and inexperienced and made an error. All I'm asking of you is that you pop the file back to our office by return, unread and this confusion can be promptly forgotten about and we can all get on with our lives.' If Mr English had hoped for co-operation from Janice he was quickly disillusioned.

'I'm afraid Mr English,' she said firmly but politely, 'as your office has been so good as to give us the file under the judge's instructions, we have every intention of keeping it. And,' she added, 'if you feel so desperate to have it back that you're prepared to return to court about it, so be it. Meanwhile we will, of course peruse it at our leisure in case it contains anything of relevance to our case.' Mr English was unimpressed and Janice heard him swear quietly under his breath before he exploded with: 'This is totally unreasonable, Miss Everett, totally out of hand. You are to return the file to us immediately.'

'I'm afraid I'm not prepared to do that,' Janice retorted, 'unless a judge instructs me to do so.'

'This is by no means the end of this matter,' Mr English almost screamed down the telephone before he slammed it down, making such a racket that it caused Janice to wince before she too replaced the receiver.

Since then they'd heard nothing at all from the CPU, who were clearly suffering from a severe amount of egg on their faces, and Janice had wondered whether the ill fated Miss Greenhowe was still in their employ. However, the file was in the possession of Dixon, Dixon and Partners and even if the CPU did take them to court to retrieve it they'd be unlikely to achieve it before Nick's case, as it was only a week away. The episode sounded alarmingly stressful as Janice related it to me, but I was so thankful that if need be the documents Trevor Westward had stumbled on could be used.

I also enquired about Jo and Ruth's statements. No, Janice hadn't heard anything. The statements had been submitted to the prosecution but there had been no come back. This worried me somewhat as Jo was in Malawi and Ruth in Israel. If the prosecution refused to accept their statements the evidence was invalid unless they flew back to court, and who would pay for that? Janice said they'd probably hear Thursday or Friday which seemed alarmingly near the actual case but I realised there was, as usual, no arguing with the system.

Another query which bothered me was, would Nick be kept on remand for the duration of the trial? Thankfully Janice didn't seem to think so; and so came the final question that had been troubling me, what should Nick wear? In some ways it seemed trivial, but I was desperate for the right impression to be given to the jury, and knew I could rely on Janice's expertise. The reply was very much as expected, a suit, if Nick felt comfortable in one, or smart casual. There would be breaks during the trial, Janice reassured me, when Nick would be able to chat to me, and he'd probably be permitted to pop out at lunch time for a bite to eat with me too.

Putting the telephone down, it felt to me as if, perhaps, we were at last getting there. Anita's abuse as a child, or, if not experienced personally, the shared information from her twin, had clearly got totally tangled in her mind and Nick had replaced the abuser. At last a sort of motive had taken shape which surely would help things along, with all the other contradictions? We both felt alternatively optimistic and pessimistic about the final outcome of the trial. One minute we felt there was so much in our favour, the next, on rereading the dreadful deeds Nick had allegedly committed, described in such graphic detail, we were filled with fear, apprehension and our confidence was knocked out of us. It was like a constantly swinging pendulum that never paused even for a second. Our minds couldn't settle to adopting one particular outcome, they vacillated between the two scenarios with the monotonous persistence of a metronome.

The next day the witness letters arrived, asking many of Nick's staunchest supporters and friends to be available the following Thursday, Friday or perhaps even the Monday. Emily received hers with stoic resilience.

'Darling,' I enquired at bedtime. 'You're sure you're happy to do this? It certainly won't be much fun.'

'Of course,' replied the determined young lady.

Dixon, Dixon & Partners *solicitors*

Miss E. Metcalfe,
6 Elmtree Avenue,
Cranleigh,
Surrey
Dear Miss Metcalfe,
RE: YOUR FATHER—GUILDFORD CROWN COURT

Mr James Bassett Q.C., the barrister representing your father, has now had the opportunity of considering all of the statements of the defence witnesses in this matter and has decided that he would like to call you to give evidence on your father's behalf.

We anticipate that this will be from Thursday or Friday of next week, 14th and 15th October 1999. However, there is some possibility if the trial progresses faster than expected, that you may be called to give evidence on Wednesday.

Alternatively, if things progress slowly it may be we will not get round to some of the witnesses until the following Monday.

I should be grateful if you could please inform me of any inconvenient times for you during this period on which it would be difficult for you to give evidence. I would also appreciate it if you would supply me with a telephone number on which you can be contacted at short notice during the Court proceedings.

May I take this opportunity to thank you once again for your assistance in this matter. Please do not hesitate to contact me should there be any problems in respect of the above.

Yours sincerely,

J.A. EVERETT

'I expect it'll all be over incredibly quickly,' I said. 'You'll have to swear to tell the truth and then Mr Bassett will ask a few questions and then you'll probably be out of there, I doubt very much the prosecuting barrister will pester you, but he might. If he does, he's sure to ask you weighted questions or twist your answers, or deliberately misinterpret what you say.'

'I know Mum,' replied Emily, 'I've read enough John Grisham to know roughly how it'll run; and I can assure you there won't be any barristers getting the better of me.' I smiled, how I loved my eldest daughter's intelligent, mature approach to all this; if anyone held up well in court, I knew Emily would.

Of course, school was a bit of a problem. How would we explain her absence and what concerned Emily rather more, was what she should say to her friends? To date she'd held her tongue to perfection so that none of her colleagues had a clue of the crises at home, but they frequently commented on the fact that she was never ill. So, if she were to disappear without notice they'd be sure to wonder, and Jessica would most likely be bombarded with a plethora of questions. In the end Peter, Angie's husband, who was a school teacher, suggested the best solution. It was far from brilliant and Emily felt distinctly uncomfortable, knowing full well that her friends' curiosity would be well and truly aroused by 'Mum and Dad are going somewhere and needed Emily to go with them.' As for the excuse to the teachers, that was no better. 'Personal family reasons' was sure to create gossip in the staff room, concern in the classroom and if she were really unlucky one of the teachers would be allocated to get alongside her and root out the real problem.

On Friday I felt more positive than I had for weeks. Admittedly the nausea was still there, but I was used to that and resigned to its presence at least until the end of the trial. But I knew the big countdown was nearly over. I had to visit the supermarket for bread, cheese, milk, fresh fruit and vegetables for the following week and then I felt I'd be as ready as possible for the imminent onslaught. Friends and family were continually sending supportive cards and letters, and telephone calls came in a constant trickle. On the days I was inclined to feel overcome by the enormity of what lay ahead, we invariably received a card or telephone call to encourage me and lift my spirits.

While unpacking the shopping, and feeling full of grit, determination and resolve, the telephone rang yet again. 'Hi, it's me,' came Nick's cheery voice.

'Hi, any news?'

'Well, it's good news and bad.' he replied.

'Go on,' I said rather apprehensively.

'It's been postponed by a day.'

'What?' I was incredulous.

'Apparently, there's no judge available on Monday, so it's postponed to the following day. Janice did say she created an absolute stink, but they wouldn't or couldn't budge.'

'Oh,' I exclaimed. 'Well I suppose it's only a day, but we'll have to contact loads of people and tell them.'

'I know.'

'What about the witnesses?'

'Well, Janice says it's not worth contacting them yet as the day of their appearance is so uncertain it won't really affect them.'

'I see, so what's the good news?'

'Just that we've got another day to prepare!'

'Great! I'll have to get on the phone then?'

'Yes, if you don't mind.'

'I dare say I'll manage. Everything OK with you?'

'Yes fine, I should be home in good time.'

'Excellent, I'll see you later then.'

'Wow!' I thought. 'These things always come at you from unexpected directions. You try to think about all the possible scenarios, but we'd never anticipated even for a second that we'd get to this stage and it'd be postponed. Thank goodness it's only a day.' I duly picked up the telephone and rang the dozens of people who were involved and concerned, some of whom had even planned to come to court.

The trial commences

The weekend rolled on and hectic activity took over, preventing too much stress and anxiety. All four girls were playing the piano in a local music festival and rather than bore them to tears by dumping them there for the whole day, I chose to ferry them to and fro as time allowed. Entering the grand school hall where the event was proceeding, I gasped. Neither of us had given the festival a thought, but clearly it was one of those occasions where precious parents paraded their infant prodigies in front of the world. Little boys were done up in long trousers, white shirts and bow ties, while the girls of varying ages had long skirts, white blouses and pretty hair ribbons. I gulped; 'Oh why didn't I realise, my girls are all in Saturday casuals and everyone else is dressed up to the nines.' As the performances proceeded I realised further that these were highly polished recitals, where clearly parent and prodigy had practised assiduously for weeks on end, all for this grand occasion. I felt like a fish out of water, convinced that my girls would trail abysmally on the marks front due to lack of attention and supervision. However, as the day progressed I was relieved to learn that whilst the girls were not among the cup receivers and outstanding genii; they nevertheless held their own and scored quite adequate marks, each one receiving a certificate of merit for their efforts.

In the evening we all went to a quiz evening run by the church. It was an amusing light hearted time, made that much more fun by the fact that our team, unusually and most unexpectedly, ended up with the top score. Sunday too flew by with hustle and bustle and children. We all enjoyed a country walk and a fly on the wall would hardly have known the tension that we were quietly suffering inside.

Mainwave had arranged that the interim job Nick was doing would be completed the Friday before the trial. He had finished clearing the office out on Friday and had the following fortnight off; the theory was that after the trial he would start a new job involving a great deal of travelling and co-ordinating computer links all over Europe. That seemed a lifetime away. Consequently when Monday dawned he initially felt at a total loss. The big build up and there was nothing. No trial, no jury, no barrister, just time on his hands and a lot of frustration. I felt similarly. The shopping was done, fridge and freezer stocked, house tidy and I was ready for the off. Only nothing was happening. After a desultory coffee, we both shook themselves out of our lethargy and I went to change the bed covers while Nick fiddled with his computer and installed various programmes for the girls to use for their homework. Progress was slow changing the quilt. I dumped myself on the bed and began to talk to God. 'This waiting is tortuous, but keep Nick out of prison, please, please, please.' I felt so desperate and miserable, so low and despondent and reasonably convinced that a prison sentence would be the outcome. 'No,' I pleaded as I pummelled a pillow, 'No, not prison, it isn't fair, we've put up with so much but not prison. What about the girls?' I argued this way and that. 'How would I cope? What about our families? What about the image of the church, your image God? People'll think badly of Christians, of you, God, so don't do it please. We've taken a lot of grief, coped quite well really, but I beg you on my knees, not prison.' As I was defiantly trying to sort God out, the words 'Not my will, but yours' came to my mind. The problem was, it was the wrong way round. Jesus allowing God supremacy rather than having the choice. I didn't want to think of those words at all, anything but. I tried to tell myself Psalm 23, I tried to remember comforting quotes from the Bible that friends had sent us over the months, but 'not my will but yours' was still there. It was a huge hurdle I knew I had to get over, but I fought it all the way. I didn't want God's will if it meant prison, I was human, I could only cope with so much. But the verse haunted me. In a flood of tears I cried, 'OK God, I'll try and trust you. It's going to be really tough and I'm scared stiff. You'll have to help me all the way, but you win. Whatever is in your purposes I'll try really hard to accept.' I cannot begin to describe the peace that followed. There were no dazzling lights or visions, or angels but I knew in my heart of hearts that God was there, God did care and that he would help us through.

In the afternoon Nick's parents, and his brother who'd travelled over from Australia, came down to fill the time and say 'hello'. It was just as they arrived that the telephone rang. It was Janice. She carefully explained that the case had been postponed again until Wednesday. The sinking feeling in both our stomachs was mirrored by the strained despair on our faces. Another day of waiting, of doing nothing, of worrying. What was more,

Nick's brother, Martin, only had a fortnight in the country before he had to return to his wife and family on the other side of the world, and that time was rapidly disappearing with no sign of a trial. My parents too were already ensconced in a bed and breakfast in Guildford and no doubt would be kicking their heels. It was inhuman. Did no one understand the stress we were under? I cycled lethargically to school to collect Esther and felt totally deflated. The court authorities gaily made their decisions, but so many people were affected by this one: Nick's family, my family, our local friends, our friends in Oxted, the children, oh it was too much. A tear dropped which was hastily rubbed away as the effort was made to be composed and 'normal' for Esther. Thankfully she understood little or nothing of the strain we were under and chattered merrily the whole way home.

On returning, Nick seemed composed and resolute and I was determined to mirror that. But poor old Emily, only too aware of all that was taking place, was clearly unimpressed by the second postponement. I knew exactly what she was enduring and longed to reassure her with the maternal; 'Don't worry dear, it's going to be all right.' But of course, I couldn't, and it hurt. To see your child suffering is never pleasant but at least if they're hurting physically one can administer medicines, painkillers and be comforting; but to see the pain she was enduring and feel so utterly helpless caused me anguish. For at least the millionth time I wondered what on earth had induced the girls to make their wild accusations, and if they had any appreciation whatsoever of the pain it was causing? 'Probably not', I thought despondently.

When a new day dawned we tackled it as cheerfully as we could. Nick busied himself with the computer again and I settled down to housework. I was determined to get as much done as possible so that the house was entirely presentable when Angie should look after the children. About coffee time I suggested to Nick a walk and a pub lunch. After all, a change of scenery and some exercise couldn't come amiss. Nick, of course, was pleasantly compliant, it was almost as if he'd given up fighting. I knew that whatever I suggested he'd agree to, as the waiting strain began to tell. Nevertheless, the sun shone as we ambled along the local roads and discussed unemotionally the sort of house I would buy if Nick was no longer around. It would be modern, with minimal upkeep and a small garden. Three bedrooms would be fine, for both pairs of girls could share. By selling our five bedroom house we'd recently moved into, Nick reckoned there'd be no mortgage, legal fees could be repaid to our kind supporters and if I could get a half decent job, that would just about cover bills and food. In Cranleigh there was a huge variety of semis and we pointed out to each other which ones we liked. We had a pleasant walk and an enjoyable lunch. Could anyone make bigger bacon baps? Nick relished the fare at The Horseshoe and seemed relatively cheerful. Once home again we continued with our respective jobs each willing the telephone to ring, for it to be Janice, assuring us that Wednesday was 'the day'. But I set off to Esther's school with no news and began to hope that at last we could get to grips with this foul situation once and for all.

As I opened the front door, with Esther merrily chatting away behind me, I heard Nick on the telephone and knew in an instant it was Janice. 'Please God, let it be OK, let the trial start tomorrow.' Esther was fussing about needing a drink and biscuit, so I was able to catch little of the conversation; but in a moment of quiet I heard Nick say in a resigned voice: 'Oh well, another day of doing nothing then.' And my heart sank. Could it really be true? Were we in for another day of waiting, wondering and worrying?

Once Esther had been seen to and Nick was off the telephone, he elaborated. 'Apparently, there's a case at Guildford that's taking longer than anticipated, points of law keep being raised and the court have to stop to consider them. Janice is absolutely wild and so is Mr Bassett. He contacted the court and protested, so it's supposedly postponed 'til Thursday. Janice says she's never known anything like it and is so cross. But there doesn't seem to be anything at all we can do about it.'

'Nightmare,' I sympathised, 'shall I ring everyone?'

'If you don't mind. I think you do it better than me.'

'Rubbish, it's only 'coz everyone wants to talk to you that the calls take so long.'

After collecting the other three from school I was summoned into the study by Nick with the comment, 'I've had another phone call.'

'What now?' I wondered.

'Janice rang again to say the prosecution have asked for a postponement.'

'What?' I exclaimed.

'Apparently they've got problems with their witnesses, one's at university and one's got a hospital appointment. But Janice wasn't having any of it.' Nick hurried to reassure me. 'She told them that we also had witness problems but were ready for the off and wanted no delay.'

'So that's Penny who's ill and Debs who doesn't want to come back from university?'

'I would imagine so, but Janice says anything like this can only be to our advantage.'

'Good.'

Nick paused, then pulling the back of his hand across his forehead muttered, 'This is becoming so unreal, I feel as if I'm losing my momentum, and I'm so fed up with it.'

'I know exactly how you feel,' I assured him. 'But if the girls are getting wobbly, it can only be a good thing.'

Wednesday rolled on. More domestic chores, more tidying of the study. Another walk to a pleasant cafe. Arm in arm we sauntered back to the house. Would it ever get started? Shortly after we returned the telephone rang. Janice. Yes, it was definitely tomorrow. Be at court for 2.pm but don't expect miracles was the advice. Courts are renowned for delays, long waits and the consequent stress.

Telling the girls that evening was, for once, a pleasant task. Yes, it really was going to happen. Yes, it really would start tomorrow. Angie would pick them up from school and get their tea, and we'd at last start on my menu of meals already in the freezer. Nick was positively cheerful, cracking jokes and obviously delighting the girls with his buoyancy. I too felt better than I had done for days, now that at last things were getting going.

Surprisingly we both slept well, delivered the girls to school, pottered around, had an early lunch and then set off to Guildford. I was equipped with a book to read, pen, paper, water to drink, the essential Nurofen and some liquorice All Sorts to keep Nick going on the way home, his favourite. The road was clear and we arrived in plenty of time. Gazing up at the impressive stone structure of the Crown Court building, I wondered what the future held, how many days we'd go through this routine and what would be the outcome? I flinched and grasped Nick's arm tighter. What if it meant prison? But with an effort I refused to let my mind go down that alley and forced it back to the present. Soon we were through security, had checked the listings and found we were to be in Court 1. Janice and Mr Bassett appeared and I had my first glance of him. He was middle aged, grey haired and balding, short and round in stature, spoke in a cultured voice and seemed pleasant. He was soon introduced to me.

'Sorry about all these delays.' he said.

'Oh, it's not your fault.'

'I know,' he continued with a wry grin, 'but I'm apologising on behalf of the judicial system of this country, because no one else will!'

'Oh thanks!'

'Now,' he went on in a businesslike voice to Nick, 'I don't expect we'll get much done today from what Janice tells me. Have you eaten? Good, good. Well I'm just off for a bite of lunch.' With that the solid figure marched off leaving us to talk to Janice. 'I think we'll get the jury sworn in today,' she said, 'the other case is still going on, but I think we made such a fuss, the authorities felt something had to happen to shut us up!'

Sure enough a while later 'All those concerned with the case of Nick Metcalfe' were duly summoned to Court 1 by an anonymous voice over the tannoy. Various friends and relatives, including both sets of parents, scuttled off after Nick to Court 1. I was left sitting on my own amidst an interesting assortment of bags and coats. An hour or so later the cluster of supporters reappeared and then Nick and his legal back up. The jury had been sworn in and that was all that would happen today.

'What did you think of them?' I anxiously asked Nick.

'Oh, I don't know, OK I think, it's hard to tell.'

'What happened?' I pressed, only too aware of my vast ignorance of courtroom procedure.

'Well, the potential jurors were asked various questions, like did they live in Oxted, did they go to the Oxted church or did they know it, did they work for Mainwave and when they all answered 'no' they each took a number from one to sixteen from a hat as it were and then those with the numbers one to twelve are the jury.'

'And you think they'll be OK?'

'Well, I don't know, I hope so. There was one large lady I didn't like the look of, not because she was fat,' Nick added with a grin, 'but she had a really mean face, but thankfully she wasn't picked; oh and one bloke had problems reading the card swearing them in, but that doesn't mean he's got no common sense.'

We went for a cup of tea with my parents who were staying in a guest house for the duration, and then set off home. At last it had started, we'd be back tomorrow to hear what the girls had to say. That wouldn't be much fun, but at least the way things were at the moment, we would have the weekend off to recover. There had been no question of putting Nick on remand, which was a huge relief, so now we just had to grit our teeth and get through it all.

The girls were thrilled to see us, and we summarised the events as precisely as we could. Dinner was happy enough, the mood lightened by the start of the onslaught. The two littl'uns wonderfully unaware of the potential stress, and the older ones riding it very well. 'Have you washed my PE kit?' from Jessica, and 'I need £1 for The Guide Dogs for the Blind,' from Felicity reminded me after dinner that somewhere out there at the end of a very long twisty and confusing tunnel there was a real world ticking along in a normal fashion. I wondered if I would ever become part of it again. At that particular point in time, it didn't seem at all likely.

The trial underway

We were able to deliver the girls to school before making our way to Guildford. At least that end of the day resembled normality for them, even if the other end of their school day was rather bizarre. Once again friends and family were waiting for us outside court or soon appeared as we entered the building. The whole situation struck me as verging on the fantastic or ludicrous. There were our closest friends and family assembled all together from all over, not just this country but from all over the world. Under any other circumstances it would be party time, but instead they were all anxiously concerned with only one thing; clearing Nick's name.

Predictably, the previous case continued throughout the morning, and it wasn't until after lunch that the announcement came and Nick and the supporters scuttled off to Court 1. I knew I was in for hours and hours of waiting and tried to settle down with my book. But, as I had rather expected, I could hardly concentrate. My eyes had only skimmed half a page before my mind was back to, 'What was going on? What was Anita saying? Was she being convincing? How were the jury reacting? How was Nick?' I shed a tear as I imagined him sitting there in the dock, caged in like an animal. With a concerted effort I blew my nose, had a drink of water and dived back into *Pride and Prejudice*. It was a slow afternoon.

[I only learnt afterwards from court notes of all that took place. For the sake of continuity, I have inserted the events in their rightful place.]

Meanwhile in court the gruesome procedure had commenced. Nick, penned in with a guardian beside him, sat in the dock, while the family and non testifying friends in the public gallery listened initially to legal wranglings between the prosecuting barrister and the judge. The astonished audience in the public gallery suffered considerable confusion as the number of counts to be levelled at Nick was discussed and tossed around. The judge asked whether there were specific incidents or whether they were sample counts as in the indictment. The prosecuting barrister explained that the indictment could now be amended as the particulars had been clarified. They wanted to leave it at twelve counts of sexual assault, each being a specific incident but demonstrating a frequent tendency of the defendant.

Mr Bassett, even at this early stage, was keen to score a point, and explained how the defence were concerned that the initial arrest had been made for triple rape, then it was reduced to single rape and now it wasn't being mentioned as rape at all. Surely the witness was of partial truth rather than the whole truth? Even the judge admitted the situation was confusing. The prosecuting barrister then rose and attempted to clarify things by explaining that in the rape instance there was no evidence that the witness had physically tried to stop him. So the prosecution would therefore have to prove she was not consenting and because of the words in her statement, the crown would have difficulty doing that.

Was there just the faintest hint of a smile on the judge's face as he exclaimed: 'So we're left with the position that there was voluntary sexual intercourse during which she was indecently assaulted?'

'It's just that I can't prove rape,' persisted the prosecuting barrister.

With a slight expression of frustration the judge then turned to Mr Bassett.

'Your case is that none of this happened?'

'Yes. Your honour, I can only speculate as to why this girl has lied. With the other two, you could put it down to wilful misunderstanding.'

'Well,' continued the judge, 'I can only think this confusion would assist you.'

'It does, your honour, but it's only a tactical advantage, it'll be difficult to ensure justice is done.'

After a few more legal technicalities the jury finally came in and the prosecution barrister explained the case regarding the rape. They were nothing if not confused.

Then Anita was called. She came in looking a little apprehensive and when asked whether she would rather sit or stand she opted for sitting, which resulted in her head only just peering over the edge of the lectern and meaning those in court could hardly see her. She sat there looking slightly nervous and twisting her hands together. Her short cropped dark hair and dark rimmed spectacles gave her an academic appearance and one received the impression that she had made the effort to dress smartly in a navy jacket, tight fitting lilac top and matching plain trousers. She filled in details as to her family background, where she lived, which school she went to and which university she was attending, as she was by now twenty years old. Then the questions became more specific. How well did she know the Metcalfes? How often did she attend the youth group? Was it Nick or her parents who took her home after the meetings?

'Often Nick would take me home and come in for coffee and a chat. Initially he would touch my leg.'

'Where?'

'In the car. I thought I was imagining it.'

Anita then elaborated, much as in her statement, how upset Nick would get, how he cried, how he'd ask for hugs. She then gave details of his hands up her shirt and various other gropings.

'Did this happen often?' asked the prosecuting barrister.

'I don't remember dates,' Anita replied. 'But it went on for weeks maybe months.'

The judge checked her age: 'You were twelve or thirteen? So it happened after you'd started the group?'

Anita nodded. She then went into great detail about how Nick had wanted to retrieve some books which he needed for the youth group; how he'd gone up to her room and had intercourse.

'It hurt, I was afraid and didn't know what to do.'

'Did you say anything?'

'No.'

'It stopped when my parents came home. He appeared as if nothing had happened.'

'Did you carry on going to the youth group?'

'Yes, all my friends were there, I didn't want them to know anything had happened.'

Anita elaborated on a variety of other instances of assault in great detail, but confirmed that despite these repeated assaults she continued going to the group for five or six years. Then she explained how she eventually went to the church leaders and complained about Nick and finally to the police. Yes, she'd seen Nick at her friend Alice's wedding, Deb's sister, and had said 'hello' to him there, but she hadn't seen him since.

She held together well and made quite an impact on the public and jury alike. Mr Bassett stood up for his cross examination. First he homed in on the confusion of whether there was an alleged three rapes or just one. Anita admitted she had been confused the first time she went to the police. Then he tried to pin her down on dates; but Anita maintained it was difficult to remember. 'What I do remember is that it happened.' He quizzed her on ages, when she joined and she became increasingly flustered. He also asked a series of seemingly illogical and non-sequitous questions all with a view to contradicting them later on in the proceedings. No doubt the onlookers were confused, however one or two of the jurors were assiduously taking notes, so that they could keep good tabs on things.

Mr Bassett hinted that the strong drugs Anita had taken after her foot injury in the Charity Swim might have affected her. He asked her about continuing in the group after all these assaults and she was adamant it was because her friends were there. She felt pressurised to continue coming by Nick, Melanie and the people at church. Mr Bassett then moved on to questions about her use of Nick's computer.

'Did you use Mr Metcalfe's computer regularly?'

'Oh no.'

'It was at his house?'

'Yes, but I never used it of my own choice. Nick pressurised me.'

Mr Bassett then asked if Mike Cunliffe had any reason to lie. 'No.'

'But he says you spent hours round there, using Nick's computer.'

'Well, I didn't.'

He proceeded to question her about the alleged rape. Why didn't she tell her parents? Why didn't she tell anyone? Why did she leave it so long, quite literally several years, before mentioning anything to anyone?

Anita struggled, went red and shed tears. There was a dramatic pause as she removed her glasses, wiped her eyes and blew her nose. The time scale baffled her. She hadn't realised she'd left it so long before telling anyone. Mr Bassett asked about her boyfriend. Yes, he was anti-church; no, he'd never met Nick, but disapproved of him because of what he'd done, he said it was disgusting. There were a few further questions about Mr and Mrs Islington, their friendship and their handling of her complaint, also her friendship with Alice and Debs, their daughters, and then as time was ticking on and Mr Bassett clearly had further questions, the judge requested she reappear on the Monday. She did not really have any choice; although she seemed surprised and flustered by the request, she had to acquiesce.

About 4.45 pm the whole group, Nick and his supporters, came traipsing down the stairs towards me. Instinctively I leapt up. 'How's things?' The relatives looked serious. This was the first time they'd heard in any depth the wild allegations. Certainly the parents must have been shocked. Explicit sexual details were not common parlance for them and probably offensive. Nick seemed OK.

'You can't really say,' he replied to my anxious questioning. 'We knew the prosecution bit would be horrible and it's not much fun. Anita's finished relating all the dreadful things I've supposedly done and Mr Bassett's questioning her. He's doing a great job. She appears singularly confused about any details such as dates, months or even years but is absolutely adamant that I did it. She nearly jumped out of her skin at the end when the judge said: 'I think we'll stop there Miss Simpson, and perhaps you'll be good enough to return on Monday?' Obviously she'd not been expecting that. We've also warned her that we're going to bring up Jasmine's allegations about her family.'

'Oh, wow!' I exclaimed. 'I wonder what on earth she'll make of that? I should think it'll put the cat among the pigeons in their house over the weekend, wouldn't you?'

'Yes, well, maybe, I just don't know,' responded a clearly tired Nick. 'I'm beyond knowing how or why she says what she does.'

Although worn out Nick seemed on relatively good form and I was so glad we had the weekend together to recover a little and gather our strength. The girls were again delighted to see us and relieved to have Mum and Dad to themselves for a couple of days.

Much to Felicity's delight, Saturday was an open day at Emily and Jessica's school. My parents came over from their guest house in Guildford and we had an expedition to see the whole set up. The grandparents were thrilled to have the opportunity to look round the senior school, were riveted by every detail, and Grandpa had to be continually hauled out of classroom after classroom after entering into intense conversation with the staff on 'the wrongs of schooling today.' Jessica was in the geography department demonstrating the use of the computer, and we visited her and were able to procure her assistance for the rest of the tour. This included a trip to the dining hall where, much to Felicity and Esther's delight 'free' doughnuts and cream buns were on offer as well as coffee and squash. Felicity's greatest pleasure was the party's last port of call, the science block. There was a wide range of 'hands on' experiments and she homed in on them like a bee to honey. Eventually as the open morning was about to close, she was hauled away, having decided that with a science department like that it was definitely a school worth going to when she was eleven.

On our return home we were surprised to find the table laid, bread buttered and cakes all set out. Emily had returned from a successful lacrosse match and had set to and prepared lunch. I was impressed at her caring approach and hugely appreciated her assistance.

The grandparents did not harp on about the case; but it was so weird conversing as if life would continue normally when we felt our future was incredibly uncertain. Inevitably the conversation involved events at Guildford and my parents were gently encouraging. 'We do think things are going quite well,' my Dad stated. 'There have been such a number of contradictions in that girl's statement and your barrister is excellent. He's picked up on all the inconsistencies and is doing a great job.' We both wished we could share his optimism, but felt that with an English jury anything could happen.

The day flew by and felt faintly normal. Although it seemed to me that life was chaotic and disjointed, my mother commended me on keeping everything running smoothly, and it was nice to be praised and supported a bit. I felt weary and frustrated, but solaced myself quietly that the ordeal would not last for ever; and whatever the outcome, one day we might be able to begin to put our lives back on track. I hoped to goodness the outcome would be good, but recognised that there was yet much ground to cover.

Sunday was a day we all needed, together and quiet. A friend rang to invite us out for a walk and we politely declined. Today was going to be time for us, just us; absolutely essential, vital time to potter, sit, read, play or snooze, whatever was required.

The trial continues

With resolve, we felt strangely calm, almost happy on Monday. This week, at last, would get to grips with matters. 'The jury will have an opportunity to hear our side of affairs,' I thought, 'and hopefully they might be finished by Friday.' Another late start was frustrating and 'All those involved in the case of Nick Metcalfe' weren't called until 11.40 am. Before that, an atmosphere of concern spread among the ranks. Although the relatives and friends didn't know the inside story, they sensed that we were seriously worried. The prosecuting barrister had informed Mr Bassett that Anita had told her sister what had come up regarding unearthing Jasmine's allegations against her father, and apparently Jasmine was planning on saying that it had been Nick who had assaulted her, but she'd reported it as her father. Nick couldn't believe his ears when he was informed, it seemed so outrageous, but was nevertheless concerned, and indeed I was too. How many more girls were going to lie about him?

The supporters and Nick duly went into court, leaving me alone. I could hardly focus on my book. 'Please God, don't let Anita be convincing, please let her lies become obvious.' Each minute felt like an eternity and every time I looked at my watch, less and less time had passed. I was briefly intrigued by a barrister at the adjacent cluster of chairs, trying desperately to explain the simple principles of theft to a rather uncouth looking young man. But he totally failed to grasp them. I admired the barrister's perseverance and patience, but found myself wondering, not for the first time, what I was doing in such company. Many of the characters I'd seen looked like villains, but Nick wasn't one. Nick was innocent.

Time dragged on. A weeping lady paced the corridor in front of me, comforted by an older companion. 'What was the problem?' I pondered. 'Nasty divorce? The custody of a child? Shoplifting?' A whole world of crime was unveiled here every day.

In court Anita was doing her best to describe Nick's crimes to those present. She appeared very distressed, not composed as she had been on Friday. She was told she'd be needed for several hours yet, and was then shown the printout Nick had prepared of the hours she'd spent using his computer. She was asked if she'd discussed the case with the other girls and was adamant that she hadn't. Mr Bassett pointed out that Deborah Islington's statement suggested differently, reading out one or two exerts to make his point. Then came the bombshell as Mr Bassett asked Anita about Jasmine's visit to the police, alleging problems with her father. Anita stuttered, tried to compose herself and then spluttered; 'Jasmine said it was my father but it was really Nick Metcalfe who did it.' Mr Bassett appeared duly aghast and commented to the judge that these allegations from Jasmine were the first his client had heard of them, there'd been no mention of them in her statement. There was a short discussion between Mr Bassett and the judge and then the questioning continued.

It was an uphill struggle for Mr Bassett as each question posed was answered by confusion and a torrent of tears. There were repeated pauses as Anita removed her glasses and mopped her face. Everyone waited apprehensively. Anita was however absolutely certain that she'd witnessed Nick put his hand down Deb's trousers. 'I know he did that, I saw him and I saw his face. He looked so shocked that he'd been caught out. I'll never forget it.'

'Deborah Islington denies that anything like this happened. Are you sure you saw Deborah assaulted?'

'Yes.'

Having made his point Mr Bassett swung back to her use of the computer. She maintained she hadn't used it much, if Nick or Mike Cunliffe said she had, they must have meant someone else.

'Did you ever have a key to the Metcalfe's house?'

'No.'

'Mavis Winger, the Metcalfe's next door neighbour says she lent you one quite regularly at one stage.'

'I might have had one to use the computer. I forget little details, but I'll never forget what happened to me.'

'So you went to his house regularly, used his computer and played his organ?'

'I had to use his organ because ours was broken and I was taking grade eight. I only used his organ once. I didn't want anyone to know what was happening to me. I wanted everyone to think things were normal.'

Mr Bassett then indicated to the court usher, a middle aged lady with large blue spectacles and grey hair, that he wished to use the video machine. She stood up, went to it. It was large and on wheels, and reminded Nick of those used in schools. Inserting the cassette she switched it on, only to be met with a crackling sound and black and white lines darting erratically up and down the screen. The judge looked unimpressed. The lady fiddled with the various buttons, but to no avail. In fact, if anything, the situation worsened as the crackling crescendoed to an ear piercing screeching. The judge said in an exasperated tone: 'We'll have to call a recess until this thing is fixed.' So the court usher ordered the court to rise, the judge exited through his door at the back and Anita and the jury were also escorted out. The bemused onlookers wondered what would happen now and whether there was such a thing as a court engineer or technician.

However there was no need for any such person. Nick, who'd been quietly sitting in his cage watching the proceedings, was pretty sure he knew exactly what the problem was. Once the judge and jury had gone, he rose, let himself out of the box and went to the flustered official's assistance.

As he approached, she was clearly dubious about allowing the 'criminal' near her and the machinery, but he said something to her, exactly what the curious onlookers couldn't catch, and she stepped back and allowed him to look at it. The problem had been diagnosed correctly and within seconds the awful noise ceased, the screen went blue and then a picture appeared of Anita fooling around with Nick on one of the Italian trips. The court official looked relieved and her flushed expression calmed down. Nick returned to the dock where he locked himself in and the judge and jurors were summoned back again.

Once everyone was settled again Mr Bassett indicated to the official that the video was to be shown and the machine was duly switched on. For twenty seconds Nick looked pleased with himself that his electronic skills hadn't completely failed him despite the pressure he was under, and then his mind turned again to full concentration as the video was watched and Anita questioned. The film showed the young people on board a cross channel ferry on the journey to Italy. There was a clip of Anita sprinkling water over Nick from her drinking bottle, and Nick retaliating by making as if to throw her overboard.

'Have you seen this video?' Anita was asked.

'Yes, a month ago.'

'Was this prior to giving evidence?'

'No, my boyfriend wanted to watch it.'

'He's your first serious boyfriend?'

'Yes.'

'Twice your age?'

'Yes.' Anita replied with indignation. 'It makes no difference, he doesn't make me do anything I don't want to.'

'When you first went to the police station you didn't allege rape or mention Mr Metcalfe's visit to your bedroom, did you?'

'No.'

'But two months after taking up with your boyfriend it then crops up?'

'Yes, but he didn't put words into my mouth.'

'Might it have been that he wanted the relationship to go further than you did?'

'No.'

Another video clip was shown of Anita happily chatting with friends on her second trip to Italy.

'Why did you trust Nick enough to go to Italy a second time?'

'My only friends were in the church.'

'Jasmine didn't go.'

'No, she'd left the group.'

'Exactly, she didn't feel pressurised to stay.'

'I can't explain, no one understands. He makes you feel guilty, he needs to be liked.'

'The video looks like four happy girls chatting without any worries.'

'He wasn't in the room at that stage.'

Mr Bassett then changed tack once again. 'In your statement you said after Mr Metcalfe had raped you in your bedroom he then started reading a book?'

'I meant looking at a book. I was upset, I just wanted to get out of the police station.'

'But you've signed to say this is accurate. You've also signed to say you were a victim of triple rape in your bedroom.'

'No, I said there were other occasions of assault but only one rape in my bedroom.'

'Miss Simpson, you are an intelligent woman, currently studying at university, are you too stupid to make it plain to a police woman?' Mr Bassett's voice was firm.

'I was very upset.'

'He was arrested for triple rape.'

'I didn't know what they said to him.'

'So you didn't show you wanted to be alone with him?'

Anita struggled, looking thoroughly confused, she replied, 'I said nothing because I was afraid, I felt guilty, he made me feel guilty. I was young, I was a child.'

At this point Nick felt his stomach tighten, he knew that card was sure to be played, and sure enough there it was. He glanced across at the jury and wondered whether it had made the intended impact. Anita was in full swing as Mr Bassett continued: 'When he touched you, you never indicated he shouldn't?'

'I never said he could do the awful things he did to me. It's not just clear cut that I didn't say anything to him.'

'But you'd had sex education at school?'

'I was young and too impressionable to know what was happening to me.'

Mr Bassett then moved on asking whether they had locks on their bedroom doors at home and the answer was 'no'.

'Was there any abuse in the family?' Again, 'No.'

'Never had any indecent handling?'

'No.'

Mr Bassett then finished up his questioning with: 'I put it to you that Mr Metcalfe did come into your room twice. Once to collect books you'd borrowed and once to admire the wardrobe your dad had made for you and that was all he did.'

'No, that's not true. I wouldn't ever tell lies. It's unforgivable and disgusting to lie. Unthinkable.'

Anita was clearly agitated and anxious, but before she could step down the questions continued.

'Had you any idea Jasmine had made allegations against members of your family?'

'I had no idea, she didn't tell me anything.'

Mr Bassett questioned her further on her relationship with her sister, with Deborah Islington and Mrs Islington. He repeatedly brought her back to discussions she'd had with them about Nick. He then returned to the confusion over the alleged three rapes becoming one incident. Nick got the impression he was trying to hammer home to the jury Anita's unreliability. Eventually after a few more brief questions from the prosecution, Anita was allowed off the stand and the jury went out. Mr Bassett rose quickly to his feet once more and reported to the judge that the complaint he'd made earlier of colluding among witnesses must be noted, because he felt sure Anita and Jasmine, the twins, had conferred over the weekend. Nick assumed the previous conversation between his barrister and the judge had been in private for it was the first time he or any of those in the public gallery had heard of it.

At last around 1 pm the crowd came down the steps, and although I was out of earshot, I could tell by their gait that all was not well. Shoulders sagged, faces looked serious and Nick looked haggard. I hurried up to him.

'How's it gone?'

'Oh hopeless.' replied Nick. 'I'll tell you more over lunch.'

At McDonalds, amidst the bustling mothers, screaming children and trendy students he explained how Anita had wept on and off all through her questioning. She'd been singularly unhelpful and vague about things but hammered the point that whilst she didn't have a good memory for dates and things, she did know what he'd done to her. My heart sank. The jury would be convinced, I knew they would, I mean who wouldn't? A weeping twenty year old girl against a business man? It must seem obvious he'd done something wrong, otherwise he wouldn't be in the dock. I gulped as Nick related the mornings events, and bit my lip in order not to cry. The old angry determination welled up inside me, I'd stand by him come what may, whatever anyone said; he'd have a loyal wife and I wasn't going to let him down now by blubbing.

All is not well

However once court was back in session after lunch and everyone had gone again, the tears began to fall. I sat there with *'Pride and Prejudice'* on my knee, unable to read a word as the tears streamed down my face. I tried not to sniff in order not to draw attention to myself, but I felt totally and utterly miserable. The pain was indescribable, I wanted to scream about injustice, to talk calmly to Anita and Penny, to wring the policeman's neck; well actually, just to lie down quietly and die seemed quite an attractive alternative.

'Mrs Metcalfe?' A voice interrupted my misery.

'Yes.' I mumbled hastily dabbing my face and wondering who on earth knew who I was.

'I'm from the witness support group,' explained a friendly looking middle aged lady. 'We're a group of volunteers who come in each day to help in court. Each day we're allocated different cases and we just help where we can.'

'I see.' I said, rapidly collecting myself and hoping sincerely that the recent gush of tears was not too conspicuous.

'Are you all right?' The well meaning lady enquired.

'Moronic question, or what?' I thought. 'It's patently obvious, isn't it, that I've come here for the fun of it, that it's a laugh a minute and there's nothing in the whole world I'd rather be doing than stressing myself out about what Penny and Debs are saying about my poor husband?'

Out loud I said, 'Yes, thank you, I'm OK. It's just that well er, this is all rather horrible.'

'Yes, of course dear,' cooed Mrs Benevolent, sitting herself down next to me.

'Please don't hug me, I don't know you. You're very nice and all that, but I can cope with my own tears my own way, if it's all the same to you,' I thought as I shrank back in my seat. But the witness support lady was well trained and didn't gush. She talked gently to me about what she did each day and how they were allocated to different cases on each occasion so that they didn't get too involved with the individuals concerned. But, yes it was all very interesting, and sometimes one did get absorbed and want to know the outcome even though one was supposed to keep a distance.

After a time of gentle chit chat the lady was called away and I was relieved. However she'd done a good job of stemming the tide of depression that had threatened to overwhelm me and of briefly distracting me, and I knew that my tears were done for that day. I settled down with my book as best I could, and awaited the end of the court session.

Meanwhile the afternoon session was well underway with Deborah Islington being sworn in and questioned by the prosecuting barrister. Debs, tall, broad with dark eyes and short dark hair seemed a little nervous but composed. She looked smart in a loose blouse, with a pretty, contrasting skirt. The questions started, as they had done with Anita, with background. Yes, she'd come to the church when she was about twelve with her parents and was now studying geography at Plymouth University.

'Did you attend the youth group?'

'Yes.'

'Who ran it?'

'Nick and Melanie.'

'How did you get home from the meetings?'

'Sometimes my father came to collect me, sometimes Nick would give me a lift and sometimes other helpers.'

'Did anything happen between you and Mr Metcalfe?'

'Sometimes he would touch my leg, in the van, instead of the gear stick. Once he touched the back of my legs.'

'Was this the first instance?'

'Oh no, the first was about a year after I'd joined the group.'

The questioning was fast and intense. Brief questions, short answers. Deborah was adamant she'd felt uncomfortable, protested once and never consented to any 'touching'. After nearly half an hour Deborah then had a pause and a drink of water before Mr Bassett took over.

'You were a regular attendee?' he asked.

'Yes.'

'Mr Metcalfe gave you hours of time, helping you and others with problems?'

'Yes.'

Mr Bassett clearly had his own agenda, asked specific questions, received brief concise replies and moved on rapidly. Nick shifted his position and felt suddenly bored. He was fed up with all this nonsense, tired out and cheesed off. A wave of exhaustion swept over him, but he fidgeted a bit, took a sip of water and forced himself to continue concentrating on the proceedings.

'In Italy, you were a difficult teenager?'

'Yes, I was a bit stubborn.'

'You wouldn't eat?'

'I didn't get on with Italian food.'

'Nick and you had a row about not eating and you went off and climbed a tree?'

'Yes.'

'Not because he had touched you indecently?'

'No.'

'Was there any question of you being touched indecently in Italy?'

'No.'

'In February 1998 Anita went to see your mother to back up your story of indecency?'

'Not that I'm aware of. I had mentioned to my parents that he sometimes made me feel awkward.'

'And that's as far as it goes?'

'Yes.'

Mr Williams the prosecuting barrister, then asked half a dozen further questions and Debs acknowledged that when Nick had gone on at her about not eating, Anita had comforted her in the ladies' toilets. For a minute everyone thought Debs' testimony was over, but an idea must have leapt into Mr Bassett's mind for he stood up and suddenly asked her; 'Did you see Anita comforting Mr Metcalfe after he'd become upset with you?'

'Yes.'

'Did you see her hug him?'

'Yes.'

'Thank you very much, Miss Islington.'

The whole court could now take a breather while Debs stepped down and Penny was called. She appeared in her short rust coloured mini skirt and matching top, her dyed dark hair twisted up elegantly behind her with a big clip, looking composed and resolute. She chose, like those before her to sit rather than stand. Again her head was hardly visible to those in the public gallery. Almost before she was under way, there was a point of law and the jury were marched out. But it was quickly dealt with and the group came traipsing back in again. Soon the questioning turned to incidents in Italy. Yes, the second trip had been a stressful one. Yes, the van broke down, and Nick spent much of the time trying to get it fixed.

'Nick was stressed and upset, and gave me a hug and thanked me for the moral support I'd been. He put his hand on my right breast for a couple of seconds. He acted as if nothing had happened. I pushed him away, someone came in and he acted normal.'

'How did you feel?' asked Mr Williams the prosecuting barrister, sounding concerned.

'I felt very uncomfortable and wanted to be with other people, not alone with him.'

'Did it happen again?'

'On another occasion in Italy, he was plumbing in some showers and asked me to help him, when I handed him a tool he put his hand on my bottom and left it there.'

Nick peered out from his glass cage. He didn't know whether to laugh or cry. 'Would people really believe all this nonsense?' he deliberated. 'It is sheer fantasy.'

The questioning continued. Penny seemed very calm and in control. Mr Williams asked her about the time lapse between the 'assaults' and reporting them.

'Why have you complained now?'

'Because I heard Nick was moving away and I wanted people to know what he was like and I didn't want him to do it to other kids.'

Nick felt momentarily nauseous. 'Was she trying to make out he was a serial child molester?'

Penny had remained tranquil throughout her questioning and seemed quite ready for Mr Bassett as he took over. He plunged straight in. 'You're friends with Anita Simpson?'

'Yes.' Once again it was apparent he knew where he was going.

'When did you start talking about these incidents?'

'Two years ago. On quite a regular basis ever since, because sometimes it got too much and it was good to talk.'

'You had a recent meeting in the pub? And you discussed all these issues?'

'Oh yes.'

'Were you a regular attendee at the youth group?'

'Yes.'

'Most Saturdays and Sundays?'

'Yes.'

'No one forced you to go?'

'No, but if I didn't go Nick would get upset.'

More quick fire questions. More brief answers.

'Some of these touchings. Could they have been accidental?'

'No. They were deliberate.'

'Why didn't you complain?'

'We thought we wouldn't be believed.'

'But you continued going in November 1998 after you knew of Anita's accusations?'

'Yes.'

'You decided to back her up?'

'Yes, she's my friend.'

Nick glanced across at the jury. One of the women was fishing something out of her pocket and another glanced at her watch. 'This must seem so tedious to them,' he thought. The endless questions continued.

'Did you use Nick's computer?'

'Yes, once.'

'Did Nick show you help and kindness?'

'Yes.'

'Did you arrange with Tony Brookes to buy Nick and Melanie's leaving present?'

'Yes.'

'Did you sign the leaving card?'

'Yes.'

'Is this it?'

'Yes.'

'Can you find your writing?'

'Yes.'

'Can you read out what you wrote?'

Penny looked a trifle embarrassed, but read clearly: 'Dear Nick and Melanie, thanks so much for all you've done, we'll miss you. Do come and see me, I'm only down the road. Loads of love, Pen.'

'Why did you write that?'

'Nick had done a lot for me. If I'd not written in the card, people would have been suspicious and I wanted to keep it to myself.'

'You wrote to Nick regularly on email?'

'Yes.'

'You always sign it 'love Pen'?'

'Yes. I always sign emails and letters like that.'

'But he doesn't write 'love Nick?''

'No.'

'Let's consider these emails a little further,' said Mr Bassett, holding a thick wodge in his hand. Mr Bassett read out one after another. Much of it was teenage nonsense but it was all affectionately phrased with not a hint of animosity. Every now and then Mr Bassett interjected to Penny; 'You confirm you wrote that?' And she, blushing and gazing down at the floor mumbled a feeble, 'Yes,' in response. Mr Bassett was determined to hammer his point home as he read one after another, but just when the jury were beginning to look a little bored and mesmerised by the whole process, he changed tack.

'You let him visit you at college after assaulting you?'

'I couldn't not let him come.'

'He assaulted you there, but you didn't tell anyone?'

'I could have done, I didn't because I just wanted to be friends with Nick. We all did.'

'Why do you say 'we'? I think you've discussed this a lot? It would be too much to carry on your own? How many times have you and Anita discussed this?'

'About twenty.'

'You wrote to a friend, 'It's not nice when your Dad does things like that to you', meaning sexual assault?'

'Yes.'

'Perhaps you transferred what your father did to you, to Nick?'

'I've never had a good relationship with my father, but the two are unrelated.'

'But something did happen to you?'

'Whatever happened with my father,' Penny burst out indignantly, 'was a long time ago, before I met Nick. We get on well now.'

'Thank you, Miss Finch.'

You could have heard a pin drop, the public gallery were dumbfounded, no one on the defence team could believe that Penny had been trapped into admitting sexual assault by her father. This was a second major breakthrough, there was now confirmation that there had been sexual abuse (or allegations of) in both Anita's and Penny's families. While no one was pleased about these facts that had now emerged, everything was beginning to make much more sense to Nick, and the reasons for the false allegations more logical.

The prosecuting barrister then tried to redeem the situation a little by saying: 'It's been suggested you made up these accusations?', but Penny was adamant.

'No I know what happened, and', looking across at Nick, 'he knows too.'

On that rather vehement note the session was closed.

Hearing a murmur of conversation some while later, I looked up and saw my parents, the in-laws, brother in law and several friends descending the all too familiar stairs. Their heads were high, shoulders back and there was a spring in their step that hadn't been there at lunch time. Before Nick appeared, my father had a word. 'A good afternoon, my dear, a good afternoon. That tall broad girl, not the one with glasses, the other one, more or less said she hadn't wanted to bring charges and the other one was well caught out, I can tell you, well caught out.' Simon Winger, our next door neighbour in Oxted for nine years and family friend joined in. 'A positive start I'd say,' he confirmed. 'Your barrister's excellent and certainly started sorting those girls out, excellent.'

I could feel my spirits lift. If people were so positive at this stage when the prosecution were the people calling the tune, surely it must get better and better? Then I thought back to Jasmine. Well, that was a hurdle yet to get over. Nick still had to endure further nonsense from that direction. Nick appeared with his usual cheery school boy grin and I felt tranquil. He was OK, I was settled. In the car he'd tell me a bit about it and tomorrow was another day.

'How did it go then?' I quizzed once we were alone.

'Well you know I'm not allowed to say much as you're a witness, but I'll give you the bare bones. Debs was OK. I think she told the truth as she saw it. I mean, her allegations are totally pathetic and yes, I may have tickled the back of her leg, but it certainly wasn't sexually motivated. Anyway, she was OK, but when Penny came on I tell you it was a different matter. She was so cool, so smooth, I thought, this is it, I'm done for. She related all the different incidents most convincingly and I was sure the jury were swallowing it hook, line and sinker.'

'So how come you all came out so chirpy, then?' I asked.

'Oh, you should have been there at the end,' said Nick. 'Mr Bassett didn't half do a good job.'

'Go on.'

'Well, he produced the card the Young People gave us when we left and gave it to her. Then he asked if she could find her writing, and then he asked her to read out what she'd written. You remember it, don't you? All about thanks for all you've done, how much she'll miss us and do visit her at university as she's not far away. She read it all out but looked well embarrassed and when asked why she'd written all that she was stumped. Then we had the emails. Mr Bassett read out loads and loads of them and she nearly died. You know she'd said in her statement that I'd written how much I loved her in them, well of course I hadn't, not once and a copy of all of them's been passed to the jury. Mind you,' Nick added with a chuckle, 'I did catch your Dad's eye when he read out 'I've hidden myself in the study to keep out of the way of the in-laws for a bit' but I don't think he minded!'

'Wow,' I grinned. 'I'd no idea he'd read out things like that. Poor old Mum and Dad. Still it sounds as if Mr Bassett did a great job. It's so good we've got him.'

'Yes,' agreed Nick, and then changing the subject slightly, he added, 'you know it's really weird, in fact it's quite a farce really.'

'What is?' I enquired.

The News; Monday, October 18, 1999

NEWS IN BRIEF…
COURT TOLD OF SEX ASSAULTS

CRANLEIGH: A man indecently assaulted three teenage girls; a court was told. Computer manager Nicholas Metcalfe, 41, of Elmtree Avenue, denies 12 charges of indecent assault on three girls aged 13 to 16. Richard Williams, prosecuting, told the jury at Guildford Crown Court that Metcalfe had touched their breasts and bottoms.

(proceeding)

'Apparently it is essential that the jury only ever see me behind the glass screen in the dock. So whenever they come in, there I am sitting good as gold. But before and after court sessions I come and go almost as I please.'

'How do you mean?'

'Well, I'm supposed to have a guard with me, to make sure I behave myself,' he added with a smile, 'but half the time he's not there or he turns up late, so I let myself into my cage before the session starts and lock myself in. Then I let myself out when it's over and the jurors have gone. It's quite mad.'

'Absolutely ridiculous,' I agreed. 'But that's the least of our problems, isn't it?'

The newspaper article reproduced here appeared in the local press on Monday night. It caused me a considerable upset and a few tears envisaging that life would be made difficult for the girls at school. But in God's mercy we were not aware that anyone picked up on it.

'Indeed, but so far, so good, though I'm not happy about tomorrow's antics with Jasmine.'

'No, it could be awful, though at least to date it's OK.' I said, determined to maintain the positive mood, 'let's worry about tomorrow, tomorrow.'

Prosecution complete

It upset Nick, but more particularly me, to see DC Stevens each day at court talking assiduously with Penny and her friends. It felt as if it was all one huge conspiracy backed by the British police represented by DC Stevens. I had always believed that the police back the truth, but felt that on this occasion truth was irrelevant and a conviction was what was eagerly sought. It made us feel most uncomfortable walking past Penny, her friends and DC Stevens each day into court, and now Penny had done 'her bit' she was free to sit in the Public gallery which she did most persistently from the moment she'd completed her testimony onwards. At lunchtime Penny would meet up again with DC Stevens and it was an ongoing stress for both of us to see the pair of them in such close cahoots. Fortunately the other two girls Anita and Deborah made themselves scarce and were not seen again once they had given their evidence.

On Tuesday the prosecution were still calling the tune with Deb's parents first; Jeremy, Deb's boyfriend next, followed by Alice, Deb's sister, and Anita's parents. The case had changed court and so the prosecution witnesses were pacing the floor right near where our group was based. It was embarrassing, awkward and extremely stressful. Once the court was in session, I was the only one who watched the comings and goings behind the protection of *'Pride and Prejudice'*, everyone else was in court. The prosecution witnesses paced the floor outside in turn and were clearly anxious about giving evidence, but then I didn't exactly relish the prospect myself.

Deb's mother was a tall lady, broad like Debs, with permed curly hair. She was dressed smartly and appeared calm. She chose to sit in court and her head and shoulders were clearly visible to all in court. She summarised briefly her involvement with the church and that of her daughters Alice and Debs. Then she mentioned how Anita had come round in tears one evening and explained what Nick had done, how the church officers had been concerned and had talked to Anita. Mr Williams' questioning was quickly over and Mr Bassett mentioned the family meal to which Nick had been invited on Alice's exam success. He asked whether Nick had been the only non-family member who attended, and Mrs Islington had to agree. There were a few more enquiries, and Deb's mother explained that they'd now left the church.

'Why?'

'Because the allegations were far worse than we'd ever imagined.'

'Thank you very much, Mrs Islington.'

Those listening felt that little had been added to the case and wondered whether her husband would change that at all. Deb's father was shorter than his wife, had a thick beard and glasses and looked studious and intellectual. He appeared nervous and fiddled with his fingers incessantly, twisting them backwards and forwards. Mr Islington was asked how well he knew Anita and how he'd heard about the allegations. He explained how he'd spoken to Nick about the original comments Anita had made when she said that Nick was too pushy, and that Nick had agreed not to telephone at all if she missed the group. This had happened six months or so before Nick and his family moved but there had been no indication of any wrong doing or of any sexual assault. Nick had assured him of his full co-operation. 'The following week, Nick spoke to me at church, he said he'd never had an enemy in his life and wanted a reconciliation. I said Anita was busy doing A levels and it would have to be after that. Nick was rattled because I was unwilling to arrange it earlier.'

After other questions Mr Islington explained that he'd told the church officers, and had arranged a lunch with his wife and Anita in order to discuss it.

Once again Mr Bassett followed on.

'What Anita complained of was touching and emotional dependence?'

'Yes.'

'Was it a continual problem?'

'Yes.'

'Touching her arms and legs?'

'Yes.'

'And emotional dependence?'

'Yes.'

'Nick was very upset, because he felt responsible that she'd left the church?'

'Yes.'

'And was anxious for a reconciliation?'

'Yes.'

'He was upset because he wanted to push it on faster than you?'

'Yes.'

'Then Nick, Penny and Anita met at Penny's house and made up?'

'That's right.'

'Who told you about this?'

'My daughter Alice, and I contacted Nick and Anita to confirm this.'

'Anita said it was all sorted?'

'Yes.'

'She mentioned nothing of a sexual nature?'

'No.'

'If she had, would you have gone to the police?'

'Yes.'

'Not until Penny was involved did things take a turn for the worse?'

'Yes.'

Jeremy Buckley was next, Deb's boyfriend. But his time in the stand was very brief. He confirmed he'd attended the youth group, enjoyed it, that Nick had helped him with problems, supported him when he'd been nervous about starting sixth form college and that he'd helped with a little painting at our house at one time. He also said he'd finished with Debs and made it quite clear that, despite being a prosecution witness, he had nothing against Nick whatsoever. The supporters in the public gallery were relieved.

Then came Alice, Deb's sister, who confirmed what she said in her statement; she'd attended the group from the age of fourteen to seventeen and a half, and had enjoyed it very much. Mr Bassett asked her how old you had to be to join, 'Fourteen', was the answer. He asked when Anita joined and how she came, 'On Alice's invite because they were friends at school', and how old Anita would have been when she joined, 'At least fourteen and a half'.

Nick breathed a sigh of relief; from day one he had maintained he had not met Anita until she was at least fourteen, so it would have been impossible to rape her when she was thirteen. Why wouldn't anyone believe him? Having someone from the prosecution confirm this encouraged him that things might not all be going their way. Alice's time in the witness stand was brief. She'd enjoyed the youth group and had not witnessed anything of a dubious nature. Mr Bassett decided there was no more mileage in having Alice on the stand, so he politely thanked her for her evidence, and as the prosecution barrister had no more questions Alice was then permitted to leave.

Jasmine was the next to be summoned. Nick's friends and family were staggered at the similarity between the two girls. The prosecution barrister questioned her first.

'Did you attend the youth group?'

'Yes, for six to eight months.'

'How did you get home?'

'Nick gave us lifts in his van.'

'Did he come to your house?'

'Yes, he'd turn up unexpectedly quite often.'

'After you'd stopped attending, Anita continued going to the group?'

'Yes.'

'Did Anita tell you what was going on with Nick?'

'I knew she felt uncomfortable with him. Sometime round her hospitalisation her mood changed. I know her very well. I comforted her.'

'Was this before or after her hospitalisation?'

'It's hard to remember, I don't know.'

'How often did Nick visit?'

'Weekly. Then when Anita went to university he asked for her address. I didn't give it to him and there was no more contact.'

Mr Bassett then asked her why she left.

'Nick had touched my leg and I knew it wasn't right so I decided to leave.'

'Have you had any problems with Nick?'

'Just one. On the way home when I was on my own with him, he pulled over in a lay by and came on to me, I said 'no' and he was very embarrassed.'

'When was this?'

'When I was thirteen.'

'Did you complain?'

'No, I should have.'

'Do you make allegations easily?'

'No.'

'But we note when you were seventeen you made allegations to the police about your father?'

'Yes, but I was traumatised by Nick.'

'So what you said about your father was wrong?'

'Yes.'

'A lie?'

'Yes.'

'As bad a lie as you can tell?'

'Yes, and I have to live with that for the rest of my life.'

'When did you tell anyone about this?'

'I told my Dad at the weekend. I knew you'd find out. I'd planned to be in America and not here.'

A faint but audible gasp came from the jury box. Someone was struck by the lengths Jasmine had taken to try and avoid coming to court.

'You mean you told your father about the allegations you made to the police three years ago after Anita heard on Friday we were going to mention it in court today?'

'I haven't spoken to my sister. I should have gone to the police in the first place.'

'You told the counsellor that full penetration hadn't occurred but everything else had and that your father had been involved?'

'I hardly knew what I was saying, I was too stressed.'

Mr Bassett waited a few moments, then suddenly changed tack. He asked Jasmine about her mother's health ensuring that Mrs Simpson's schizophrenia was mentioned. He then reverted to

'You were thirteen when you allege Mr Metcalfe tried it on with you?'

'Yes.'

'Seventeen when you complained about your father?'

'Yes.'

'You and your sister seem to go in for making false allegations.'

'I believe her, of course I do.'

Those in the public gallery recoiled from the strange information presented and struggled to concentrate as Anita's mother took the stand.

They felt, and no doubt the jurors felt the same, that they needed a break, a coffee, a chance to work out in their own minds exactly what Jasmine had alleged and how her story had changed. It seemed that she complained to the police about family abuse but was now maintaining Nick was the culprit. The onlookers' heads spun. After being sworn in Mrs Simpson looked around blankly. My mother, a former midwife, wondered what medication she was on, for she looked as if her mind really wasn't on it.

Her session was short as she confirmed her statement and said Nick did visit a lot. Then Mr Bassett asked whether Nick visited before or after Anita went into hospital. She wasn't sure.

'Did you come back from the pub on any occasion and find Nick and Anita upstairs alone?'

'No.'

'They were always on the ground floor?'

'Yes.'

'Dishevelled?'

'No.'

'Did Anita ever come down distressed, followed by Nick?'

'No.'

'Did you ever see anything suspicious?'

'No.'

'How did you get to know Nick?'

'He would bring Anita home from the youth group and stop for a coffee.'

'Was this before and after Anita's hospitalisation?'

'I don't know, it's a long time ago.'

Mrs Simpson seemed genuinely confused and was soon dismissed, then her husband stepped up. He confirmed that everything was as per his statement, but the prosecution barrister probed.

'What did you and your wife do on a Sunday night?'

'We'd go to the pub and Nick would bring Anita home.'

'Did he stay late?'

'Yes, sometimes eleven to eleven thirty.'

'Did you ever notice anything?'

'Yes, he seemed over attentive, I felt it was inappropriate.'

'Were these visits before Anita went into hospital?'

'I don't remember.'

'Did Mr Metcalfe visit her in hospital?'

'Yes.'

'Frequently?'

'Yes.'

Then Mr Bassett took over.

'You are a shop keeper?'

'Yes.'

'But enjoy gardening and DIY?'

'Yes.'

'You had conversations with Mr Metcalfe about DIY?'

'Yes.'

'Nick regularly brought Anita home; you were grateful for that?'

'Yes.'

'Did you ever find him upstairs?'

'No.'

'Always downstairs?'

'Yes.'

'Thank you, Mr Simpson.' To everyone's relief a recess for lunch was announced.

After lunch DC Stevens took the stand. He was asked several questions regarding the facts of Nick's arrest and then he went laboriously through word for word Nick's original interview and the subsequent one on the day he was charged. The prosecuting barrister reading Nick's part and DC Stevens reading the police interviewer's lines. Nick found this role play most unnerving. Initially he was a little concerned that the barrister might try to change the sense of some of the things he had said by the way it was read, but as the re-enactment of the interview went on, he was impressed by the acting ability of the barrister and with the final result. He was so relieved that in those early interviews he had not lost his cool, but had been totally co-operative on that first dreadful day; not realising that every word uttered then would be used in evidence. Nick's Dad glowed with pride as he heard the way his son had managed to give such coherent responses on that intimidating morning of his arrest. God *had* been in control from day one even though we'd not been aware of it.

Chapter 28

Then the jury were dismissed while Mr Bassett and the judge had a complex legal argument. Mr Bassett asked the judge if three of the charges could be dropped. Why? Because the incidents hadn't been mentioned by the girls or substantiated; there was therefore no concrete word on which to back the charges. The point of law took a lot of wrangling, with Mr Bassett stating various cases from a large red tome he had in front of him, the judge countering it with other cases and the prosecuting barrister interjecting occasionally, fighting his corner that all the charges should of course remain and be left to the jury to sort out. However, much to Nick's relief, and those in the public gallery who were rooting for any charges to be dropped, after several hours of verbal crossfire it was concluded that counts 3,4 and 9 could be disregarded. It had sounded like technical mumbo jumbo to those in the gallery and they struggled to piece it together. But they eventually gathered that two of the counts of sexual assault on Debs and one on Penny were being disregarded because they'd given no substantiation of them in the witness box. Mr Bassett fought tooth and nail: 'This case is full of inconsistencies,' he protested. 'Transferred allegations. I'm sure we were all disturbed to hear Jasmine's allegations this morning. Penny Finch has also admitted to being interfered with by her father. Some cases simply are not safe to continue.' The judge did not accept this for one moment, but he did concede that the three counts discussed could be ignored as unsubstantiated.

At the end of the session I heard a brief summary that was faintly encouraging. Alice, I gathered, had been honest. Nick was relieved. Deb's parents were clearly doubtful as to Nick's integrity, but had nothing much to say, not having witnessed any of the alleged dreadful deeds. Deb's boyfriend was positively supportive of Nick, which both of us found most consoling. If the best the prosecution could do was produce people like Alice and Jeremy who had nothing negative to say about Nick, then surely that might influence the jury a little?

Anita's parents had been adamant they'd never come into the house when Nick and Anita had been upstairs, a fact that Anita had assured the court they had, and the only criticism Anita's Dad had of Nick was that he seemed to have a crush on his daughter. Of course, it wasn't true, Nick was just the caring type, but at least that wasn't a crime for which one could be jailed.

The biggest worry that day was, of course, Jasmine. But the Metcalfe friends and family had been absolutely appalled by the obvious errors in her tale and felt the jury too would most likely notice the multiple inconsistencies.

The defence

By Wednesday we were feeling tired. Thankfully we were sleeping adequately and the arrangements for our daughters were working out smoothly. Angie was doing a great job and the children seemed as settled as they could be. Emily was clearly getting twitchy as she knew now that the prosecution case was complete she would at some point have to take the floor. But she gave the impression of being calm and perhaps even a little excited at the prospect when we informed her on Tuesday evening that Wednesday would be a day off school and a trip to Crown Court instead.

All the defence witnesses were duly primed to appear at court on Wednesday, just in case. It seemed unlikely that Nick's grilling would be short but Janice wanted to cover all eventualities. The session was slow getting underway, and by lunchtime Nick's questioning had barely started. The atmosphere outside the courtroom in the sitting area now took on a very different feel. A whole crowd of Nick's friends from a variety of walks of life congregated in their Sunday best, all ready to witness to his good character. There were youth group members, church members, the next door neighbours from Oxted and of course Emily and myself; alongside the stalwart family members who had sat in the public gallery supporting Nick from the start but who were not directly involved. Coming from all over the country they were introduced to each other, though most knew a little of the other folk, jokes were cracked, amusing memories retold and Nick's antics as a youth group leader repeated.

I found the situation bizarre. It was like something in a crazy dream. There I was hosting a party, greeting each person as they arrived, after all I was the pivot point, the only person they all knew and could relate to, enquiring after their journey, their health, their family etc. but all the while I was rooting desperately for my husband being quizzed in detail on every aspect of his work with the youth group, his relationship with the three girls and (as I afterwards discovered) his relationship with me, right down to intimate details. It was equally weird for those in court as every now and then when the door opened to let someone in or out, the party atmosphere was audible and momentarily pervaded the solemn and austere proceedings within.

Emily sat detached, trying to get on with some school work while I endeavoured to laugh at the jokes, be interested in the new baby, or the house move, feeling that at any moment I might totally lose concentration or embarrass the person concerned or myself by coming out with 'I'm sure your baby's cold is very traumatic for you but at this precise moment I really couldn't give a monkey's. My husband's in there being grilled to death about a crime he hasn't committed and any moment now I might have to go and take the witness stand. I can't bear it, I can't concentrate and I wish to goodness you'd shut up!'

Nick, meanwhile, was standing in the witness box having his chance to say something. He made his oaths confidently and stood erect and alert, knowing that now was his chance, his only chance, to account for himself. Having sat through hour after hour of hostile material, and suffered day after day, week after week and month after month from the lies concocted against him, he was relieved at last to be able to vindicate himself: to explain his actions and refute the allegations. He knew that now, more than on any other occasion, he needed to keep his wits about him, answer the questions honestly but shrewdly and be wary of the very words he used lest they had an alternative meaning or could be rephrased in a different light.

Mr Bassett asked him about his family and beliefs initially, and then all that he'd done in the past with young people. Nick explained he'd worked in a variety of capacities, assisting with music, water sports and as a canoe instructor.

'Has it ever been suggested you were involved in improper behaviour?'

'Never.'

'You've had some letters of support?'

'Yes. Several hundred.'

Nick then gave details of the family's move to Oxted and how in 1991 he was asked with me to take up the church youth work. He explained how the youth group ran, when the three girls joined, who gave lifts and was then asked:

'Have you ever been in Anita's bedroom?'

'Yes, twice. Once to retrieve a book and once to admire a wardrobe her father had built her.'

The questions came fast and furiously. Nick could feel his pulse racing.

They reverted to Anita's hospitalisation and his acquaintance with Jasmine.

'What about this incident in the lay by?'

'I was astounded by it, I've never heard anything so ludicrous.'

'After Anita was hospitalised, you gave her lifts home?'

'Yes, as did Brian Darnell our co. leader, Tony Brookes and my wife.'

'These 'touchings', were they for sexual satisfaction?'

'No.'

'Were they indecent?'

'No.'

'If she'd complained, would you have stopped?'

'Yes, of course.'

The questioning was high powered, intense and pressurised. Although Nick knew Mr Bassett was on his side, he felt threatened and insecure. He was then quizzed on how well he knew Anita's family, the DIY dad, the friendly mum and what physical contact he had had with Anita. Mr Bassett then leapt, as he was prone to do, onto another subject.

'Have you taken any professional training courses outside work?'

'Yes. Life saving, which I refresh every two years, first aid, minibus driving and cycling proficiency.'

'In those courses physical contact would be involved?'

'Yes. We were advised to be very careful and in life saving always get a witness.'

'Tell us about Deborah Islington.'

'She came in spring '93. Initially she was a difficult young lady with massive mood swings. But she improved over the five years.'

After a few questions on how he got on with Deborah there were further comments on activities of the youth group and a couple of questions regarding Jeremy Buckley, before Penny's name was raised. 'She joined in 1995,' Nick told the court. 'Had a good voice and played the clarinet.'

Nick's dad was leaning forward in the public gallery. Perhaps he couldn't catch all that was being said? It was more likely though that the physical gesture was a subconscious outward indication of how much he was feeling for and supporting his son. The questions were relentless. Was Nick musical? Did he accompany her sometimes?

'Did you pressurise her to play with you at church?'

'No. I sometimes asked her to accompany me, but she'd always say if she'd rather not.'

'In Christmas '95 she says you touched her bottom.'

'That's rubbish.'

'Did you ever handle Miss Finch indecently?'

'No.'

'Did you ever say anything of an indecent nature to Miss Finch?'

'No.'

'Did you take her home?'

On and on it went. Had he assaulted her at university? What about the emails?

'Is there anything improper in the emails?'

'No.'

Nick's head was spinning, he felt hot and sweaty and was most relieved when a lunch break was announced. Once out of the courtroom I thought he looked tired and haggard, but he managed a cheery exterior and we lunched at McDonalds with a number of friends. Then it was back to the all too familiar courtroom for Nick and more tense waiting outside for Emily and me.

Once lunch was over Mick, now 25 and an ex youth group member, began to pace the floor.

'I've got to get to Latvia tomorrow for an important business meeting. If I'm not on today then I'll miss my chance to stand up for Nick. I really want to do my bit.'

The message was passed on to Janice and to Mr Bassett. He then interrupted the proceedings and once the jury had been ushered out, he requested that whilst it was a very unusual request, could he please bring Mick on to give evidence now interrupting Nick's testimony? Much to everyone's surprise, the judge agreed. Nick's roasting was then suspended in order for Mick to take centre stage.

Pressure

Mick was tall and dressed smartly. Although at present working for a Christian charity, he had in fact done a law degree at Oxford, so Nick felt confident of the impression he would give. Firstly he explained how he had to go to Latvia the next day; then how he'd gone to school and church in Oxted and knew Nick as a nearby neighbour, a church member and youth group leader. He was enthusiastic about Nick's abilities using words such as 'brilliant' and 'amazing'. He said Nick gave everyone much care and sacrificed himself a lot on the young people's behalf.

'He was a real role model for me. He taught me loads about living as a good person, and I never heard him raise his voice. He was always calm and caring, concerned for our welfare, and ran an open house.'

Asked if Nick was reliable, he answered: 'As to truth, impeccable. His life always lived up to what he preached and I never noticed any improper behaviour.'

'Did you know Anita, Debs and Penny?'

'Yes.'

'How well?'

'Penny not very well, Debs was quite a bit younger than me, but Anita quite well. Penny was always round at Nick's house.'

'Always?'

'60% of the time I popped round she'd be there.'

'How did the relationship seem?'

'They seemed good friends.'

'Did he relate better to girls than boys?'

'The girls tended to initiate a warmer friendship. Anita, Penny and Debs were like puppy dogs around him, he was fun to be with, always laughing and joking.'

'These teenagers could have had a crush on him, if so would Nick have been aware of it?'

'I don't think so, he was a bit naive about bad things.'

The prosecution barrister then took the floor.

'Emma Winger was very friendly with Nick?'

'Yes, she lived next door, came to the youth group, baby-sat and had loads of fun with the Metcalfes.'

'Did you have any concern about their relationship?'

'No.'

'Do you think Emma had romantic inclinations towards Mr Metcalfe?'

'I should hope not!' Mick said in a shocked tone.

'Why's that?' Enquired the barrister.

'I was going out with her at the time!'

A ripple of laughter ran round the court, the prosecution barrister was clearly irritated that he had been made to look foolish and realised that he had clearly underestimated Mick. There was a smug little smile on a couple of faces in the public gallery. Nick felt it was so good to hear the prosecution barrister being put in his place.

However Mr Williams quickly recovered.

'Did you ever see Penny at Nick's house?'

'I'd often pop round and all sorts of people would be there. Once the young people went to sixth form college, they'd pop round to the Metcalfes for a coffee in their free periods. Penny, Debs, Anita, Andrew Townsend, Natasha Darnell, loads of people. But Penny was the most regular by far.'

'But you were at university, how could you see on a regular basis?'

'Because I was home every seven weeks or so.'

'I think you're exaggerating.'

Mick's law training kicked in, he refused to be bullied into changing his evidence, 'I wouldn't say so, if I saw her at the Metcalfes every time I was home, there was unlikely to be a change when I wasn't there.'

As Nick had predicted, Mick was 'on the ball' could anticipate the line of questioning and made an excellent witness. After several further attempts to undermine what Mick had said the barrister finally gave up, realising there would be no joy from this witness.

Meanwhile outside the courtroom the chat and laughter continued, but I felt relieved that Mick had been squeezed in and pleased for Nick that he'd had a brief break. I felt for him under all that pressure. Every action, every word, every motive queried, doubted and whenever something in his favour emerged, it was promptly turned on its head by the prosecuting barrister.

Mick reappeared, looking satisfied and confident and gave those outside a quick summary of the procedure. Nick was no doubt back in the witness box, but shortly afterwards he and those in the public gallery all came out. What was going on? 'Apparently,' explained Nick's brother, 'one of the jurors has a migraine and is afraid she might be sick, so today's proceedings might be postponed.' Instantly several of the supporters opened pockets and handbags, producing a variety of pain relief from aspirin to Nurofen, surely the tortuous procedure needn't be halted? I could hardly believe my ears. The whole affair was agonising; a delayed start on Thursday, followed by long waits, prolonged legal proceedings, long lunch hours and now this. But the break was not long: after ten minutes or so Janice approached us to explain that the juror would plough on a bit, but there was no chance of any other defence witnesses being done that day, it didn't even look as if Nick would be finished with.

Nick was back being questioned about the initial allegations, his reaction to them, what the youth group gave the Metcalfes when they left Oxted, their move and their new church in Cranleigh.

'What happened when you were arrested?'

'I was in shock for about a week. I cried when the police marched me away and I saw my four girls all crying. I've never come into hostile contact with the police before.'

'You have a clear conscience?'

'Yes, I've always been of good character, and I can't believe the girls would lie like that. I have a totally clear conscience.'

The prosecution lawyer now set to. It was his job to undermine all that Nick had said, and Nick sensed it as soon as the questioning began. Implications were in every question. You like to touch people? You regularly sent emails to Penny? You gave Anita more attention than the others?

Nick was alert and anxious not to be caught out. He reminded himself that he must, whatever happened, keep his wits about him.

'Why do you touch people?' The questions were relentless.

'Because a touch can say more than words.'

'Do you treat men and boys the same?'

'Yes.'

'Are you affectionate to your wife?'

'Yes.'

'Do you have a happy marriage?'

'Yes.'

'Do you show affection to her in public?'

'Yes, we hold hands walking down the road, but we don't stop every ten minutes and kiss.'

'You have no problems within your marriage?'

'No. She is very supportive of me and we work well as a team.'

'Are you supportive of her?'

'Yes.'

'Did you indicate you weren't happy with her to anyone?'

'No.'

'Or that all was not well in the marriage?'

'No, I did not.'

'Or that you didn't love your wife?'

'No. Of course I love my wife.' Nick was getting cross. 'It's a complete lie. I've never said to anyone that the love had gone out of my marriage.'

'Did you have a good sexual relationship with your wife?'

'Yes.'

'Regularly?'

'Yes, and we always have had except when the children were born.'

A chair shuffled in the public gallery and Nick glanced up. Perhaps someone, his mother in law possibly or his father, felt uncomfortable at the line of questioning. He refocused quickly. As the questions moved on to lending Anita books, *'Joni'* in particular was mentioned which had been lent to Anita when she was in hospital, the barrister obviously felt he had found a crack in Nick's story; if Nick was so sure that he had lent it and later retrieved it, why could he not produce it? He even suggested the whole book lending was a fabrication by Nick as a cover story. Nick resolved to find the book as soon as he got home that day. The time was 4 pm; Nick was feeling tired and to his relief the session was closed for the day.

Meanwhile, while Nick was suffering in the courtroom, my stomach churned and I wanted to scream. Poor Nick, another day of cross examination. He'd looked jaded at lunch time, how on earth would he look when he finally emerged today? The answer came shortly afterwards and confirmed my worst fears. He looked drained, pale, haggard, as if he'd been psychologically shredded by some vicious animal. But before I'd given him more than a quick hug 'Will all those concerned with the case of Nick Metcalfe please return to court 3,' boomed out over the loud speakers.

'What now?' I asked out loud 'What on earth is going on?'

The crowd of witnesses waited anxiously outside for what felt like an eternity, before the courtroom door swung open again and out erupted a bubbling mass of people all simmering with something, something sort of positive, it seemed. What could it be? The explanation wasn't long in coming. One of the jurors had a funeral to go to tomorrow. The person in question hadn't realised that they couldn't just miss a day until the migraine incident had occurred. At the end of the proceedings the juror, a lady, had told the judge about the funeral she had to attend, and the court had had to be reconvened to explain the situation. As the judge explained to the lady in question the inconvenience and disruption that would be caused, she burst into tears.

'Whose funeral is it?' Asked the judge.

'My mother in law's,' replied the agitated lady. 'I didn't realise it would cause so much trouble,' she said. Then looking Nick straight in the eye, she said to him, 'I'm so sorry.'

The judge was instantly alert: 'There's no need to talk to the defendant,' he said. 'If necessary court can run with eleven jurors or be postponed twenty four hours.'

Mr Bassett advised Nick not to accept a session with only eleven jurors and consequently the case was now adjourned until Friday.

When I heard all this, I had mixed emotions. More delays and messing around. Not to mention more inconvenience. It was awkward asking all the witnesses to come back not tomorrow but Friday, and then there was Emily, of course. Did she go back to school for one day and then off again? But looking across at the pale drawn face of my husband I decided that over all it was a good thing. He'd taken a pasting, he could have a break. He might even get a good night's sleep knowing he wasn't going to be questioned the next day. Yes, it had to be positive. We'd wondered how we were going to cope with five full days of court, and now we had a day off. I could catch up on housework and he could chill out a bit.

Defence continues

Emily, anxious not to miss out on any of her beloved schooling, returned to school with the appropriate note explaining that the sore throat was now much improved and feeling an utter fraud. Like her father she was an upfront, honest girl who felt very villainous having a day off for a sore throat that normally she'd hardly have noticed. Nick spent the day in the study fiddling with his computer equipment and I pottered round the house achieving little but thoroughly appreciating a day when my brain could go into neutral, when I didn't have to practise my social skills and hide my emotions. It gave our dear friend Angie a break as well. So sad though the funeral was, I felt it had been most beneficial for us.

Realising that the book '*Joni*' which we had lent Anita so many years ago was now becoming central to the prosecution's questioning, we hunted for it assiduously Thursday evening. It wasn't where it should have been, but on questioning Emily and Jessica, Jessica announced, 'Oh I think it's in my room. I've been reading it. I'll go and get it.' Sure enough there it was large as life. I remembered reading in Anita's statement that her boyfriend had destroyed it and sighed as I realised that that too had been yet another fabrication.

On the Friday morning I took '*Joni*' and the other two books I remembered lending Anita whilst in hospital '*Words of Comfort*' and '*Words of Joy*', up to court and Nick handed them over to Mr Dixon. Janice had a holiday booked in the States and although she'd tried to change it, her boyfriend had reminded her that the whole reason they were going at that time was because it was her nephew's birthday who lived out there. Therefore, if they postponed the holiday, the said occasion would be missed. Consequently Janice had very reluctantly said 'goodbye' to us on the Wednesday and Mr Dixon himself had come to court. An unusual occurrence and we felt honoured.

There were further gruelling questions for Nick once court was in session again on Friday. The barrister was again harping on about books, how many were lent and when Nick went to retrieve them.

'Did you go unannounced on the Sunday when you went to collect the books?'

'I never dropped in unannounced on a Sunday because I was always giving Anita a lift home from the youth group. If invited I'd go in for a coffee and leave about ten thirty.'

'Did you fancy Anita?'

'I tried to deal with all the young people the same. Her character was attractive. She's a pleasing person to be with and talk to. But I didn't single her out for special attention, only when she was in hospital, because I felt responsible for her injuries. She also showed signs she might have made a good leader in the future; so when she wanted to stay on after she was eighteen we suggested she became a helper. She seemed a happy person and regularly baby sat.'

'How did she get to your house?'

'Once she could drive in '97 she came under her own steam. Before that she was usually brought and I gave her a lift home.'

'Did she use your computer?'

'Yes. Quite regularly, I've done printouts of all her work on it,' Mr Bassett duly produced them, and Nick continued; 'There are twelve pages and I haven't edited them.'

'Why not?'

'Because I didn't want anyone to suggest I'd tampered with the evidence.'

There then proceeded a long discussion between the prosecution barrister and Nick about these. The barrister continually suggesting that being so computer literate, Nick had tampered with them. But Nick stuck to his original story and explained adamantly, using technical jargon that that was not the case. At one point he glanced across at the jury and saw that a chap of similar age was following closely and obviously understood the computer speak. He felt fractionally encouraged. As the futile line of attack continued, the judge intervened.

'Have you any evidence that Mr Metcalfe tampered with the evidence?' He asked in a slightly irritated tone.

'No, your honour.'

'Then I suggest we move on.'

'Yes, your honour.'

The questioning moved on to the trips to Italy.

'Did Anita object to physical contact?'

'No. Not at all. We had a lot of fun and she enjoyed the whole trip.'

'She stopped being a leader?'

'Yes. Once when she didn't want to go on a trip and Melanie told her she'd let us down, she said she didn't want to be a leader any more as it was too much of a tie. We saw less of her then.'

'But you pursued her?'

'I was concerned, we saw less and less of her. I rang up a few times and spoke to Jasmine her sister, but never really found out what was going on.'

'In Christmas 1995 you stroked Deborah Islington's leg?'

'No. I might have tickled her leg, but I wouldn't caress someone, it would be inappropriate and indecent for a youth leader.'

'When you went to Italy, you again stroked Deborah's leg?'

'No. She was difficult and sulky, stroppy and wouldn't eat and at one point I held her hands to stop her running away from me when we were talking; but I certainly had no other physical contact.'

Nick felt irritated by the assumption of guilt that the questions implied. Someone in the public gallery coughed. Perhaps they thought the same?

'You pleaded with Penny to go to Italy the second time?'

'No, Tony Brookes lost his passport so my wife rang Penny up and said she could come. She'd been round the night before saying how much she wished she was coming.'

'You chose Penny to go with you to the garage in Italy when you had trouble with the van.'

'No. She didn't like the practical work and was a good map reader, so I suggested she came with me. I did not choose her.'

'In Italy you brushed Penny's breasts?'

'We were working in close confines. I was trying to put some piping in. I may have brushed passed her but I did not touch her indecently.'

The questioning went on in the same vein and Nick repeated again and again that he hadn't fancied Penny, that he hadn't assaulted her sexually, and that he couldn't remember the alleged incidents because they didn't happen. The emails were examined in depth and every possible innuendo suggested.

'You didn't sign that one, why?'

'You said 'hi, it's me again' how often did you write to her?'

'Why don't you mention your wife more often?'

'On the one 2.12.97. You say 'I do love you really' what did that mean?'

Nick was frustrated, but managed to keep cool.

'It's a turn of phrase. I love my wife which is different from my love for my children and I love spaghetti bolognaise, they're all different.'

'The emails of 6.4.,7.4.,16.4.,23.4.,16.5.,18.5.,9.6., and 10.6. Penny doesn't sign off in the usual way. Why?'

'I am sorry but I have no idea, you are reading something into nothing.'

Suddenly the questions jumped back to Anita again. Nick reiterated;

'I didn't cry with Anita, I didn't ask for hugs, I might have given her a hug good bye, that's all.'

'You were concerned when you didn't see her when she'd left the church and youth group?'

'I was distraught when I feared she'd left and I might have been the cause of it, but she stopped contact with all Christian groups including the sixth form college Christian Union. I run my life on strict principles and I like to be on good terms with everybody. If there's a problem in the youth group or someone stops coming, we try to find out what the problem is. The phone calls I made to Anita were only with that in mind.'

'Did your wife know you were following her up?'

'Yes. She did and we shared everything. I was completely open with my wife.'

To Nick's intense relief the prosecuting barrister then concluded with; 'No further questions.'

Mr Bassett then took the stand. He firstly read out a couple of emails that had been read in part. The whole picture gave a more healthy impression of Nick's relationship with Penny than had been suggested.

'Have you the support of the church leaders at Oxted?'

'Yes. Their full support. They've issued a statement to that effect.'

'Thank you Mr Metcalfe, that is all.'

Nick finally emerged from court at lunch time looking totally exhausted. If he'd just run the London marathon he couldn't have appeared more shattered. But there was an element of satisfaction in his demeanour.

He'd done his bit. Those from the public gallery were quick to congratulate him; his father, in particular felt he'd held together supremely well and praised him for his consistency. Despite the fact I hadn't heard a word, I felt sure he'd kept his wits and held his own. He was a quick thinker, could anticipate a line of questioning well and, I was convinced, wouldn't have tied himself in knots, despite the best efforts of the prosecuting barrister, because there was nothing to hide and no lies to substantiate. Now I had the prospect of being called in myself and I felt myself tense up at the sheer thought. Of all people, I knew I must not let Nick down.

Other people had been so wonderful and supportive, I felt the responsibility weigh heavily on my shoulders as Nick's wife. But then my mind wandered over the innumerable occasions of exceptional support. God hadn't let us down yet, so surely he'd uphold me too? A young man had appeared at court one morning before proceedings were underway, introduced himself to Nick, for they'd never met, and said he'd come to express his firm support for Nick, and was most sympathetic and concerned for the situation Nick found himself in. He was a friend of Andrew Townsend's brother, and a teacher. One of his pupils had made false allegations against him, which had, of course, threatened his whole career, so he knew a little how Nick felt and the difficult situation which surrounded him. Every time I thought of this young man coming all this way to uphold Nick, despite having never met him, it warmed my heart.

Also unbeknown to Nick and myself about this time my father had consulted an accountant and was sorting out financial arrangements for the girls and myself should the worst befall. Despite the intense pressure of everything I knew deep, deep down that God was there, God did care, and God would provide.

During lunch at McDonalds, Nick became brighter and brighter and when I asked him about it, he said; 'I've done my bit. It's up to everyone else now. Whatever happens from now on it's completely out of my control, so at least I can relax a little and hope.'

Relaxing he certainly was doing, cracking jokes and entertaining Emily and our friends with anecdote after anecdote. Perhaps it was all the strain, I wondered. Whatever it was, there was some truth in what he said. His bit was all over. How would the other witnesses cope with the strain?

Support from friends

Ianticipated that Emily and I would be next in line, for Mr Dixon had assured us that we'd be questioned early on so that we would at last get into court and share the ordeal with Nick. As the crowd of witnesses and supporters sat around waiting and wondering who would follow on, a court usher unexpectedly appeared and said in a loud penetrating voice; 'Andrew North please.'

Andy, who'd been pacing the floor in a world of his own, nearly jumped out of his skin. For twenty seconds his usual composure abandoned him and the 'under control' twenty five year old looked startled and scared. But it was momentary. All in one action he grabbed his jacket, slipped it on and strode confidently into the courtroom.

Having taken his oath and elected to remain standing, he explained that he was a sales assistant for an electrical firm in Oxted and had known Nick since 1991.

'How would you consider Nick Metcalfe?' 'When did you first have contact with him?'

Andrew explained that he'd been with him on the first trip to Italy, that Nick had achieved a lot, worked hard and there'd been no problems. Andrew had also seen him in his family. Nick was a warm, loving and caring man who always gave up his time for his wife and children. 'I have never had any problems with him, he upholds his Christian principles, is concerned for the truth and I have spent many evenings at his house.'

'Was he a tactile person?'

'No, not particularly huggy, but into practical jokes and that kind of thing. I've never seen anything to give me concern. He was always one hundred per cent committed to what he did. A happy effervescent sort of person.'

The prosecuting barrister asked; 'Have you ever seen Nick hug anyone?'

'Yes, when they were upset and he was comforting them.'

'No further questions, your honour.'

Andy felt shell shocked. The big build up, the nights lying awake wondering how he could give Nick his full credentials without giving the wrong impression at any point, and suddenly it was all over.

As he walked out, Aaron Howlett was summoned, the friend from Liverpool who'd attended the church for a while and helped with the youth work. He was now married but still a firm friend of ours. A surge of anger welled up inside this normally placid young man as he walked into the court room, at the injustice of seeing his friend and fellow youth worker shut up in a monkey cage behind a glass screen with a guard seated beside him. He was genuinely angry and had to bite his lip hard to control it. He deliberately took a deep breath before answering any questions. He was asked about his knowledge of Nick and replied that he had an excellent relationship with young people; never spoke down to them and was an example to young people of today.

'Did you know Deborah Islington and how she related to Nick?' Mr Bassett asked.

'Yes, I knew her quite well. She played up to Nick to get attention. For example in the summer of '97 there was a crowd of us in Nick and Melanie's kitchen and she shouted out 'Nick, stop touching my leg'. Melanie asked what was going on and so did I. Nick was talking to people behind and we all laughed it off as a joke.'

'What about Anita?'

'Anita was a bubbly person and popular with the group and loved being at the Metcalfes. She had a key at one point and used to be round there when I popped in.'

'Penny Finch?'

'Yes, I also know her, she plays the clarinet and played at my wedding. I used to accompany her sometimes because I play the piano. Penny was quiet and everyone knew she didn't get on with her parents. Nick would do anything to help any of them, any of the youth group.'

The prosecuting barrister questioned Aaron about minibus trips and inappropriate behaviour, but he was adamant there'd never been any with Debs, Anita or Penny or he'd have witnessed it.

Clearly there was little headway to be made for the prosecution and Aaron was dismissed and Brian North came in, Andy's dad, who'd also helped on a trip to Italy. He described Nick as a fine upstanding young family man; a very successful and very popular youth leader. Asked about

Italy he said it had been a successful trip, much had been accomplished and all he remembered was that Deborah Islington had been rather difficult. He was not cross examined.

Mavis Winger followed, our next door neighbour from Oxted. Although apprehensive about testifying, she strode into court with a confident step and looked determined to save the world if it lay within her power. She stood erect, one hand either side of the lectern and explained clearly in the voice she used for leading the ladies' meetings that she now lived in Tunbridge Wells where her husband was a minister and that Emma and Georgina were her two daughters; they'd all lived next door to the Metcalfes for many years in Oxted. She told the court how she'd got to know us once we'd moved next door.

'They were a great family. Nick is a super guy, a totally honest, reliable and dedicated Christian, he's good and kind and will do any thing to help. He was fantastic to my girls. They went through teenage difficulties and he and Melanie were always there for them, being a listening ear. He cared for my girls, maintained their cars, hugged them if they were down, he was like a big brother to them.'

Mavis rattled on and Mr Bassett had to gently interrupt her stream of praise to focus her more specifically.

'Did you know Anita Simpson?' He asked.

'Oh yes. I visited her in hospital, I was the church sick visitor, and Nick used to visit her too, didn't you, Nick?' She turned to Nick and addressed him directly causing just the hint of a smile to twitch the corners of the judge's mouth.

'Did you have a key to the Metcalfe's house?'

'Oh yes. The young people often used to call to borrow it to use the church photocopier, or play the piano or organ there. I know I lent it to Anita and Penny several times, I'm not sure about Deborah, possibly not.'

'Have you ever been cross with Nick?'

'Oh yes I have,' she responded forcefully. 'I was Nick, wasn't I?' She looked him straight in the eye and grinned; Nick could do nothing but grin back.

'Once they, Emma, Georgina and Nick that is, had a huge water fight across the garden fence and some water got in through an upstairs window and damaged my wardrobe. I was furious!'

A variety of amused expressions appeared on the jurors' and those in the public gallery's faces. This was a considerable improvement on the tedium of the previous days. This was positively entertaining.

'How would you describe Nick as a person?' The questions went on.

'A fantastic husband, fun loving, very generous, he and Melanie ran the youth group and never asked for expenses.'

At the 'Thank you Mrs Winger', Mavis started to step down from the witness box and a court usher had to jump up and say quietly, 'Just a moment please, there might be a few questions from the prosecution.' 'Oh yes, of course.' Mavis was flustered and instantly resumed her stance. Not only those in authority, but those on the jury, were thoroughly enjoying her performance and appreciated her 'faux pas' with shared little knowing smiles.

The prosecution barrister began. 'Emma and Nick were very good friends?'

'Yes. But I never worried about them, he was like a big brother to her. Both families were good friends and we lived in each others pockets, didn't we, Simon?' At this point Mavis lent over to look into the public gallery to catch her husband's eye. This done, he nodded and she continued; 'We'd go there for meals and they'd come to us. I miss them now we've both moved. While they were away we had free run of their house and used their furniture or whatever we needed and while we were away it was visa versa.'

The prosecution barrister brought Mavis back to the here and now with; 'Is Mr Metcalfe a tactile person?'

'Sometimes, not to me, I'm not a huggy person. Though he was with Emma and Georgina. I've only hugged him once and that was when all this came up.'

The prosecution barrister continued in his vain attempts to get Mavis to suggest that anything Nick had done or said was unsuitable or improper. Mavis was genuinely horrified at that concept and vehemently refuted that there was ever a hint of impropriety. He then went on to ask about lifts home after the young people's group. Mavis was clearly baffled that the barrister was expecting her to know who had been given lifts, who sat in the front etc. eight years previously just because she lived next door. Again realising that he would make no headway with this ardent supporter of Nick, Mr Williams gave up.

As Mavis was dismissed she fairly scampered out of court, burst through the doors and emerged the other side shaking like a leaf and crying. Those outside were startled by her eruption but water was fetched, a chair given and Emma, her daughter, hugged her, reassuring her that all was well and that she was sure she'd done a fine job in there, absolutely sure.

Before Mavis was completely calm Natasha Darnell was summoned. Brian and Joyce's daughter and also at one time a keen member of the youth group. Being short she opted to stand and still only her head and shoulders were above the lectern. At twenty one and a legal secretary, she looked neat and stylish and though visibly nervous she too explained how she'd enjoyed the group and how Nick had made it fun. She also told how she'd been friends with Anita, Penny and Debs and the others in the group and never seen anything dodgy. Though she did think Anita fussed about her foot after the swimming accident to get attention from Nick. She explained that her dad often gave the Simpsons lifts home and often other parents would too. If no one else was available then Nick would be taxi. She was not cross questioned.

Natasha Darnell emerged from court and burst into tears, which I found harrowing but Richard, her older brother hastened to reassure me that Natasha always burst into tears after any ordeal. 'It's the stress, you know,' he said reassuringly. 'Nothing to do with what happened in there.' I felt faintly comforted and hoped to goodness no one had accidentally let Nick down.

Emily was then summoned. In many ways it was a relief for the fourteen year old to get the ordeal over and done with. She walked tentatively into court. She'd lain awake the previous night wondering whether she'd know where to go, but it was all perfectly obvious and before she knew it she was standing in the witness box, looking neat in her navy top and cream trousers, taking the oath. Her session was brief and to the point. Her aim was to explain to the court that she had an insight into Metcalfe family life, being one of them and that her mum and dad had an excellent relationship. She regularly saw Anita, Penny and Debs at the youth group on Saturdays and Sundays and they often popped in during the week. The visitors were always friendly to the four Metcalfe girls, Anita and Penny would help Emily with music and often baby-sat.

'Anita was our favourite baby-sitter.' Emily explained. 'We loved her, she was like a big sister to us, we never ever saw anything wrong. When Mum and Dad needed to go out they always rang the youth group girls, and Anita was most often free and willing.'

Predictably she was not cross examined and emerged looking satisfied with her performance. Tony Brookes then took his oath. His testimony was even briefer than Emily's, but he affirmed that once he'd learnt to drive he'd frequently given Anita lifts home, that he'd liked her and her bubbly personality. That it was he, Brian Darnell, her parents and Nick who shared the transport after a Saturday or Sunday meeting.

The day was drawing to a close. Mr Bassett was aware that the jury were tiring and losing track of who was who, but he decided to bring on the Winger sisters to round things off. After all, Mavis had been an excellent witness, guileless almost to a ludicrous extent, she'd amused them all and he was confident Emma and Georgina would also be excellent.

Emma, petite, smart, pretty and composed, stood up straight and told the court how she was a manageress of Marks and Spencer now and was married a couple of years ago. Asked about Nick, she described him as a fun loving person. 'We had loads of water fights over the fence and played jokes on each other when we lived next door.'

'Does he hug you?'

'I greet him with a hug, no more.'

'Did you like having him as your youth leader?'

'Enormously, he was fun, but taught us a lot. I nannied for them when Esther was born and once when they were out late I stayed over-night, but I had no worries, there was no impropriety.'

'Did you know Anita, Penny and Debs?'

'I knew them a little. They were younger than me.'

'You told Anita to keep away from Nick?' Mr Bassett asked.

'No, I never told Anita to keep away from Nick. Why would I? There's not a word of truth in that.' The jurors were baffled by the question, but Nick recalled that in her statement Anita had said that Emma Winger had warned her to keep away from him. He was reassured to hear that nonsense so clearly contradicted. Emma continued: 'But as I went to university I had very little to do with Anita, Penny or Debs.'

She was then cross examined with the now standard questions from the prosecution trying to trip her up. When asked whether Nick had had any influence on her life, she even surprised herself with her answer and heard herself replying, 'Well, I think I'm rather a nice person actually and I feel Nick was in some ways responsible for this.' One or two faces in the gallery broke into gentle grins. Again the prosecution eventually gave up, seeing not one chink in the defence's armour.

Georgina Winger, Emma's older sister then came in. She was also short and smartly dressed. Her vibrant personality exuded from her. Now a shorthand secretary and mum, she, like her mother and sister before her, seemed prepared to take on the world. She proclaimed clearly how she'd known Nick as a friend and neighbour, but had never been in the youth group as she was too old. She described him as a totally trustworthy, good friend, always willing to help others, very truthful and honest. She too mentioned the endless practical jokes and water fights.

'Would you describe Mr Metcalfe as tactile?'

'Sort of, he always gives me a hug to greet me but nothing improper at all or inappropriate.' She closed with 'He's a good and loyal friend and totally dependable.'

There was no cross questioning. It was 4.15pm and clearly both the judge and Mr Bassett felt it was a good point to end the day.

I had found it an interesting experience watching our various friends being called into court and then a few minutes later emerging looking either shattered, relieved or completely dazed. But I was relieved when the session was over and Nick finally came out. He looked tired and jaded, but had a little more life in him than he'd had when he'd been testifying.

Taking the witness stand

Having a weekend's breather didn't bother me too much, after all testifying in court wasn't exactly something you could prepare for, like an exam; so I could go home, get on with life and enjoy the children, then come fresh to it on Monday. I anxiously listened to Nick in the car going home summarising how our various friends had held up. 'Was I OK, Dad?' queried Emily in a concerned tone. 'Great.' replied Nick. 'Absolutely wonderful. You didn't have to say much, but what you did say was really good.' 'Are you sure?' Emily desperately needed reassuring that she'd done her best for her father, that she'd fought his corner and stood firm for him. It would go with her for the rest of her life, and she needed to know categorically that she'd handled it well. Nick gave her the required reassurance and was adamant that she'd been a star. I so hoped she'd accept his comments and not torment herself with doubts and anxieties.

Another bizarre weekend lay ahead. Another period of time when the stress factor was on hold and somehow life had to continue more or less as if there was none. Thankfully Saturday was well taken care of as a family meal had been arranged at a local Mexican restaurant at midday. The table had been booked days ago as Martin, Nick's brother from Australia, had his flight booked on the Sunday. He'd arranged to be in the UK for a fortnight, the duration of the trial he'd assumed, not wanting to be away from his wife and family any longer than necessary. But with the many delays and hold ups he found himself in the exasperating position of having to fly home not knowing the final outcome. The family meal had been arranged hoping it would be a celebratory one, but now it was more an expression of unity and support for Nick and farewell to Martin.

However, it was a good diversion for all the family and gave us something to focus on. The girls had never had Mexican food before and whilst Esther was apprehensive about trying something new and inclined to go for chicken nuggets and chips, the adventurous Felicity was indignant that the only 'different' item on the children's menu was chicken tortillas and she planned to indulge in something far more exciting than that. Many happy minutes were spent perusing the menu and eventually settling on a dish, and the process was delightfully repeated when Granddad announced that the drinks, as well as the food, were on him; consequently the wide selection of non alcoholic cocktails demanded considerable attention.

We rarely went out for meals, we couldn't afford it; and if we did it tended to be a quick McDonalds on a journey. So this luxurious occasion with no limits on expenditure was a real treat. All four girls seemed thrilled with the occasion, it was unusual and pleasant to have all three Metcalfe brothers together again with their parents, and we were well distracted. As in court, it bemused me that what should be a unique party event fell somewhat short of that because of the clouds of uncertainty hanging over us.

Nevertheless, it was a good send off for Martin and an excellent diversion for us. By the time the prolonged luncheon was complete and farewells said, it left only a little time before our two youngest were due to go to bed. We each occupied ourselves well, had a modest bite of tea, being still very full from the meal out and Felicity and Esther trundled off to bed. The older two had homework to complete before they too followed suit.

A little later Nick and I flopped in front of the telly. Eventually when the film had ended neither of us had any idea what it had been about; our exhausted minds had collapsed straight into neutral. We hadn't chatted, nor fallen asleep, just sat in a comatose state and let two hours drift over us in a much needed condition of as near relaxation as was possible.

Sunday meandered by in much the same manner. The girls were tranquil and after church we enjoyed a Sunday roast. The thought that this might be the last family Sunday for a long while haunted me, but I didn't voice my thoughts and hoped I didn't betray them either and somehow we got through the day. Once the girls were in bed, time was taken up getting food out of the freezer for the next week's meals, preparing the lunch boxes and generally getting organised for another onslaught at court. 'At least,' we both thought, 'unless something goes drastically wrong, we'll be done this week. Finished, the ordeal over, but what then? One dreadful stage would be complete, but would it be the start of an even more tortuous period of our lives?'

We were soon up to court again, and there was Penny chatting to DC Stevens and the prosecution barrister once more. She looked smart, attractive and confident. It was most unnerving. It felt as if everything was against us and my heart sank. I had yet to testify, but what could I say to convince everyone that these allegations were outrageous? How could I explain to the jury that Nick may be fun loving and occasionally quite mad, but never irresponsible and so would never ever commit the foul crimes Anita and Penny were suggesting? It was good to see the familiar faces of friends and relatives at court and I was assured that I'd be on first thing so I'd have a chance afterwards to sit in the public gallery and at least witness the final proceedings even though I'd missed so much.

I had deliberated long and hard as to what to wear. I wanted to look fresh and smart, but not too businesslike. After all, I was a mother of four and a housewife, not an executive. In the end I opted for the long green cotton skirt Nick had given me for my birthday, and the matching black and green striped top. I hoped the impression I gave was favourable, though inside the smart outfit my heart was racing and my legs felt like jelly.

Almost as soon as the court had assembled I was summoned. As usual the gallery was full to capacity and I had my first glimpse of the inside of the courtroom. To my surprise as I walked up to the witness box, I didn't feel particularly nervous, I think I was relieved at last to be able to have my say and survey all that took place. The court was a large room with the judge on a raised platform at one end. A quick glance at him showed a middle aged intelligent face, grey hair and almost a glimmer of humour on the side of his face. Nick was behind a glass panel at the opposite end of the room, the barristers and their assistants were in the middle and the jury on the far side. I peered across at them, hoping I looked friendly and acceptable. 'You may sit down Mrs Metcalfe,' broke in on my reverie, but bearing in mind Nick had recommended standing, I declined the offer. I was quickly sworn in by a bored looking court official who probably went through the same routine dozens of times a day. Then the questioning began. Mr Bassett went through my statement and quizzed me firmly, politely and genially on my background. How I came to meet Nick, how long we'd been married and when we moved to Oxted. I described Nick's personality as fun loving and boyish but also very responsible, caring and committed to the family and youth group.

'Tell me about the youth group.'

'We ran a programme three out of four Saturdays and every Sunday. Sometimes Nick would take the young people away for the weekend. We provided listening ears for the girls and fellows, and if they were ill we'd send cards, phone or visit. We also visited people in hospital, Amy, Jack, Tony Brookes and Anita.'

'Tell us about Anita's accident and the books that were lent.'

Mr Bassett was careful in his terminology leaving it open for me to respond as appropriate and as he wanted. I explained all about Anita's accident and then added: 'I'm the reader in the family and I thought the book '*Joni*' would be suitable for Anita as it was about a girl who had a swimming accident and was left paralysed. I gave it to Nick to pass it on to Anita. Months later we were doing an evening on Christian autobiographies and I needed it back so I got Nick to go and ask for it. Anita was renowned for being forgetful so it wasn't at all unusual to have to ask for things to be returned.'

To the consternation of the prosecution barrister, Mr Bassett then produced the book and got me to confirm this was the same book that had been lent and returned. The prosecution barrister practically snatched the book from Mr Bassett and examined every inch of it in the hope of finding some evidence that it was not the original book. He was clearly disappointed having obviously been told by Anita that the collection of the book had been a fabrication and that her boyfriend had destroyed it.

What struck Nick, which he never had an opportunity to point out, was that he had from day one maintained that the only reason he was in Anita's bedroom was to retrieve the book '*Joni*'. The book was about a girl who had been in a swimming accident which is why I had lent it to her in the first place. Yet Anita maintained (in order to make the alleged incident as young as possible) that this had all occurred before her swimming accident. Inwardly he screamed, 'Can't anyone see this is just a pack of lies. Unless I have the gift of prophesy, why did I lend her the book?' As his mind ran at 100 mph he missed the next few questions to his wife.

'Did you see a lot of Anita?'

'Oh yes. We ran an open home, so the youngsters were welcome to pop in anytime, and she called in a lot when she was at sixth form college.'

'How often?'

'Several times a week; they'd bring their sandwiches and I'd give them a drink and a cake.'

'Who baby-sat for you?'

'Any of the girls in the youth group, but most often Anita, though also Penny and Debs. I don't remember how frequently Anita baby-sat, once or twice a month maybe, that's from memory, I've no written record.'

'How did the young people get home after the meetings?' Old ground was being covered again, no doubt Mr Bassett's sole purpose was to reiterate to the jury that the truth was being told as this question had been put to a number of different witnesses all with the same response.

'Who gave Anita lifts?'

'Brian Darnell always offered and Tony Brookes. But I think Tony fancied her and she wasn't keen, so she always said it was all right she'd go with Nick. Very occasionally I drove the girls home if Nick was away but I don't like night driving.'

'Where did the girls sit?' I managed a faint smile before I responded.

'Nick and I used to joke about the teenagers. If I was driving, the girls sat in the back and I always had a fellow beside me, whereas if Nick was driving, it was always girls who sat in the front, usually Anita and Debs, and they claimed they got travel sick in the back!'

'How did Debs behave?'

'She was a typical moody teenager. One moment very happy and larking around and the next, silent and sulky and hugging a cushion in a corner.'

'What about Penny?'

'She seemed to have quite a lot of problems and frequently asked to speak to Nick on his own in the study. We always left the door open at least an inch or two.'

'What happened when Anita stopped coming to church?'

'We were very surprised and tried ringing her. We saw her once and she said she was looking after someone's horses. We then sent her a little card. Nick wrote it saying we missed her, which was perfectly true.'

'Would you say you had a happy family life?'

'Oh yes. When the police woman asked me that on the morning Nick was arrested, I said we were the happiest family in the world until ten minutes ago.'

'Thank you very much, Mrs Metcalfe, no further questions.'

Then the prosecuting barrister stood up and I wondered what on earth was coming. Wrapped in a smooth, almost seductive tone and with a smarmy smile came question after question implying that the only reason Nick ran the group was to form friendships with the young girls.

'Was the card you sent to Anita posted?'

'What an idiotic question,' I thought, but replied out loud, 'I can't remember. I might have put it in the post, or Nick might have dropped it off. Anita lives on a main road and Nick travels a lot.'

The questions ranged from when Anita came, to how long Jasmine had attended.

I felt alternately irritated and exasperated. The questions seemed so ridiculous. Occasionally I grabbed a little thinking time by saying 'I'm sorry I don't understand the question.' But it wasn't a very satisfactory way to proceed as the barrister seemed incapable of rearranging his vocabulary and simply repeated the question with a touch of irritation in his voice.

I became further frustrated when the barrister began harping on about books.

'What books did you use in the youth group?'

Bemused, I responded; 'The Bible.'

The prosecuting barrister then produced with glee three others and held them up for the court to see, *'Operation World'*, *'Ultimate Questions'*, and a *'One Minute Bible'* and pronounced; 'I suggest there were many occurrences when you lent Anita books.'

I retorted indignantly, 'You can suggest what you like. I remember lending her three in hospital. We *gave* her *'Ultimate Questions'* and possibly the *'One Minute Bible'* too.'

'Did you ever go to her house?'

'Yes, I ran Anita home sometimes and was always invited in. I tended not to go in as I'm not as sociable as Nick, I prefer to go home.'

There were more questions on the time the youth group finished, what time people left, how long it took to drop everyone off and what time I would expect Nick home. Ridiculous questions, as the times varied on every occasion, it was impossible to be specific. I was baffled. They were a sort of 'how long is a piece of string' questions, and it wasn't always girls he took home anyway. There were then further questions as to when Anita had stopped coming and why. 'What exactly was the problem?'

'I gather Nick had hugged her and she didn't like the physical contact.'

'Was this typical behaviour for your husband?'

'I've seen him giving a hug to a youngster when she was upset or demoralised.'

'Did he hug Debs?'

'I don't remember in particular, he may well have done.'

'Do you remember her saying 'Don't touch my leg'?'

'No.'

'Have you any problems in your marriage?'

'No. We were and are incredibly happy. At times I wished Nick had been around a bit more when he was so busy with the youth group.'

Irritated, but not particularly flustered I clawed my way through three quarters of an hour's questioning and was then allowed to leave the stand. I walked resolutely out of the court room and it was only once back with the others outside that my strength momentarily failed me and for a horrible second I thought I was going to faint. But surrounded by friends, a chair was provided, a drink of water administered and I became more composed. 'No,' I reassured everyone's anxious

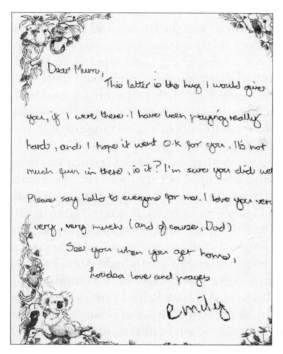

Dear Mum,

This letter is the hug I would give you, if I were there. I have been praying really hard, and I hope it went O.K for you. It's not much fun in there, is it? I'm sure you did well. Please say hello to everyone for me. I love you very, very, very much (and of course, Dad) See you when you get home,

loadsa love and prayers

Emily

Above: Emily gave this note to me the day I testified. My instructions were to open it when it was all over and I'd emerged from court again.

enquiries, 'it hadn't been too bad, not too bad at all.'

Emily gave this note to me the day I testified. My instructions were to open it when it was all over and I'd emerged from court again.

After five minutes of recuperation, I was then keen to join the others in the public gallery, and at last be as involved as I could in the final proceedings.

It gave me a sense of participation to join the friends and family in the public gallery. I felt properly involved at last as I was able to watch the events myself rather than have snippets of information relayed to me second hand. I eyed the jury cautiously, what had they thought of me? Had I done OK? Had I accidentally contradicted something Nick had said? I hoped with fervent desperation that I hadn't said anything that was somehow incriminating. The jury looked a friendly bunch; a good range of ages and types. But what were they thinking?

There were only five more witnesses after me. Richard Darnell was first. He was a computer engineer and now aged twenty four. The immediate impression one received was a favourable one, as he stood straight and tall, well over six feet, looking smart but a little nervous. It was the same line of questioning. What did he think of the youth group? Of Nick? There were similar answers as before. Richard was full of praise and admiration for Nick, his truthfulness, integrity and leadership. He thought Anita had had a crush on Nick, but Nick had never put himself in a compromising situation. Asked about Penny, Richard said Nick helped Penny come out of herself, and with his sense of fun, he cheered her up. Did he know Debs?

'Yes, but she was known to be moody which I can't handle very well, so I tended to keep my distance.'

'Did you go to Italy?'

'Yes. Everything went very well and Nick did absolutely nothing to cause concern.'

On cross questioning Richard became flustered with the year Anita joined. 'But anyone would,' I thought. 'It shows he's human and hasn't swatted it all up.' Soon Richard was dismissed and Andrew Townsend called. As a youngster Andrew had been renowned for his timidity. I was apprehensive as he took the stand. I imagined Andrew looking down at his shoes and muttering that he thought Nick was a nice bloke, and then being shredded by the prosecuting barrister, who'd been nicknamed the Rottweiler by those of us waiting outside. I couldn't have been further off the mark. Mr Bassett questioned him thoroughly, working from his statement, and he answered clearly and confidently. 'Yes, he had enjoyed the youth group; no, he'd never seen anything dodgy going on and yes, he trusted Mr Metcalfe absolutely as a man of total integrity'. I breathed a sigh of relief; what a fantastic testimony. The 'Rottweiler' clearly felt he'd gain nothing by quizzing him, and released him quickly after a couple of questions.

After Andrew came David Darlington. A shortish round looking man, a member of the Oxted church who'd always looked as if he had foreign blood in him. He'd run the youth group for eleven to fourteen year olds in Oxted with his wife and had been outraged by what had happened to Nick.

He confirmed his confidence in Nick's honesty and integrity and that both his daughters and his son had been through the youth group, with no problems and enormous enjoyment. He also substantiated the fact that Anita, Penny and Debs had been very happy at the Metcalfe's; for often when he'd arrived to fetch his children and had offered them lifts they'd refused saying that they'd go with Nick later.

'What do you know of Penny Simpson?'

'She used to like private chats with Nick and on a couple of occasions told us she had problems with her parents. We were concerned, but when we suggested we talked to her parents, she backed off and said no, it was only a joke.'

Kirsty Sinclair, a girl from the youth group came next. Tall, slim and blond she made a striking impression in court and although obviously nervous she spoke clearly about what a good friend Nick was and how he'd helped her with some family problems.

'Have you had any physical contact with Nick Metcalfe?'

'He hugged me across the shoulders. It was nice to feel comforted.'

'Did he hug girls and fellows?' Asked Mr Bassett.

'Probably more girls, as they show their emotions more.'

'Did Nick give you lifts home?'

'Oh yes, often. But I've never felt threatened by him. I've often been alone with him in the car.'

'Nothing inappropriate happened?'

Kirsty looked surprised: 'No, never.'

The prosecution barrister asked a couple of questions which didn't seem to achieve anything and Kirsty was done. She looked relieved. I had to admire her, after all she was only sixteen and prepared to go through the nerve wracking ordeal of testifying in court for the youth leader; that took some courage.

Lastly came Martin Knighton. He was now a school inspector, had been a teacher and a deputy head. He strode into court with confidence, took the oath and spoke loudly and clearly. I could see immediately why Mr Bassett had left him until last. After the slightly nervous young people he seemed sure of himself, his views and all he had to say. He told the court how he'd had forty years of working with teenagers and had often had to make judgements about school teachers' integrity. He'd known Nick since he'd joined the church and trusted him totally. Nick did a superb work with the teenagers.

'Have you ever noticed anything untoward in Nick's behaviour?'

'Never. The church photocopier was at the Metcalfe's house and I used to turn up at all sorts of times to use it, and was always made welcome. I saw how the family ticked and the youth group integrated with them.'

'Does Mr Metcalfe have the full support of the church leaders?'

'Yes. We've spent considerable time trying to understand these allegations, but they don't fit with Nick's character at all and he has our total support.'

Mr Knighton was then dismissed and Mr Bassett prepared to read a large number of letters of support for Nick from a wide range of friends and relatives. The prosecution barrister didn't seem too happy about it and a short legal volley went to and fro. Ultimately the documents were read and the court broke for lunch.

Prosecution summary

T he public gallery had been filling up rapidly, for as each of Nick's witnesses testified they were then anxious to join those watching the proceedings. Consequently after lunch the public gallery was so full that it was arranged for the extras to go down and sit in court along the wall underneath the spectators. As I took my place actually in the court, once again, I felt pleased to be at last in the same room as Nick, trying to absorb all that was going on. Again I peered over at the jury. They were clearly taking things very seriously, some took notes occasionally, some looked a little bored; but then that was understandable, this thing had been going on nearly a fortnight, and I felt quite sure they had better things to do than listen to all this nonsense.

The jury were dismissed and then some legal wranglings began. I couldn't follow it totally, Mr Bassett was requesting that copies of the letters he'd just read out in court should be handed to the jury. The 'Rottweiler' didn't want any of it and quoted a case from his law book where it was laid down that letters should only ever be read out in court and copies not passed physically to the jury. The judge listened patiently and then pronounced: 'You may pass copies of the letter to the jury, Mr Bassett. I know, Mr Williams, about the article you mentioned, but if they've been read out in court, I see no reason why the jurors shouldn't have copies, I always thought that was a silly law anyway.' The prosecution barrister was indignant; 'I'll be complaining tomorrow.' He said with a note of frustration. 'That's your right,' replied the judge. 'But you might as well save your breath.'

I could feel a smile creeping over my face at that point and hoped it wasn't too conspicuous. Mr Williams then again fiercely disputed the dropping of three of the twelve charges but Mr Bassett once more had his way. Complex legal arguments continued and my concentration lapsed several times but in essence I gathered that the 'touchings', or at least some of them, were definitely going, as they'd not been specifically referred to by the witnesses. One of the counts didn't fit with any of the dates that had been specified. Corroboration was also mentioned and the judge said he would draw the possibility of it to the jury's attention. Mr Bassett hammered on, stating cases from his big red book of so and so v. someone else, sometimes the prosecution barrister chipped in but the judge stuck firmly to his guns that there was a case to answer on nine counts but that he would allow the other three to go. Mr Bassett wasn't quite done. If the assaults on Penny *had* happened, he argued, then she must have consented as she hadn't voiced a protest, and so there would be no charge. It was only because the defendant was adamant they hadn't happened that there was a charge. The judge, of course, understood, but said it was up to the jury to decide what had and what hadn't happened.

3.30 pm arrived, court was adjourned and everyone shuffled out looking rather tired from the mental gymnastics involved in trying to follow the complicated court discussions. But with a quarter of the charges eliminated I felt gratified but still anxious, as we drove home that night. The stress was beginning to tell, we were both mentally and physically exhausted and relieved that the end was drawing closer. Almost regardless of the outcome, neither of us felt we could handle many more of these intense court room sessions.

Mr Bassett and his assistant seemed calm on Tuesday. Mr Bassett was philosophical.

'Well,' he said, 'as a defence team we've done all we can. All we can do now is pray.'

Whether or not Mr Bassett believed in prayer, he had taken on board our situation and realised how very significant prayer was. People in Oxted were praying round the clock, as were friends in Cranleigh. Indeed the word had spread far and wide, but we didn't really appreciate just how far and wide until long after the event.

'What exactly happens today?' I enquired, knowing that I was displaying my legal ignorance once more but also feeling that I was beyond caring. The legal team were gentle in their response and far from patronising. 'Well,' explained Mr Bassett, 'the prosecution barrister sums up, then I sum up, and then the judge does a final summing up.'

'How long will that take?'

'I guess we'll be finishing the case tomorrow and the jury will go out then.'

'Oh, I see, thank you.' I felt a little bewildered. How could summing up take over a day? I'd always been taught at school that a summary was a brief presentation of the whole. Still, I'd soon find out.

Nick's case was called once again and everyone clustered to the public gallery, once more overflow was allowed in the court itself. Mr Williams took the floor and held everyone's attention; he was a fine orator. 'Members of the jury,' he addressed them, ensuring one hundred per cent attention from everyone as he fixed his eyes on them and seemed to demand allegiance, 'our concern today is whether any of these alleged incidents occurred.

'*He* says he never touched them indecently at all. *You* will be sure of what occurred. You have heard Mr Metcalfe is a man of good character, a good guy; there is no reason to doubt him. Many of the references came from the church and members of the youth group, which we need to put in perspective. They are a very close knit group, a close community. Those who spoke were very supportive of him, but put yourselves in the position of these young girls, teenagers, trying, wanting to speak out in the face of that church. They are confused, not sure what to do, they are fearful of being ostracised by the church who, let's face it, are not supportive of the accusers, not open minded. I invite the jury to have an open mind. Just imagine, knowing the church would back a church man, who ran the group, who ran the music etc., etc. Each girl is very reliant on the church for friendship, music, teaching, and they enjoyed it and didn't want to give it up. So it is not surprising they didn't speak up. Each girl felt a lone voice. That is not now the case. Let's consider which witness is reliable and credible.

'Anita. When she was cross examined, we had the opportunity to observe her at close hand to see her reactions. She is now twenty years old and didn't know certain dates and times. She said she wasn't good at remembering dates, that's not unusual. Don't criticise her for not remembering each incident, date and time. She went into hospital in March '94, and said all the incidents of an indecent nature occurred before hospital. That's important. She was a member of the group with her sister, who left abruptly. The defence are trying to extend the time Jasmine attended.

'Anita said she went regularly, was very involved early on, the defendant gave her lifts home, and came into her house for coffee. These lifts home, the defendant said he didn't give her lifts before '95, only after she'd been in hospital. Why is he telling that lie? Anita says before hospital it was a regular thing. He would come in for a chat because she was the last person to be dropped off. Her sister says "he dropped us both off at home," her mother is adamant that he came to the house both before and after Anita was in hospital, her father says before and after. But perhaps as family they are bound to support her? The defence witness Tony Brookes said she was given lifts before she went into hospital by Metcalfe. Richard Darnell said Anita didn't join until '95 but he could have been wrong, Natasha Darnell quoted her diary that in March '93 she, Alice Islington and Anita had bought the Metcalfes a wedding anniversary card, which proves she was well involved and a regular attendee, this one year before going into hospital. This is a matter agreed by a number of defence witnesses as well. He has not told you the truth because he wants to distance himself from those visits. He has blanked them out of his mind, because they were things a youth club leader should not have done.'

Mr Williams was forceful and determined. He spoke of dates and lies with a conviction that was convincing. Those listening wavered fractionally in their assumption of Nick's innocence. Someone in the jury moved some papers and a sheet fluttered down into court. An usher picked it up and the barrister continued.

'Anita tells us that Metcalfe, when in her house, was pleasant over coffee and spoke to her about a number of personal matters one would not expect a man of his age to chat to a young girl about, his wife, his family, his work. Yet it would be extremely unusual for Anita to have made it all up.

'Mr Islington said Anita complained of the way Metcalfe spoke to her. He was emotionally pushy. Again it would be an unusual thing to make up. She repeated it in 1998 and has done so again before a jury.

'It was the "happiest of marriages", "no frustrations at all". Again we must get this in perspective. He worked hard, was a family man. Did all he could for his daughters, he ran the youth group. He ran the music at church, helped people with their computers, he was an extremely busy man. It is common sense that with the stresses of being very busy, responsible, people looking up to you and looking to you for help that the stress would get to him. He sought a shoulder to cry on, Anita's. He cried, asked her for a hug. He's a tactile person, he would hug people, put arms round them. But Mrs Winger said in her evidence that he never touched her, he didn't appear tactile. Only if he was playing a game and being boisterous would he touch, but not generally every time they saw or left him.

'Why would Anita make up the story of the hug? It's harmless, at first it went no further. He touched her breast and later, on a number of occasions he touched her bottom. There was the incident in the bedroom. She was lent many books, she couldn't remember the books but did remember it was before her hospitalisation, so they couldn't have been the books we've seen here in court. Metcalfe said he'd lent her one book, then in the end he retrieved it. Then he said he didn't know about the books, his story was changing. Anita said when they went to her room to look for books she had been raped. At the time of sexual intercourse she may have led the defendant on, or may have given him that impression. If she may have, no jury can be sure of what the defendant knew or believed, whether she was or was not consenting, and for that reason the crown are not proceeding on the rape charge.

'But, she was under sixteen years and cannot consent to indecent assault. We've heard her say that after the sexual intercourse, he yet again sexually assaulted her. She remembers her parents coming home and going downstairs to greet them. Her parents can't remember the defendant being in the bedroom. But in her evidence there are two questions which arise to do with the bedroom incidents. She says Mr Metcalfe behaved as if nothing had happened at all. Why? Because he was blanking it out. He had a public face to maintain, he made everything appear normal. The second time he went to her bedroom, we don't know why, he lay down on her bed and took her clothing down. "Suddenly he just stopped" and that was it, and he went downstairs. Why? Maybe his conscience got the better of him? If Anita was making it up, she could have made it so much worse, she could have exaggerated it, but she didn't.'

My stomach tightened in a knot. Our supporters were tense. None of us had anticipated this fine and very convincing speech. But then none of us were familiar with court protocol at all. Mr Williams carried on.

'In her first statement she states there were two further incidents but in her evidence she said there was one further incident and two further lesser incidents. She corrected the mistake in her second statement, because it was fairer to the accused, or because it was the truth?

'She spent a year in and out of hospital and Metcalfe was an extremely regular visitor, because he had built up a close relationship with her, not because he felt responsible for the accident and injury. Their relationship had started long before. After hospital Anita was depressed and missed her friends at the youth group so went back. Metcalfe continues visiting her but there are no further indecent assaults. She was more aware, she arranged lifts with other people and used her moped as soon as possible. She carried on attending because it was her life, her friends were there, she needed the computer and her friends were always around. Incidents only occurred when there were only two people there, Anita and Metcalfe.

'Anita knew Metcalfe was so highly thought of that it was almost impossible to make a complaint. Mrs Islington approached her, she wasn't ready to speak out, she wanted to brush it aside, and the church had made promises to sort it out. Mr Islington saw the card left for Anita at her home. He said it was an inappropriate card to send to a young girl in those circumstances. This card was indicative of Metcalfe's mood. He felt extra sad at losing Anita and was worried she was growing in confidence and might speak out. Mr Islington tells us Metcalfe was annoyed that he was giving her priority because of her exams, he wanted to speak to Anita sooner rather than later. Or was he annoyed because he was desperate to speak to Anita to see if she was going to speak out?'

'I'm annoyed now,' thought Nick, 'that you're talking such utter rubbish.' But the diatribe continued.

'The defendant had a short meeting with Mr Islington not even admitting he'd been tactile, let alone emotionally pushy. Why did he say he was devastated by Anita's absence? They had no contact at Alice's wedding and then sent an email to Penny because he didn't have Anita's address. He was worried that she was going to speak out. We haven't heard from the church officers about what happened after the complaints. We've heard from Penny Finch that she'd wanted it dealt with within the church, but because of their inactivity she'd been to the Police. Why haven't we heard about that?

'Anita went to the police, she accepted she hadn't said everything when she started in September. That's no surprise, she was still undecided whether she had the courage to speak out. Why did she bother to go to the police eventually with the whole story and subsequently to court if it wasn't true?

The first suggestion is that her sister had made allegations in the past about her family. She was informed on Friday by the prosecuting counsel about the allegations but not who they were against, she had no idea. Jasmine's evidence is a side issue. Even if Jasmine is not telling the truth about what happened in '95 it doesn't mean that Anita is not telling the truth. She is not transferring what happened with Metcalfe to her family.

'Another suggestion is that she had a crush on Metcalfe, and that these are imagined incidents. Nonsense. Why pick on Mr Metcalfe, he'd done nothing but good for her? Unless of course, he had assaulted her.

'Deborah Islington: we've not heard many nice things about her. But surely she was a normal teenager? Perhaps her behaviour was because something was happening to her, something she didn't like? She didn't say anything to Metcalfe, she thought he would pass it off as a joke. Her father was a church officer, no one would believe her. Metcalfe caressed the back of her leg at his home, it was indecent and she spoke out, "stop touching my leg" but the defendant has no recollection of any complaint. Mrs Metcalfe has no recollection. Metcalfe has blanked it out of his mind. Aaron Howlett hadn't seen the touching, it must have happened when they were on their own. Kirsty Sinclair, according to Andrew, was behind them but he must have been wrong because she would have remembered the incident.'

Someone coughed in the public gallery. Mr Williams, undisturbed and unperturbed, ploughed on.

'Deborah is a girl who didn't have the courage to speak out. She even said "Maybe he thought it was a joke." But no, it was for his sexual satisfaction. In Italy she recalls the incident differently from Anita. But there was clearly an upset between Metcalfe and Deborah on that trip, Deborah went on the second trip and we've seen the edited video of that. The content may not be important, they were just joking about, but it has been edited, the defendant is trying to put a different slant on events and that's important to remember.

'Penny Finch: she left quickly after returning from the trip. Why? She was concerned about Italy, she too carried on going to the group because it was her life. At the end of the meeting Mrs Metcalfe was in bed and Metcalfe thanked her for all her support on the trip and touched her breast. The previous Christmas she'd gone to assist him, knelt on the stool beside him and he'd put his arm around her and his head on her shoulder. He apologised for something earlier and ran his hand down to her bottom, stroking her bottom. She says, "I didn't know what to do, how to react." Also in Italy there was the incident in the pastor's house, and the incident in the showers. How come she can remember them so specifically if they didn't happen? He was under stress, the van had broken down. He says he copes with everything, but like with Anita, when under pressure he turns to a young girl for support. On his public face, everything is fine.

'Penny Finch says she and Metcalfe had a good friendship, but he went beyond it. He still wanted her friendship. After his visit to her university, Penny still went to their house because she had affection for the whole family. She tried to put the bits she didn't like out of her mind. Touching her waist in the halls of residence, touching her bottom on the tube, she tried to put these to one side so that she could keep up friendship with the family and the church. She didn't want to complain, she went to the police with Anita, but didn't say anything. She went to the church, and it was when they did nothing that she then went to the police. She was the supporting friend. It would have been most unusual if she hadn't talked about it with Anita, her best friend. Church members have discussed it, it is human nature to talk about it.

'It has been suggested that she had problems with her father and is now blaming Metcalfe. Yes, she says she did have problems with her father. She told the Metcalfes, it was no joke. So her fear got out of control and she blamed Metcalfe? Why pick on Metcalfe and not her father or someone else, unless it had been him who had taken advantage of the situation? It was put to Penny that Metcalfe would do more for any one than expected and she'd answered "way beyond". Why blame someone who would go so far beyond the call of duty unless it were true?

'I put it to you that Metcalfe, on the whole, is everything he's been said to have been, but under pressure he resorts to a variety of indecent approaches and assault on young girls and therefore, having heard the traumas and terrible experiences these three girls have been through, it leaves you, the jury, with no alternative but to find Metcalfe guilty on all counts.'

He had portrayed Nick's case in the worst possible light. I felt increasingly uncomfortable as he had regaled the jury with suggested motives for this assault and that offence, explaining carefully and powerfully why things had happened, how such an upright man could have committed such acts and why despite the many testimonies and letters to the contrary as to his good character, he was convinced that Nick Metcalfe had done all that he was alleged to have done and why the jury had absolutely no alternative but to find him guilty.

As he proceeded I felt my stomach get tighter and tighter and wave after wave of despair swept over me. Once he had finished his speech the court was dismissed for lunch and I had no option but to fly to the 'ladies' and sob silently in the privacy of one of the cubicles. But determined to maintain a brave face to the outside world I quickly washed away the tears, shoved a bit of make up on and brushed my hair, still managing to emerge before Nick had left the court having had a quick chat with Mr Bassett.

Defence summary

We had a quiet lunch in a church hall coffee bar and to my immense surprise Nick seemed relatively chirpy. 'Wasn't that awful?' I said.

'Yes,' replied Nick. 'But it was a pack of lies, he got quite a few of the facts wrong and hopefully the jury will see that.'

'But what if they don't?' I questioned anxiously.

'Worry about it when it happens,' Nick said with a grin, biting hard into his cheese and pickle roll.

'We've still got Mr Bassett and the judge to go yet.'

'I know,' I muttered doubtfully.

That afternoon we witnessed a totally different approach. Mr Bassett was not out to convince the jury by the power of oratory and the force of his voice. Standing up he too turned to the jury, but started off in a gentle persuasive almost discussional tone. 'Members of the jury, I am appealing to you as fellow human beings. I would request that you put yourselves in my client's position, put yourselves in his shoes just for a moment. Woken one morning by the police and arrested for sexual crimes that you've never even heard of. How do you defend yourself? How would you, in that position, convince a jury that you were not guilty? Remember, we have no specific date to work to, even the years are hazy, the allegations change somewhat as time progresses, but it is nonetheless essential that you prove your innocence. Well, you start looking for evidence, anything that will contradict the allegations, you pull out all the stops, you find old cards, emails, photographs; anything that will substantiate the fact you did not commit these crimes.' It was a totally different approach, fresh, appealing and less intimidating.

'You, members of the jury, have an arduous duty, an important one and one in which it is important to use both common sense and fairness. You must judge on the evidence and we must rely on you to judge fairly. The climate of opinion has changed dramatically over the years for this type of case. You may feel that false complaints are filtered out nowadays, but these are grave allegations and easy to make.

'Consider Jasmine: hers is a case where wholly false and wicked allegations have been made. You see an illustration of the accuser and the accused. Of course all young people must be protected from unwanted attentions. But the experience of the court over centuries is that these type of allegations can easily be made, because it is one person's word against another's. But how does an innocent man protect himself? He relies on the burden of proof, the evidence. I don't know if you've been taking notes, but you are the judges of the evidence, you don't convict him on speculation as in the prosecuting counsel's speech. Mr Darlington's testimony for example. Prosecution speculated that something must have been done in Italy because Penny left early on their return. Miss Finch was not asked about this, we must keep a steady head and look at the evidence. I and my assistants have kept notes, and I try to get it right, and not misrepresent evidence.' The emphasis on hard facts appealed to Nick and he hoped to members of the jury.

'It has been suggested that it is not just the girls on trial, but the whole Oxted church on trial. No, these groups are not on trial, the defendant is on trial.

'How many times have they been referred to as young girls? They are not young girls, they are young women. If we hear about young girls, it is our natural reaction to want to protect them, and we would expect them to get things wrong. Miss Simpson is twenty years old, Miss Islington is nineteen and Miss Finch is twenty. They are not young girls. Anita was a teenager at the time, Miss Finch was of an age to give consent, over sixteen years old. She attended the group frequently and was not a young girl unable to say what has happened to her. You haven't got a duty to protect them, you have a duty to judge the evidence.

'These are wild allegations, how do you protect yourself? Jasmine's may be a side issue but what else is there? First he was accused of rape, sexual intercourse and two further times of intercourse. This was totally denied. Anita was twenty years old when she then alleged that she had got it wrong. It started with triple rape, he was arrested for something that happened years ago and has now been dropped. She said she'd been raped three times and now says, "oh no, I got it wrong." The prosecution counsel say she might have led him on, which gives us a flood of light on what the prosecution think of Anita and her reliability.

'We've heard four accounts of crimes; of crimes that Mr Metcalfe hasn't committed. Obviously we need more detail, and precise dates. But we're now down to nine indictments. There has been a weeding out process, and there are some left for you to consider. Think about the defendant's position. Wouldn't you want to know when it happened and where? We've heard about digital penetration, but that is the only specific allegation. What exactly were the "other touchings"? Miss Islington called out when her leg was touched, Miss Finch referred to specific touchings on her breast and bottom. You have been allowed evidence on other counts, though it is limited, but these are nothing to do with counts nos 1—6.

'When Anita was asked for specific details we saw floods of tears and comments such as, "I'm not much good at detail," so we have to rely on the jury to make deductions. Anita gave us no details but was adamant it happened. Plainly she didn't enjoy giving testimony, she was clearly distressed. But false allegations can be made up for lots of reasons and the defendant doesn't know why. We just have to look at the burden of proof. You may conclude this trial is unusual as the defendant hasn't said "you prove it", but has set out his evidence to disprove it. Don't fall into the trap of saying that Mr Metcalfe hasn't proved he is innocent, for the prosecution have not proved their case.

'Anita falsely alleged intercourse on three occasions, and tried to explain it as a mistake. Another case of pure invention was in Italy, when she says she saw my client with his hand down Miss Islington's trousers and that Mr Metcalfe's face was a picture. On another occasion she says "his face was a picture, he knew he'd been caught." This is pure fabrication. Miss Islington tells us herself that nothing at all happened in Italy. She accepts that she was a difficult teenager, but there are no hints of indecency. This is not a case about Mr Metcalfe having difficulties with teenagers, or hugging them, or being emotionally pushy, it is about indecency. He may have been huggy, and emotionally pushy, which may explain why complaints were made, but that is not what he's accused of, he's accused of indecency.

'On her own evidence when the judge asked when Anita had last seen Mr Metcalfe she replied, "Not for at least a year". She was forgetting Alice's wedding, and the reconciling meeting of ten minutes duration. She was under stress and forgetting? But this is the young woman who says she was indecently assaulted by my client. Consider the realities of what she's said. How do you defend yourself about "touchings" in which you are given no details, just tears?

'These are serious offences and there would be physical signs, pain, blood, tears, yet when her parents returned she spoke to them while Mr Metcalfe read a book in the bedroom. (Which has changed from an earlier story of looking for a book in the bedroom). How can this be an account of a young girl's deflowering; she would have been a virgin at the time? She claims to have been a thirteen year old, and raped upstairs. Her parents came home when he was on her, but on their evidence there was no distress, no upset, they never saw him upstairs. Her story is unsupported, there is nothing to back it up. The prosecution say, "Convict on this!" How can he defend himself on the other allegations other than say repeatedly, "I didn't do it." Anita has been proved to be wrong. She said "Emma Winger warned me to look out for Nick Metcalfe," but Emma claims, "I never warned her about Nick Metcalfe. He's a very good friend of mine. We've had lots of fun together. He never touched me sexually. I would hug him now." Miss Anita Simpson was fabricating evidence.' I let out a silent sigh of relief. This was more like it. This was what I'd longed to hear.

'Natasha Darnell has nothing but good to speak of Mr Metcalfe. She tells us Anita would try to get attention by saying her leg hurt after her hospitalisation. We're told that the accuser might have had a crush on Mr Metcalfe. Mike Cunliffe says she and Penny Finch followed him around "like puppy dogs." Anita has no explanation as to why she continued to seek out Mr Metcalfe's company. Why she still belonged to the club, why she went frequently to their house, why she baby sat, used their computer and their organ. She has no answer.

'Her twin wasn't a member of the club, they are very close. Jasmine had no problems leaving. If the church are so dominating what do we make of Mr Islington's role? He was an officer of the church and listened to her complaints with his wife, so how can she argue that she couldn't complain to the church leaders? It's unsupported and ridiculous.

'Then one asks, how long has she been saying these things and when were they first said? What is the history of the complaint? It didn't surface until '98, after Jeremy Buckley made the Islington parents aware, and there were no complaints of indecency at this stage. This card we've heard so much about, we haven't seen it, but we've been told it's important and was inappropriate. Anita was nineteen and a half at the time. The card came from both Mr and Mrs Metcalfe. Of course Mr Metcalfe was upset, the whole purpose of the club was to provide support for young people, spiritual and moral. She'd left the club with no warning, and the card was to say, "We're missing you, come back." Is that so very sinister?

'He used the word devastated? Yes, of course he was upset, he felt he'd let her down, he felt he'd unwittingly and innocently caused her so much offence that she'd left the club.' As in his questioning Mr Bassett jumped around from topic to topic. His tone was discussional, as if he were carefully trying to analyse the situation from every possible angle.

'Regarding books. There's a good account in the interview, conducted on the basis of three rapes, there's a suggestion that he said he'd only lent one book. But if you look at page 34 of the first interview you'll see DC Stevens asks; "She borrowed books?" (plural) Mr Metcalfe replies; "Yes, books, they rarely come back." Further on you'll find a further mention that he "lent her books" that before her hospitalisation he hadn't lent her books, nor had he been to her house before that. Then when she was in hospital and was bored, he lent her *'Joni'*, later he constantly asked for it back but it was not returned. Surely with allegations of this gravity you're not going to convict on whether he lent her a book or books, are you? The evidence is that he went into her room to recover a book he'd lent her, that's why the book is important. The defendant lent her books because she was in hospital, after she came out of hospital he went to retrieve it. *'Joni'* is the relevant book because it's to do with a swimming accident, as Joni was injured similarly to Anita. Anita says it was his excuse for coming in the bedroom. Mr Metcalfe and his wife have proved that they collected the book after Anita came out of hospital. The truth is plain. The Metcalfes lent the book. If Anita is right, then the Metcalfes lent her a book about a swimming accident before she'd had one! Are you satisfied that Anita's explanation for the book is truthful? It may seem a small point, but how else is an innocent man to defend himself?

'Another detail: what about this reconciliation? If Anita had been raped and indecently assaulted, would she have wanted a reconciliation? It doesn't make sense. There was a meeting in July before Alice's wedding where Alice met with Ruth Knighton and protested that "it was all a mistake", a misunderstanding, no assertion of anything improper. Mr Islington heard about the reconciliation meeting from Anita, he was told that all was well.

'We hear of slight friction on the night of November 5th. Mrs Metcalfe was short with Anita for letting the group down, she was anxious at the responsibility of being in charge of the youngsters without a female leader, but Anita was nineteen years old and Penny also eighteen or nineteen. To an adult this event was trivial, to a teenager events like this can fester. Harsh words were exchanged and "immediately" after that Anita stops attending. Not a hint of anything indecent.

'Then in 1998 Anita starts going out with a man twice her age who doesn't approve of the church. And then a few months later the allegations appear. I can't prove it's why she lied. I can't prove she transferred her family's abuse onto Mr Metcalfe. But I can't dismiss it.' An ambulance siren penetrated the courtroom for a moment. Mr Bassett paused and it quickly passed.

'The sisters, of course, have a close relationship. Anita says the first she heard of the alleged abuse of Jasmine was at court on Monday, but Jasmine says "it was Sunday when I first mentioned it." When Jasmine was asked by the police if she had any complaints against Mr Metcalfe she replied, "no, no complaints, I met Mr Metcalfe lots of times, it was always pleasant." Then she tells us in court that "one time he pulled over in the van, and touched my leg when my sister was there," and "he pulled over in a lay by and came on to me, I pushed him off." But she had never mentioned either of these incidents before, despite having been given every opportunity. She has told us she made false complaints about her family.

'Miss Finch has told you that her father interfered with her too, "doing things to her". Jasmine's strange assertions are not substantiated by Anita's parents. Their answers were wholly unsatisfactory and unusual. Jasmine said there is a history of mental illness in the family. This was apparent when Mrs Simpson gave evidence. These parents don't prove the case against Mr Metcalfe.

'Remember Jasmine was prepared to make wholly false allegations against her family and then implicate Mr Metcalfe to explain it; the sisters are alike, Anita's allegations could be wholly false too. Where Anita can be tested and checked she can be proved wrong, where she can't, it can't possibly be safe to rely on.

'Penny Finch alleges there was an incident on the underground, but there is no one to back it up and it has been denied. There is no evidence to support it. If Mr Metcalfe was abusing her we have to ask ourselves why does she stay in the club, go to the house and follow him around? She brought the Metcalfes their leaving present and signed their card, this has been substantiated by Tony Brookes, who seems a nice trustworthy young man.

'Mr Darlington has told us that Penny Finch often wanted to see Mr Metcalfe privately in his house, he said she was good at winding him up, pretending she had problems she didn't really have. He saw Penny Finch and said she'd often be in the study. They'd offered to help once and talk to her parents, but she backed off, his conclusion was that she had wound him up.

'The defence witnesses don't have to prove anything at all. If you, the jury, are not wholly satisfied that Penny Finch is truthful, then that can end the case with her. Why does she stay on at the club after allegedly being assaulted in Italy?

'Anita says she only used the computer once when others were there. But we've seen the computer print out. It's been suggested by the prosecution that this was fabricated, as they suggested the video was unfairly edited, but these items were taken by the police, so if there was any truth in those wild suggestions they have had ample time to prove it. Metcalfe said the police have the original, just as he had the original leaving card. Yet despite having the means, the opportunity and the invitation they have not produced anything different from those we've been shown, but they ask you to convict on this basis. Remember common sense and fairness must be applied. You have the computer printout before you, it shows Anita used the computer for twenty seven hours in total, but she said she only used it once because she had to pass her A levels!' I glanced up at the public gallery and saw my father rub his hands together, probably unaware he was doing so. It was simply an outward expression of inner satisfaction as Mr Bassett carried on.

'The emails too are clearly set out. Penny says pressure was applied to her in the emails, but they show nothing improper at all, just an affectionate friendship. It's been suggested there is something sinister in an older person befriending a younger person. Check the emails, there is nothing.

'The questions to my client about the sexual relationship he has with his wife were offensive and ludicrous.

'Penny Finch regularly went to the Metcalfe's house, she went to the club, to Italy, she was welcoming at university. Why did she seek this man out? There is no answer. But the prosecuting counsel say Penny Finch admitted she'd chewed over the evidence with other women. Anita says she talked on twenty occasions, she talked in the pub.

'Deborah Islington: we've looked at each complaint separately, and I must say we can't say Deborah Islington is a worry. But it is important to look at it the other way round, they may have tainted each other's evidence, they talked before they went to the police and they talked after they went to the police. The collusion is not necessarily improper, but they have plainly colluded. They have come to some agreement. We can't say that what comes from Miss Simpson is not tainted by Miss Finch and so on.

'The emails show a perfectly normal and affectionate friendship.

'Deborah Islington: Miss Finch, you may think she is lying; whereas Miss Islington is plainly lying, in that there was no indecency. She has acknowledged herself, see counts 7 and 9, that it could all have been a joke. The only time any of the girls complained is when she called out. The prosecuting counsel says she "recollects Metcalfe caressed her", that is *NOT* what Miss Islington said. She made it quite plain that there was only one incident and it was at his own home with people in the kitchen. This was clearly an opportunity for the prosecution to collect evidence. But you've heard Aaron Howlett, the one from Liverpool, he is plainly a truthful, reliable man, he said "Deborah Islington came to the door and said 'Nick, stop feeling my leg' I had a clear view, nothing had happened. It was a joke, she laughed it off. I would have seen a deliberate touch. It was a jovial remark, she used to joke about these things." We've also heard she used to dress provocatively in mini skirts. But Howlett is adamant my client didn't even touch her. How can you be satisfied? It is an example of the lengths the prosecution have to go to pin something on him.

'We've also heard that Deborah Islington liked to sit in the front seat of the van and to change gear. She liked Nick's attention, she was strong willed, it was easier to agree with her. From Mrs Metcalfe you've been told how Anita would tie Nick's shoelaces together, have fun with him. Mr Darlington says Anita would seek his attention in horseplay.

'Let's consider the allegations in order of gravity. Anita's are first, then Penny's and finally Deborah's. Deborah's are in a different category. The other two families both have a history of abuse.

'If you decide he is not guilty of crimes against Anita, and not guilty of crimes against Penny, don't think you'll find him guilty with Deborah to teach him a lesson for being an idiot. Don't forget they are separate allegations, each must be treated separately, and each witness must be treated individually. We don't want any compromise verdicts here.' I agreed wholeheartedly. I was so worried that Nick would be found guilty of a couple of the charges and the jury would assume that there was no smoke without fire.

'Miss Islington tells us on the subject of complaining to the church, that she couldn't complain that Nick was tactile because her father was an officer. But she was the best placed to complain with easy access to an officer, her mother and sister being church members. Deborah's sister Alice says she brought Anita into the group, that the Metcalfes were excellent youth group leaders, that she confided in Mrs Metcalfe. That Mr Metcalfe was tactile and she told Anita to say something if she felt uncomfortable with his touching. The prosecution say the indecencies took place when Anita was twelve or thirteen. Anita says; "I was twelve, I think, when I started the group ..." That is a lie. We know she couldn't join until she was fourteen years old. (She was fourteen in November '92). Alice Islington said she joined in September '92 and Anita joined after that. In the twenty years of her life, how can she attribute incidents to when she was twelve or thirteen, which couldn't have happened until she was fourteen or older? If she won't give details, how can we judge?

'If Miss Islington is a victim of indecent behaviour, can you think of her older sister inviting the abuser to her wedding? She insisted Metcalfe came to the wedding.

'The prosecution say the church was a tight knit community, they shared experiences and emotions and were in each others pockets. If so, how could he get away with it for so long, for nine years? How could the others in the group not know? And not complain? The prosecution have not begun to address this. Miss Islington's parents and sister were in the church.

'Anita said Emma Winger had warned her to be careful of Nick. A mean, spiteful comment. We are left to suppose Emma Winger was so upset that she left rather than complain, it is a pack of lies. Yes, the Winger family were in favour of Metcalfe, but where does this leave Anita's truthfulness?

'The prosecution ask, why should all these little girls lie? Why? We don't know, was it because of the argument on fireworks night? We mustn't speculate. But we must remember that the two main accusers are from families with allegations of sexual abuse. Miss Finch says it was her father, Jasmine says she couldn't blame Nick, so blamed her family. Why blame her family and not a stranger?

'We've had a mass of evidence of the type of man Mr Metcalfe is; these allegations are worthless and should be dismissed. If he is innocent why doesn't he say so? He plainly wants to say so. My learned friend has criticised him and said he's been laughing a lot, why? A clear conscience being faced by wild allegations for the first time in his life. He is flabbergasted, gob smacked. If he's told the truth, he's a man who's been under strain for a long time, he suffered a dawn raid, was taken to the police station leaving his wife and children in tears, his computer was seized, accused of triple rape, then one rape charge, which was later abandoned. He hears a mountain of untruthful allegations. He's been supported by having many friends and family here, who've no doubt come because of the seriousness of the allegations.

'Mr Metcalfe has selected from hundreds of letters some twenty three character references that go back right from his teenage years through to Oxted and his employment. There is an astonishing array of people who speak nothing but good of him. Consider the "live" witnesses. How many of us could call on so many to testify that we led a good life and were of good character? Are they all liars and fools? They all gave him praise such as one usually only finds on tombstones, granted that the church wears its heart on its sleeve.' How I hoped the jury were listening to this. This was the truth. Nick was innocent. I clenched my fists and prayed fervently that they were taking all this in.

'Look at Mike Cunliffe, he says the girls followed Nick around like "puppy dogs," that Nick was a brilliant, great guy, a role model etc. impeccable with the truth, an excellent upright Christian. Mrs Winger, a pastor's wife and great friend, says her daughter Emma wouldn't have reached her potential without him. We have to call on his character, it helps with his credibility, why shouldn't you believe him? He's reached forty years of age with no allegations against him.

'The prosecution say he "blanked it out" for himself so that is why he gives convincing denials. But this is not something you blank out. If you were a small child you might, but not an intelligent adult, so he must be deliberately lying. He says he went twice into her bedroom, once to retrieve books and once to admire her wardrobe. Do you believe him? There have been intrusive questions, suggestions of falsifying the computer records.

'His wife was put through the mill. Intelligent people say a wife knows if her husband is going elsewhere. If she knew what was going on, would she lie? Why shouldn't you believe Mrs Metcalfe?

'There's a mass of witnesses, Kirsty Sinclair said the defendant is a nice, friendly, kind man. He would give her a friendly hug over the shoulders to comfort, it was nice. Martin Knighton was very helpful. He's been dealing with young people since 1960, and is an officer of the church. The court didn't hear from the other officers, but Mr Knighton clearly spoke for all the officers. He put forward the view that Mr Metcalfe had the continued confidence of the officers and was a man of high moral standing. Is he such a cunning rogue and hypocrite that the church stand by him? The prosecution have tried to imply that that is sinister and says "those poor girls" but they are actually young women.

'In this case, use your common sense and fairness. It may leave you puzzled, confused, trying to sort out all the issues. If the young ladies say they have been abused you may feel that it is the duty of the court to punish the abuser and the women can be vindicated. But it isn't the women on trial, it is Metcalfe. He has protested his innocence, called seventeen witnesses, each one has been questioned to try and catch out Mr Metcalfe.

'Is there any single evidence apart from the claimants' that support the case? These are easy allegations to make, impossible to refute and hard to defend.'

Mr Bassett had continued on for several hours in his gentle conciliatory tone and he concluded with: 'Members of the jury, I beg you to consider this case carefully and logically: to think about what has been said during this case and I would ask you as fellow men and women to find my client not guilty of any of these crimes.'

I at last felt more comfortable and let out a little sigh of relief, but Mr Bassett had not quite finished. 'And I would also urge you,' he added as a little P.S., 'not to take the approach, "Well, let's find him guilty of one because he must have done something to these girls." No,' he paused, 'that is not justice, we are not here to teach my client a lesson, we are here as I've said before, to decide whether or not he is guilty. And as I've already put to you, it is not justice to find him guilty of one charge, it is a travesty of justice. Consider carefully the evidence before you, Mr Metcalfe's good character, and I would ask you to find him not guilty on all counts.'

It was a lovely little addition and how I appreciated it. Whether the jury would take any notice whatsoever I had no idea. But one guilty charge would be so damning. Maybe not prison, but a huge blight on his record, a police record, his job threatened, possible implications for our girls and, worst of all, his name would get on the sex offenders register. It was unbearable to dwell on and I was glad Mr Bassett had added his final request.

I wondered whether that would be it for the day. After all it was 3 pm and the judge didn't ever seem keen on prolonging affairs. But no, he wanted to start his summing up and so proceeded to do so. He spent an hour or so summarising in brief the whole case, not specifically mentioning witnesses but going through what Nick was accused of and then how Mr Bassett had presented the defence. It was a clear, fair conclusion to the events and although it gave us not an inkling of where his personal inclinations lay or which party he favoured, I felt it was a very just summary. Assuming the jury would go out on the Wednesday, I was almost ready to stand up and leave the court room when the judge then embarked on an extremely detailed relation of all that had taken place since day one. He'd taken intricate notes of every detail and was reminding the jury of all the minutiae of the events as they'd unfolded which they couldn't possibly be expected to remember.

My heart sank. This was going to take for ever. Here we were on Tuesday afternoon and still going through Anita's awful testimony. At this speed it would take several more days to plough through all the testimonies; surely the judge could go a little faster? But no, he was known for his thoroughness, if not for his speed, and he was determined to remind the jurors of all that had taken place.

The verdict

It was hard to sleep that night. Despite the total exhaustion we both felt, and the strange sense of relief that we were heading up the final straight, the fear and apprehension as to the final outcome kept sleep largely at a distance. It was peculiarly unemotional. We didn't communicate much, just tossed and turned, wondered, anticipated, and occasionally sighed.

'Do you think the jury will go out today?' I asked Nick as we drove up to Guildford.

'I expect so,' He replied. 'Though if the judge is as long and drawn out today as he was yesterday anything could happen. Let's hope it'll start on time, at least.' It did. Not before Mr Bassett had had a quick word with Nick and faintly amused him with an anecdote from the 'gents'. Apparently at the end of yesterday's session, Mr Bassett had come across Mr Simpson in the 'gents' and on recognising who it was, Mr Simpson had advanced, a little menacingly, towards him and said; 'I didn't think much of what you said about me and my family in there.' Mr Bassett had kept calm and replied in a placatory manner. The contretemps had passed off without violence and Nick apologised to Mr Bassett, thankful that his Q.C. was not now sporting a black eye. Mr Bassett shrugged it off saying with a smile; 'It's all part of the job, you know. Don't you worry. I've had a lot worse, I can assure you.'

Court then resumed and the judge continued his summing up. He carefully related each prosecution witness's statements and then those of the defence. He was tortuously objective. I sat in the public gallery willing him to put a favourable light on Nick's case, but he persevered in his ponderous relation of events giving the three girls as much credence as Nick. I was worried. Wasn't the judge meant to advise the jury? Didn't he direct them? Recommend a verdict? He was the one with the legal know how, the expertise, surely he'd seen quite clearly that Nick was totally innocent? Surely it was his job to explain that to the jury? Again I felt my total ignorance of the legal system as I realised that that may happen in films, but apparently not in real life.

On and on he went, until a mixture of distaste at hearing the ghastly details related for the umpteenth time and boredom began to creep over me tinged with a touch of despair. There was no way he was recommending Nick to the jury, and probably no way he'd finish that day. But just at the point when I felt all was lost I realised he was making his last few comments to the jury. I pricked up my ears again. 'Now,' he was saying firmly and authoritatively to the jurors; 'I want you to go away and consider carefully all that you have heard. When you have done all that and have decided categorically whether or not the defendant is guilty, you may return and not before. And I don't want,' he added in a school teacher's imperative tone, 'a non unanimous decision. I don't care what you see on television or hear on the radio about split juries and 60% verdicts. I want none of it. I want you to come back with an unanimous decision. If some of you have doubts, then it's up to you to discuss them until they are doubts no longer. Is that quite clear?'

The slightly startled jurors looked back at the judge and clearly indicated acquiescence. They must have been as pleased as those in the public gallery that decision time had at last come. An usher was allocated to them and would stay with them all the time they were out. Before I realised it, the court was emptied, the jurors had disappeared into some mysterious room at the back of the court and Nick's fate was being decided. It was 12.45 pm.

All the friends and relatives looked passive; I joined Nick, Mr Bassett and his assistant outside court and anxiously asked 'What happens now?'

'Well,' explained Mr Bassett. I wondered how many times he'd had to go through this rigmarole before, but he didn't portray any irritation and with the patience of a grandfather went on, 'you'd better hang around until one o'clock; though I can't imagine for one minute the jurors will reach a verdict by then. Then court doesn't reconvene until 2.30 pm so you may go for lunch as long as you're back by then.'

'Thank you' we said in unison. Nick seemed steady, relieved perhaps that it was all nearly over; I felt more scared than I've ever been in my life. My stomach was churning, my mind was blank and my legs felt as if they didn't entirely belong to me.

One o'clock was quickly on us and we were given the all clear by Mr Bassett. It was good to get outside court, to have a bit of a break, to stretch our legs, breathe some fresh air and concentrate on the trivial matter of finding somewhere to eat. Having located a quiet little bakery I realised that eating for me was completely out of the question. As I looked at the attractive array of baguettes, rolls, quiches and sausage rolls; they had no appeal whatsoever. 'What do you want?' asked Nick. I grinned sheepishly and explained, 'I really don't think I could eat a thing, though a gallon of tea wouldn't come amiss, I've a bit of a headache.'

'Nothing? Really?' Nick sounded incredulous. 'I'll have a sausage roll and an Eccles cake please,' he said to the lady behind the counter. It was my turn to be astonished. How could he tuck into a hefty lunch at a time like this? 'Might be my last decent meal for a while,' he said with a smile. But I couldn't appreciate the humour and just retorted sharply, 'Oh don't say things like that, please.'

Across the little oak table at the back of the bakers we chatted quietly. It was relaxed in a bizarre way. It was a moment that I thought I wanted to hold on to forever, like a photo keeping a precious experience in an album for posterity. The jury wouldn't give a verdict until 2.30 pm at the earliest so until then we were free agents. 'Stop the clock now,' I thought. 'Hold it right there, as the photographers say. Let's never move forward. Let's freeze this moment. The thought of the future is just too overwhelming.'

But time crept inexorably forward and after several anxious time checks we decided that at 2.00 pm we should go back to court. We arrived by 2.15 pm and sat down ready for a long tortuous wait. Friends and relatives gathered; some sympathetic with our need to be left tranquil. Others, like my well meaning next door neighbour, trying to help by a constant stream of chatter. He was trying distraction techniques by describing in detail a chocolate cake recipe he'd made recently but I couldn't take it in and struggled to appear even faintly civil. Opposite me sat two middle aged ladies, good friends of ours, who hadn't seen each other for a while. They had a lot of catching up to do and were talking nineteen to the dozen. 'I don't know if I can hack this', I thought, 'I really don't think I can handle all these people and all this chatter.' Just as I was wondering about moving away, stretching my legs or simply screaming at the top of my voice, Mr Bassett called Nick to one side. That brought me back to earth with a bump. 'What on earth was it now?' I wondered.

The two paced up and down the far end of the corridor, hands crossed behind their backs looking deadly serious. It reminded me of a picture I'd seen in *The Lion, The Witch and The Wardrobe* of the white witch and Aslan discussing the final arrangements for Aslan's death, and I felt a morbid oppression drift over me. As soon as Nick was free I ran up to him and asked, 'What was all that about?' Nick drew me away from listening ears, looking deathly pale he said, 'Mr Bassett says that if I'm sent to prison he'll ask for a week's leave first to spend with the family.'

'Oh.' My strength failed me entirely, I couldn't drag up from anywhere an encouraging comment and I peered vacantly out of the window. We were several stories up and I thought, 'It'd be less painful to jump out of here right now than endure this, it really would.' But glancing back at Nick, I knew I had to keep him going. 'He also said,' added Nick with a half hearted attempt at a grin, 'that in one of his cases the jurors were out for fourteen days. But that was a murder case.'

'Good grief.' I exclaimed. 'Well, I sincerely hope it's not as long as that for you.'

I returned to my seat and Nick talked intermittently to one or two folk. It was tense. Even those less involved realised how critical the next few minutes or hours or, God forbid, days were. The party atmosphere that had prevailed almost throughout the trial had vanished. Everyone looked serious. My father called me over, 'Whatever happens dear,' he said, 'it's the start of a new phase and we're right behind you.' I wasn't exactly sure what he meant, but knew he intended it to be encouraging and appreciated it as such.

Sporadic chat continued, Nick looked pale and made several trips to the gents. I wondered just how long we, in particular, but also all our friends and family could cope with the intensity of stress and pressure. 'Will all those concerned with the case of Nick Metcalfe please come to court number 11,' suddenly boomed over the loud speaker system. Everyone jumped. But I was off my seat and up the stairs like a greyhound. 'I probably ought to wait and escort the friends up,' I thought briefly without even hesitating in my stride up the stairs. 'And I must look daft charging up here, but I really don't care.' Nick went off with his barrister and his assistant and the others soon joined me in the public gallery. Penny had actually shared the lift with several of our friends along with Mr Simpson and Anita's boyfriend and the icy silence had been almost tangible. She had been present every day since testifying, and had sat in the public gallery amongst the Metcalfe supporters; an embarrassing and awkward presence.

Joyce Darnell sat next to me once we were in the public gallery and was clearly concerned that I might prefer to be beside my mother. I couldn't give a thought to where I sat, I was just desperate, so very anxious to hear the outcome of the jury's deliberations. When we were all seated the jury came in. My heart was pounding and I found I was shaking from head to toe. I hadn't anticipated that, but there was nothing I could do about it. In an attempt to control the trembling I twiddled my thumbs nervously and wondered what would happen next. I surveyed the jurors, but the neutral expression on their faces betrayed nothing and the anxiety continued. Unfortunately in that particular courtroom, Nick was underneath the public gallery and I couldn't see him at all. I couldn't catch his eye, or show that I was with him in any way. It was a devastatingly lonely moment for both of us. One of fear, apprehension and isolation. I scanned the court room. Mr Williams was nowhere to be seen. Then I recalled he'd excused himself as he had another case. 'It's all a big game for him,' I thought, 'all part of a day's work.' My musing was interrupted by the jurors being asked if they had elected a foreman, and they responded positively, at which point the foreman was asked to stand up. It was a grey haired man in his forties, holding a piece of paper in his hand. The court official asked, 'Have the jury come to an unanimous verdict on all 12 counts?'

'Yes, your honour, they have.'

'Does the jury find the defendant guilty or not guilty on count one?'

'Not guilty, your honour.'

This was then repeated slowly and clearly to the clerk of the court, 'Not guilty.'

I gasped. 'Not guilty. Wonderful.' But, there were eleven more counts to go. I froze and tried desperately to concentrate.

'Does the jury find the defendant guilty or not guilty on count two?'

'Not guilty, your honour.' And repeated again to the clerk of the court, 'Not guilty.'

'Does the jury find the defendant guilty or not guilty on count three?'

'Not guilty, your honour.' And again 'Not guilty.'

'Does the jury find the defendant guilty or not guilty on count four?'

'Not guilty, your honour.' Again 'Not guilty.'

'Does the jury find the defendant guilty or not guilty on count five?'

'Not guilty, your honour.' Again 'Not guilty.'

'Does the jury find the defendant guilty or not guilty on count six?'

'Not guilty, your honour.' Again 'Not guilty.'

'Does the jury find the defendant guilty or not guilty on count seven?'

'Not guilty, your honour.' Again 'Not guilty.'

'Does the jury find the defendant guilty or not guilty on count eight?'

'Not guilty, your honour.' Again 'Not guilty.'

'Does the jury find the defendant guilty or not guilty on count nine?'

'Not guilty, your honour.' Again 'Not guilty.'

'Does the jury find the defendant guilty or not guilty on count ten?'

'Not guilty, your honour.' Again 'Not guilty.'

'Does the jury find the defendant guilty or not guilty on count eleven?'

'Not guilty, your honour.' Again 'Not guilty.'

'Does the jury find the defendant guilty or not guilty on count twelve?'

'Not guilty, your honour.' And again 'Not guilty.'

It was an unbelievable moment. I broke down in audible sobs, but not daring to believe that Nick really had been cleared on all twelve counts. I turned to Joyce Darnell beside me and through the stream of tears muttered, 'Did I hear right?' 'Yes, my love,' she responded with a huge hug, 'not guilty on all counts.' I could not control my emotions, the relief was indescribable, the tears flowed. Somehow I expected something amazing to happen: fireworks, the pop of champagne corks, a loud cheer, but the only sound penetrating the cold court atmosphere was my violent and uncontrollable sobbing.

'Mr Metcalfe, you are free to go,' came the voice of the judge piercing the stunned silence of the courtroom, and at that Nick stood, and walked out. There was no apology, no explanation, just an abrupt dismissal. As Nick stumbled out he almost bumped into DC Stevens, who grabbed his hand and muttered he was sorry they'd met in such circumstances. It was a clever move on the policeman's behalf. He'd timed it just right. Nick was too stunned to say or do anything other than take the hand offered to him and stammer something or other about it being all right. Later, he thought of a whole string of comments he would have liked to have made, but at that precise moment he was too shocked to have his wits about him.

As the Metcalfe supporters gradually surfaced from their mesmeric condition of incredulous contentment the public gallery hastily emptied. Penny had vanished into thin air. I was guided by a kind friend, for I couldn't see where I was going through the irrepressible stream of tears. The group congregated once more on the landing and I flew into Nick's arms. It was a wonderful moment. One we had hardly dared even dream of, but one which we'd never forget.

Mr Bassett called us both into a side room for a quick summing up. He and his assistant looked absolutely delighted and I apologised profusely for the tears. 'Not at all, not at all,' Mr Bassett responded in his best grand fatherly manner. 'Quite understandable, considering all you've been through. Now, I've applied for your expenses to be paid, but that all takes time I'm afraid; it'll be several months before you hear anything. And I think that's all I've got to say, except that I'm totally delighted, of course, with the outcome. It was the right one, and justice has prevailed. I've been very impressed with your testimony and indeed with the number of people that have supported you. That cannot fail to have made an impact on the jury.'

We both warmly thanked Mr Bassett and his assistant and there were repeated handshakes. Then we left the little room to return joyfully to the group of supporters. There were hugs and kisses all round. Several people were keeping me company in tears and Nick felt he wanted to pass on Mr Bassett's comments. 'Can I just say something?' He asked in a loud voice which momentarily stilled the froth and bubble.

'I just want to thank you all very much for coming.' I noticed a tremor in his voice.

'I can't say how grateful we are to all of you. And er I just wanted to tell you what my barrister's just said to me.' Nick's face began to contort, 'That, er, the jury would definitely have been influenced by everyone sitting in the public gallery and I want to say,' Nick's voice rose several decibels, his face struggled to maintain its usual shape and then the tears fell. I ran over and hugged him and stood firmly by his side as he sniffed, drew his arm across his face and just about managed to complete the sentence, 'you've all been absolutely wonderful and I can't thank you enough.'

It was an emotionally charged moment as there were more hugs and hand shakes, and the relief surrounding us was enjoyed and basked in by all. The ordeal was over, Nick was free, life could resume, the psychological effects and impact would take some getting over, but Nick was a free man, not found guilty of one of those awful allegations. Suddenly the court building didn't seem so austere, the atmosphere was no longer oppressive and I felt like dancing, like hugging friends and strangers alike, shouting to the world: 'It's all right now, he's cleared, it's all going to be OK.'

We all ambled out to the car park, relatives were hugged, congratulations repeated and we stood in a daze with a group of friends including Andy North and Andrew Townsend. We'd been through so much together and now they were here at the end. Nick was grinning from ear to ear and my heart was racing. We were itching to escape and yet, at the same time reluctant to leave the premises. The place where so much had happened, where we each, in our individual ways, had been through terrible turmoil but emerged triumphant in the end. 'Time to go,' Nick said after a moment's pause, with an irrepressible smile. 'Don't worry, I'll drive carefully. I think I'll try to avoid the police for a while!' 'Does nothing quell his spirits?' asked Andy incredulously. 'Not a lot,' I replied with a smile. Then there were final hugs and hand shakes and car engines started.

Newspaper article printed locally following the trial. One or two people from Mainwave spotted it, but it caused no problems.

CRANLEIGH / MANAGER WALKS FREE AFTER TWO-WEEK CROWN COURT TRIAL

TEENAGE GIRLS ACCUSED OF LYING OVER ASSAULT

A Cranleigh man was cleared of 12 charges of indecent assault on three girls aged 13 to 16.

Computer manager Nicholas Metcalfe, 41, broke into a smile as the jury returned their verdicts after a two-week trial at Guildford Crown Court.

Richard Williams, prosecuting, had told the jury at Guildford Crown Court Metcalfe had stroked their thighs, and touched their breasts and bottoms.

But Metcalfe, of Elmtree Avenue, told the court that the three teenage girls who accused him of indecently assaulting them were lying.

Giving evidence Metcalfe said: 'I have never been involved in any improper or inappropriate behaviour.'

Asked about the indecency allegations made by the girls, Metcalfe said: 'I am sorry to say that they are lies.'

Judge Peter Harris ordered that Metcalfe be discharged and awarded him his defence costs. Metcalfe had denied all the charges against him.

Waking from the nightmare

A s we drove home, I think we both experienced a numbness, a sense of emptiness, of unreality, and of course exhaustion. The wheels of life kept turning and we had to function; we were still Mum and Dad and still had the necessary jobs to do. A French exchange girl arrived the evening of the last day of the trial and she needed entertaining and talking to in slow, simple English.

We had joked before the trial about what we would ever find to talk about once it was all over, because it so dominated our complete existence. However, within days, far sooner than one might expect, the 'normality' we had so longed for in previous months returned. Inevitably the early weeks, when we were not tending to youngsters in one way or another, were dominated by anecdotes from the trial, flash-backs to horrid moments and laughter at the lighter incidents. Several times we repeated to each other and to our friends what Mr. Bassett had said to Nick one day in court; 'Tell me Mr. Metcalfe, can I hire your witnesses? They would be so useful in some of my other trials. They are smart, well spoken and tell the same story.' It amused and delighted us at the time and continued to do so afterwards.

We had tried to give our daughters a day to day account of what had happened at court so that they were in the picture, but it must have helped them to hear it discussed without anxiety and as a past event. Their busy lives continued, and whilst 1999 will never be forgotten, they seem, like their parents, to be happy to live as the hymn says with the 'past put behind us', and trusting God for the future.

As for us, initially I found myself mulling over whether we would have done things differently if we could live our lives over again. It is not a straightforward answer. I believe Nick's robust, enthusiastic, somewhat wild personality was used of God in the running of a very enjoyable and fruitful youth group. It was wonderful to see how he enjoyed the youngsters' company, and how they, both sexes, responded to him, his enthusiasm and dedication. Had he kept his distance and acted in more of a teacher capacity, and less as a friend, the whole atmosphere of the evenings would have been radically altered.

However, Nick's physical contact with the teenagers made it so easy to level accusations at him. With the gift of hindsight, a total 'hands off' approach would have been much safer, though inhibiting to an ebullient character like Nick's. Unable to participate fully in activities, Nick would have been frustrated and felt 'caged in'. But he would have been 'safer'.

As for taxiing young ladies around on their own, now, painfully we see how unwise this was. At the time we were ignorant and naïve. How sad that it is only safe to do this with other young people or youth group leaders in the car, thus preventing potential friendly and fruitful conversations which might arise on a one to one basis.

Nick, who seems to be exceptionally unquashable, has bounced back after his ordeal. Indeed, only a few weeks after the trial he offered a young lady a lift home after church without giving it a thought. He needs to learn the perils of this age! Meanwhile I do his worrying for him and on one occasion when he was asked at short notice to provide a car for a youth group trip to the cinema, I rang up the youth leader who had made the request and begged that Nick should have an older lady next to him, with youngsters in the back. Whether or not the youth leader thought I was completely cracked I will never know, but I was humoured and extremely grateful.

Initially, as I walked around Cranleigh I experienced the strange sensation of frequently 'seeing' Anita and Penny. It was most unnerving, anyone of their particular build and hair colour was, momentarily, 'them'. Emily has subsequently informed me that it was just the same for her. It was extremely disconcerting, and I had to pray fervently and tell myself not to be such an idiot!

As the months rolled by, I 'saw' them less and less, and the sightings are now exceptionally rare! The only lasting effect which somewhat fascinates me is the shakes. Before the trial, whenever the events were discussed, regardless who was with me, I shook. I could feel my whole body rattle, it was difficult to hold a drink steady and I used to sit on my hands to make it less conspicuous. Hopefully the shakes were not too obvious, but I was definitely aware of them and on occasions others were too. Afterwards I was intrigued to observe that the shakes were still with me. Thankfully as

1999 is discussed so rarely it is a strange and very occasional side effect of a traumatic time. I am left wondering, will the shakes ever leave me?

However in answer to all those questions: How did you cope once it was all over? Did you feel polluted? Did you feel ashamed, even though proved innocent? Did you lose your self-confidence? How did the girls manage? Was Nick all right at work? We can honestly say that we were given energy and strength to cope, as were our girls. We did not feel polluted because we had absolutely no reason to do so. Nick was fine in his new role at work and enjoys it as much, probably more than, his old one. If anything, our self confidence is higher than before, because we know for absolute certain that we are blessed with a fantastic, supportive and loving group of friends, and, what is even more important, a fantastic, supportive and loving God.

Postscript

As time moves on, we are readjusting well following our traumatic experiences. As Nick was cleared, the press made very little of it and the paragraph which mentioned his trial was merely noticed by a couple of work colleagues. Nick was transferred within Mainwave after the trial to a new job which is rewarding and satisfying and which he thoroughly enjoys.

An article was published in a popular Christian Newspaper to serve as a warning to other youth leaders in the UK and this generated much interest. One previously unknown supporter offered money to sue the girls involved, in an attempt to stem the tide of false allegations against Christian youth workers. After much prayer and deliberation we decided that it would be against our Christian principles as well as cause further heartache to our already battered household.

Nick placed a police complaint concerning the one-sided nature of the police's investigation prior to him being charged, only to be told by the internal police complaints representative that it was not the police's job to collect evidence for the defence. Horrified at the state of the UK laws which seem incapable of preventing such errors he went to his MP who was equally unhelpful and was adamant that the police and CPS had stuck to the letter of the law and consequently he felt there was no cause for further action.

Eventually, in the following April, 90% of the funds were reimbursed, so friends and family loans were at last returned to them. The final 10%, Mr Dixon informed us recently, was not going to be returned, as the court assessors deemed too much had been spent on defence costs. This news was greeted with total disbelief by both of us, before we resigned ourselves disgustedly to the injustice of the legal system, and determined not to be worn down any more by it, we resolutely tried to accept it.

The doorbell was changed at Christmas, as neither of us could live with the continuing start it gave us whenever it rang whatever time of day; it inevitably reminded us of that fateful day of Nick's arrest.

Our four girls' lives have settled down and returned to normality. Emily is relieved the stress is gone, her Dad is free and she can concentrate on her GCSEs, whilst Jessica is very thankful that the tension in the household has finally disappeared and life has normalised once again.

I too am readjusting to 'normal' life. I still find myself rushing to pick up post or answer the telephone, and having to remind myself that it will hold no hidden surprises. Perhaps rather strangely I feel acutely anxious when in the proximity of any member of the police force whether in the car or on foot. My confidence in them is shattered.

Nick has settled well to life as a free and cleared man, though if any of his friends fail to make contact when he expected them to, he is unnecessarily anxious to hear from them, from an irrational fear that no news, rather than meaning good news, actually signifies conspiracies and scheming against him.

Not surprisingly, following the trial, a number of memos were sent round the police administration department in Maidstone, where Trevor Westward worked. These were regarding the necessity of maintaining the confidentiality of material at all times. Thankfully the source of the leaked information was never traced, and Trevor has now retired.

Despite Nick having been found not guilty, his name, the names of the family, our address and his occupation were and still are totally available to the press. Whereas Anita, Penny and Debs are still protected from ever having their real names published or being identified in any way.

We continue to be mystified as to the motives of Anita, Penny, and Debs, and are overwhelmed with gratitude to our friends and family who supported us so loyally throughout that nightmare nine month period of our lives. Nor can we thank God enough for his presence with us throughout the ordeal and, of course, for the final outcome. Each October we, as a family, go out to a restaurant for a meal, to celebrate and commemorate God's goodness. We hope to maintain this tradition so that we are never tempted to forget his amazing love and care for us during the most traumatic year of our lives.

This article appeared in an Evangelical Newspaper as a direct result of Nick's Trial.

YOUTH WORKER'S NIGHTMARE

'I ask you members of the jury: how many of you could defend yourself if you were falsely accused? How many of you could produce 16 witnesses and 100 letters of reference to defend yourselves?'

So said the defence barrister in the Guildford Crown Court last October after nine days of gruelling cross examination.

The defendant had been a Christian youth worker in an evangelical church; a devout Christian and devoted family man. For seven years, he and his wife had given themselves to the church youth in the age range of 13–18. This was not just Saturday and Sunday evenings; they ran an open-house policy for the various members in the group. Whether in the evenings, to unburden their teenage frustrations and moans about parents, or at lunchtime as a haven close to the sixth-form college, there was a welcome for the youngsters.

There were also trips out for fun evenings and midnight hikes, travel abroad to help in building or maintenance projects at overseas camps or Bible colleges. All to broaden the experience of the young people and to direct them to helping others. Nothing was too much trouble.

Yes, there were occasional gripes from the young people, but there were no serious complaints; indeed for most, it was a helpful and enjoyable group.

DAWN RAID

Two girls joined the group from elsewhere and entered into everything with enthusiasm and appreciation, there was even the joy of both being baptised and one becoming a church member. Their visits to the home were probably the most frequent from the group, either at lunchtime or in the evening, sometimes babysitting. Yet these were the two who, after starting at university and drifting from the church, triggered off false accusations against the one who had done so much for them.

The youth leader knew nothing about the accusations until at 6.00 am on a January morning in 1999, when his home was raided by the police, the house searched and his four daughters, ranging from 7 to 14, were woken and questioned. Videos and computer equipment were taken away. The youth leader soon found himself in a police cell and subjected to questioning over the alleged charges, including rape on three occasions dating back eight years to when one girl was 13 and before she had even joined the group. Thankfully he was not retained in custody, but might well have been in view of the seriousness of the charges.

TRAUMATIC TIMES

The next ten months were traumatic for both the family and friends who were well aware of the defendant's upright character and dedication, and convinced of his innocence.

Fortunately his employers, a very large company, were very supportive, and could accommodate the many bad days when work was not the only thing on his mind, to say nothing of the number of days off attending court or meetings with solicitors.

The family had to adjust to the awful possibility, being duly warned by their solicitor, that they might yet have to face the wrongful imprisonment of their husband and father, the selling of their house to pay the legal bills (some £50,000), and the cloud of apparent guilt of their loved one haunting them for years. Having moved house towards the end of 1998, unpacked boxes through 1999 gave a good indication of the uncertainty in their minds of what the future held.

By the time the case reached court, the rape charges had been dropped as not possible to prove, but 12 other seedy charges remained. It was distressing to read the girls' statements and realise that, apart from the false accusations, what had been considered as pure clean fun without any complaint was now being regarded as assault. Thankfully, after ten days of court tension, the jury took only a very short time to unanimously declare him not guilty on all 12 counts.

SUCCESSFUL DEFENCE

What were the main contributing factors to the successful defence of this innocent and dedicated worker and what lessons can be learned?

a) Prayer support: Throughout the months, many people prayed. The family knew the Lord's help and strengthening during this time. During the court case, special prayer meetings were held in homes and churches as well as in the court by the wife and witnesses waiting their turn to go in to the court room.

b) Caring leadership: even if the leaders think the youth worker might be guilty, love and concern should be practically demonstrated to the brother or sister who has fallen under suspicion.

c) Consistent friendship: It is vital that friends do not steer a wide berth or dissociate themselves from the accused. In this case, there was hardly a day throughout the ten months when telephone calls or letters were not received showing love and support.

PROTECTION

We all agree it is right to have adequate protection for children against abuse by adults, but what can youth workers do to protect themselves from the possibility of those they are currently helping turning against them in several years' time?

There are recommended guidelines for youth workers and these should be in writing. They will include such rules as never being alone with a young person, but in practice these are no help where false charges are being raised. Detailed diaries can be maintained and attendance records kept for many years, but on the basis that no abuser is going to record his or her assault, such records will not count for much with the police; although they may be useful in court.

Whatever a child says must be taken seriously and followed up. The message coming from social services can sometimes appear to be that this should be done even if it means ruining the life of an innocent adult. This sadly reflects today's rejection of the fallen nature of a child but is no help to youth workers.

Even though we are evangelical Christians, we cannot rely on credit being given to us by the police, as in the view of many we are only a sect, and just as liable to do wrong as another person. This was particularly apparent in the questioning of some 40 Christians and young people by the police officer in this case. What a sad reflection of the Christian's standing in the eyes of the world, but can we say it is entirely unjustified?

Postscript

So let us recognise the increasing risks of the days in which we work. Church leaders should be in regular contact with their workers and be witnesses to what they are doing and the relationships within the group.

Youth workers should be above reproach. Let us continue to serve those whom the Lord brings under our care with love, dedication and the mind of Christ, and when false accusations are brought, pray for grace to cope and love for our accusers.